A Study of Famous World's Organization

A Study of Famous World's Organization

Manoj Kumar Singh

PRASHANT PUBLISHING HOUSE
DELHI-110094

Published by :
Prashant Publishing House
C-34, 28 Foota Road, Gali-3,
West Karwal Nagar, Delhi-110094
Phone : 011-22963970, Mob. : 9810396373
e-mail.: prashantpublishinghouse@gmail.com

A Study of Famous World's Organization

First Published 2018

ISBN 978-81-938012-8-4

PRINTED IN INDIA
Published by Mr. R.K. Jha M/s Prashant Publishing House and Published at H.S. Offset House Press, Delhi.

Contents

Preface

The United Nations (UN) is an intergovernmental organization tasked to promote international co-operation and to create and maintain international order. A replacement for the ineffective League of Nations, the organization was established on 24 October 1945 after World War II with the aim of preventing another such conflict. At its founding, the UN had 51 member states; there are now 193. The headquarters of the UN is in Manhattan, New York City, and is subject to extraterritoriality. Further main offices are situated in Geneva, Nairobi, and Vienna.

The World Health Organization (WHO) is a specialized agency of the United Nations that is concerned with international public health. It was established on 7 April 1948, and is headquartered in Geneva, Switzerland. The WHO is a member of the United Nations Development Group. Its predecessor, the Health Organization, was an agency of the League of Nations.

The European Union (EU) is a political and economic union of 28 member states that are located primarily in Europe. It has an area of 4,475,757 km (1,728,099 sq mi) and an estimated population of over 510 million. The EU has developed an internal single market through a standardised system of laws that apply in all member states. EU policies aim to ensure the free movement of people, goods, services and capital within the internal market, enact legislation in justice and home affairs and maintain common policies on trade, agriculture, fisheries and regional development. For travel within the Schengen Area, passport controls have been abolished. A monetary union was established in 1999 and came into full force in 2002 and is composed of 19 EU member states which use the euro currency.

The Association of Southeast Asian Nations (ASEAN) is a regional intergovernmental organization comprising ten Southeast Asian countries that promotes intergovernmental cooperation and facilitates economic, political, security, military, educational, and sociocultural integration amongst its members and other Asian states. It also regularly engages other states in the Asia-Pacific region and beyond. Being a global powerhouse, the central platform for cooperation in Asia-Pacific, and one of the world's most prominent and influential organisations, ASEAN maintains a global network of alliances and is involved in numerous international affairs. It is a major partner of the Shanghai Cooperation Organisation (SCO), developing cooperation model with the organisation for the peace, stability, development and sustainability of the Asian continent. It also serves as an international role model in seeking harmony and strength among diversity and differences, as well as a leading figure in international diplomacy.

The Arab League (formally the League of Arab States, is a regional organization of Arab states in and around North Africa, the Horn of Africa and Arabia. It was formed in Cairo on 22 March 1945 with six members: Kingdom of Egypt, Kingdom of Iraq, Transjordan (renamed Jordan in 1949), Lebanon, Saudi Arabia, and Syria. Yemen joined as a member on 5 May 1945. Currently, the League has 22 members, but Syria's participation has been suspended since November 2011, as a consequence of government repression during the Syrian Civil War.

This is a reference book. All the matter is just compiled and edited in nature, taken from the various sources which are in public domain.

As the book addresses this crucial issue quite deftly, it is hoped that it would prove to be a source of great information for the reader.

—*Editor*

1

United Nations

The United Nations (UN) is an intergovernmental organization tasked to promote international co-operation and to create and maintain international order. A replacement for the ineffective League of Nations, the organization was established on 24 October 1945 after World War II with the aim of preventing another such conflict. At its founding, the UN had 51 member states; there are now 193. The headquarters of the UN is in Manhattan, New York City, and is subject to extraterritoriality. Further main offices are situated in Geneva, Nairobi, and Vienna. The organization is financed by assessed and voluntary contributions from its member states. Its objectives include maintaining international peace and security, promoting human rights, fostering social and economic development, protecting the environment, and providing humanitarian aid in cases of famine, natural disaster, and armed conflict. The UN is the largest, most familiar, most internationally represented and most powerful intergovernmental organization in the world.

The UN Charter was drafted at a conference between April–June 1945 in San Francisco, and was signed on 26 June 1945 at the conclusion of the conference; this charter took effect on 24 October 1945, and the UN began operation. The UN's mission to preserve world peace was complicated in its early decades by the Cold War between the United States and Soviet Union and their respective allies. The organization participated in major actions in Korea and the Congo, as well as approving the creation of the Israeli state in 1947. The organization's membership grew significantly following widespread decolonization in the 1960s, and by the 1970s its budget for economic and social development programmes far outstripped its spending on peacekeeping. After the end of the Cold War, the UN took on major military and peacekeeping missions across the world with varying degrees of success.

The UN has six principal organs: the General Assembly (the main deliberative assembly); the Security Council (for deciding certain resolutions for peace and security); the Economic and Social Council (ECOSOC; for promoting international economic and social co-operation and development); the Secretariat (for providing studies, information, and facilities needed by the UN); the International Court of Justice (the primary judicial organ); and the UN Trusteeship Council (inactive since 1994). UN System agencies include the World Bank Group, the World Health Organization, the World Food Programme, UNESCO, and UNICEF. The UN's most prominent officer is the Secretary-General, an office held by Portuguese politician and diplomat António Guterres since 2017. Non-governmental organizations may be granted consultative status with ECOSOC and other agencies to participate in the UN's work.

The organization won the Nobel Peace Prize in 2001, and a number of its officers and agencies have also been awarded the prize. Other evaluations of the UN's effectiveness have been mixed. Some commentators believe the organization to be an important force for peace and human development, while others have called the organization ineffective, corrupt, or biased.

HISTORY

Background

In the century prior to the UN's creation, several international treaty organizations and conferences had been formed to regulate conflicts between nations, such as the International Committee of the Red Cross and the Hague

Conventions of 1899 and 1907. Following the catastrophic loss of life in the First World War, the Paris Peace Conference established the League of Nations to maintain harmony between countries. This organization resolved some territorial disputes and created international structures for areas such as postal mail, aviation, and opium control, some of which would later be absorbed into the UN. However, the League lacked representation for colonial peoples (then half the world's population) and significant participation from several major powers, including the US, USSR, Germany, and Japan; it failed to act against the Japanese invasion of Manchuria in 1931, the Second Italo-Ethiopian War in 1935, the Japanese invasion of China in 1937, and German expansions under Adolf Hitler that culminated in the Second World War.

1942 "Declaration of United Nations" by the Allies of World War II

The earliest concrete plan for a new world organization began under the aegis of the US State Department in 1939. The text of the "Declaration by United Nations" was drafted by President Franklin Roosevelt, British Prime Minister Winston Churchill, and Roosevelt aide Harry Hopkins, while meeting at the White House, 29 December 1941. It incorporated Soviet suggestions, but left no role for France. "Four Policemen" was coined to refer to four major Allied countries, United States, United Kingdom, Soviet Union, and Republic of China, which emerged in the Declaration by United Nations. Roosevelt first coined the term *United Nations* to describe the Allied countries. "On New Year's Day 1942, President Roosevelt, Prime Minister Churchill, Maxim Litvinov, of the USSR, and T. V. Soong, of China, signed a short document which later came to be known as the United Nations Declaration and the next day the representatives of twenty-two other nations added their signatures." The term *United Nations* was first officially used when 26 governments signed this Declaration. One major change from the Atlantic Charter was the addition of a provision for religious freedom, which Stalin approved after Roosevelt insisted. By 1 March 1945, 21 additional states had signed.

À JOINT DECLARATION BY THE UNITED STATES OF AMERICA, THE UNITED KINGDOM OF GREAT BRITAIN AND NORTHERN IRELAND, THE UNION OF SOVIET SOCIALIST REPUBLICS, CHINA, AUSTRALIA, BELGIUM, CANADA, COSTA RICA, CUBA, CZECHOSLOVAKIA, DOMINICAN REPUBLIC, EL SALVADOR, GREECE, GUATEMALA, HAITI, HONDURAS, INDIA, LUXEMBOURG, NETHERLANDS, NEW ZEALAND, NICARAGUA, NORWAY, PANAMA, POLAND, SOUTH AFRICA, YUGOSLAVIA

The Governments signatory hereto,

Having subscribed to a common program of purposes and principles embodied in the Joint Declaration of the President of the United States of America and the Prime Minister of Great Britain dated August 14, 1941, known as the Atlantic Charter,

Being convinced that complete victory over their enemies is essential to defend life, liberty, independence and religious freedom, and to preserve human rights and justice in their own lands as well as in other lands, and that they are now engaged in a common struggle against savage and brutal forces seeking to subjugate the world,

DECLARE:

1. Each Government pledges itself to employ its full resources, military or economic, against those members of the Tripartite Pact and its adherents with which such government is at war.
2. Each Government pledges itself to cooperate with the Governments signatory hereto and not to make a separate armistice or peace with the enemies.

The foregoing declaration may be adhered to by other nations which are, or which may be, rendering material assistance and contributions in the struggle for victory over Hitlerism. —*The Washington Conference 1941–1942*

During the war, "the United Nations" became the official term for the Allies. To join, countries had to sign the Declaration and declare war on the Axis.

Founding

The UN was formulated and negotiated among the delegations from the Allied Big Four (the United States, the United Kingdom, the Soviet Union and China) at the Dumbarton Oaks Conference in 1944. After months of planning, the UN Conference on International Organization opened in San Francisco, 25 April 1945, attended by 50 governments and a number of non-governmental organizations involved in drafting the UN Charter. "The heads of the delegations of the sponsoring countries took turns as chairman of the plenary meetings: Anthony Eden, of Britain, Edward Stettinius, of the United States, T. V. Soong, of China, and Vyacheslav Molotov, of the Soviet Union. At the later meetings, Lord Halifaxdeputized for Mister Eden, Wellington Koo for T. V. Soong, and Mister Gromyko for Mister Molotov." The UN officially came into existence 24 October 1945, upon ratification of the Charter by the five permanent members of the Security Council—France, the Republic of China, the Soviet Union, the UK and the US—and by a majority of the other 46 signatories.

The first meetings of the General Assembly, with 51 nations represented, and the Security Council took place in London beginning 10 January 1946. The General Assembly selected New York City as the site for the headquarters of the UN, and the facility was completed in 1952. Its site—like UN headquarters buildings in Geneva, Vienna, and Nairobi—is designated as international territory. The Norwegian Foreign Minister, Trygve Lie, was elected as the first UN Secretary-General.

Cold War Era

Though the UN's primary mandate was peacekeeping, the division between the US and USSR often paralysed the organization, generally allowing it to intervene only in conflicts distant from the Cold War. (A notable exception was a Security Council resolution in 1950 authorizing a US-led coalition to repel the North Korean invasion of South Korea, passed in the absence of the USSR.) In 1947, the General Assembly approved a resolution to partition Palestine, approving the creation of the state of Israel. Two years later, Ralph Bunche, a UN official, negotiated an armistice to the resulting conflict. In 1956, the first UN peacekeeping force was established to end the Suez Crisis; however, the UN was unable to intervene against the USSR's simultaneous invasion of Hungary following that country's revolution.

Dag Hammarskjöld was a particularly active Secretary-General from 1953 until his death in 1961.

In 1960, the UN deployed United Nations Operation in the Congo (UNOC), the largest military force of its early decades, to bring order to the breakaway State of Katanga, restoring it to the control of the Democratic Republic of the Congo by 1964. While travelling to meet rebel leader Moise Tshombe during the conflict, Dag Hammarskjöld, often named as one of the UN's most effective Secretaries-General, died in a plane crash; months later he was posthumously awarded the Nobel Peace Prize. In 1964, Hammarskjöld's successor, U Thant, deployed the UN Peacekeeping Force in Cyprus, which would become one of the UN's longest-running peacekeeping missions.

With the spread of decolonization in the 1960s, the organization's membership saw an influx of newly independent nations. In 1960 alone, 17 new states joined the UN, 16 of them from Africa. On 25 October 1971, with opposition from the

United States, but with the support of many Third World nations, the mainland, communist People's Republic of China was given the Chinese seat on the Security Council in place of the Republic of China that occupied Taiwan; the vote was widely seen as a sign of waning US influence in the organization. Third World nations organized into the Group of 77 coalition under the leadership of Algeria, which briefly became a dominant power at the UN. In 1975, a bloc comprising the USSR and Third World nations passed a resolution, over strenuous US and Israeli opposition, declaring Zionism to be racism; the resolution was repealed in 1991, shortly after the end of the Cold War.

With an increasing Third World presence and the failure of UN mediation in conflicts in the Middle East, Vietnam, and Kashmir, the UN increasingly shifted its attention to its ostensibly secondary goals of economic development and cultural exchange. By the 1970s, the UN budget for social and economic development was far greater than its peacekeeping budget.

Post-Cold War

Kofi Annan, Secretary-General from 1997 to 2006

After the Cold War, the UN saw a radical expansion in its peacekeeping duties, taking on more missions in ten years than it had in the previous four decades. Between 1988 and 2000, the number of adopted Security Council resolutions more than doubled, and the peacekeeping budget increased more than tenfold. The UN negotiated an end to the Salvadoran Civil War, launched a successful peacekeeping mission in Namibia, and oversaw democratic elections in post-apartheid South Africa and post-Khmer Rouge Cambodia. In 1991, the UN authorized a US-led coalition that repulsed the Iraqi invasion of Kuwait. Brian Urquhart, Under-Secretary-General from 1971 to 1985, later described the hopes raised by these successes as a "false renaissance" for the organization, given the more troubled missions that followed.

Though the UN Charter had been written primarily to prevent aggression by one nation against another, in the early 1990s the UN faced a number of simultaneous, serious crises within nations such as Somalia, Haiti, Mozambique, and the former Yugoslavia. The UN mission in Somalia was widely viewed as a failure after the US withdrawal following casualties in the Battle of Mogadishu, and the UN mission to Bosnia faced "worldwide ridicule" for its indecisive and confused mission in the face of ethnic cleansing. In 1994, the UN Assistance Mission for Rwanda failed to intervene in the Rwandan genocide amid indecision in the Security Council.

Beginning in the last decades of the Cold War, American and European critics of the UN condemned the organization for perceived mismanagement and corruption. In 1984, the US President, Ronald Reagan, withdrew his nation's funding from UNESCO (the United Nations Educational, Scientific and Cultural Organization, founded 1946) over allegations of mismanagement, followed by Britain and Singapore. Boutros Boutros-Ghali, Secretary-General from 1992 to 1996, initiated a reform of the Secretariat, reducing the size of the organization somewhat. His successor, Kofi Annan (1997–2006), initiated further management reforms in the face of threats from the United States to withhold its UN dues.

In the late 1990s and 2000s, international interventions authorized by the UN took a wider variety of forms. The UN mission in the Sierra Leone Civil War of 1991–2002 was supplemented by British Royal Marines, and the invasion of Afghanistan in 2001 was overseen by NATO.In 2003, the United States invaded Iraq despite failing to pass a UN Security Council resolution for authorization, prompting a new round of questioning of the organization's effectiveness. Under the eighth Secretary-General, Ban Ki-moon, the UN has intervened with peacekeepers in crises including the War in Darfur in Sudan and the Kivu conflict in the Democratic Republic of Congo and sent observers and chemical weapons inspectors to the Syrian Civil War. In 2013, an internal review of UN actions in the final battles of the Sri Lankan Civil War in 2009 concluded that the organization had suffered "systemic failure". One hundred and one UN personnel died in the 2010 Haiti earthquake, the worst loss of life in the organization's history.

The Millennium Summit was held in 2000 to discuss the UN's role in the 21st century. The three day meeting was the largest gathering of world leaders in history, and culminated in the adoption by all member states of the Millennium Development Goals (MDGs), a commitment to achieve international development in areas such as poverty reduction, gender equality, and public health. Progress towards these goals, which were to be met by 2015, was ultimately uneven. The 2005 World Summit reaffirmed the UN's focus on promoting development, peacekeeping, human rights, and global security. The Sustainable Development Goals were launched in 2015 to succeed the Millennium Development Goals.

In addition to addressing global challenges, the UN has sought to improve its accountability and democratic legitimacy by engaging more with civil society and fostering a global constituency. In an effort to enhance transparency, in 2016 the organization held its first public debate between candidates for Secretary-General. On 1 January 2017, Portuguese diplomat António Guterres, who previously served as UN High Commissioner for Refugees, became the ninth Secretary-General. Guterres has highlighted several key goals for his administration, including an emphasis on diplomacy for preventing conflicts, more effective peacekeeping efforts, and streamlining the organization to be more responsive and versatile to global needs.

STRUCTURE

The UN system is based on five principal organs: the General Assembly, the Security Council, the Economic and Social Council (ECOSOC), the Secretariat, and the International Court of Justice. A sixth principal organ, the Trusteeship Council, suspended operations in 1994, upon the independence of Palau, the last remaining UN trustee territory.

Four of the five principal organs are located at the main UN Headquarters in New York City. The International Court of Justice is located in The Hague, while other major agencies are based in the UN offices at Geneva, Vienna, and Nairobi. Other UN institutions are located throughout the world.

The six official languages of the UN, used in intergovernmental meetings and documents, are Arabic, Chinese, English, French, Russian, and Spanish. On the basis of the Convention on the Privileges and Immunities of the United Nations, the UN and its agencies are immune from the laws of the countries where they operate, safeguarding the UN's impartiality with regard to the host and member countries.

Below the six organs sit, in the words of the author Linda Fasulo, "an amazing collection of entities and organizations, some of which are actually older than the UN itself and operate with almost complete independence from it". These include specialized agencies, research and training institutions, programmes and funds, and other UN entities.

The UN obey the *Noblemaire principle*, which is binding on any organization that belongs to the UN system. This principle calls for salaries that will draw and keep citizens of countries where salaries are highest, and also calls for equal pay for work of equal value independent of the employee's nationality. In practice, the ICSC takes reference to the highest-paying national civil service. Staff salaries are subject to an internal tax that is administered by the UN organizations.

General Assembly

The General Assembly is the main deliberative assembly of the UN. Composed of all UN member states, the assembly meets in regular yearly sessions, but emergency sessions can also be called. The assembly is led by a president, elected from among the member states on a rotating regional basis, and 21 vice-presidents. The first session convened 10 January 1946 in the Methodist Central Hall in London and included representatives of 51 nations.

When the General Assembly votes on important questions, a two-thirds majority of those present and voting is required. Examples of important questions include recommendations on peace and security; election of members to organs; admission, suspension, and expulsion of members; and budgetary matters. All other questions are decided by a majority vote. Each member country has one vote. Apart from approval of budgetary matters, resolutions are not binding on the members. The Assembly may make recommendations on any matters within the scope of the UN, except matters of peace and security that are under consideration by the Security Council.

Draft resolutions can be forwarded to the General Assembly by its six main committees:

- First Committee (Disarmament and International Security)
- Second Committee (Economic and Financial)
- Third Committee (Social, Humanitarian, and Cultural)
- Fourth Committee (Special Political and Decolonization)
- Fifth Committee (Administrative and Budgetary)
- Sixth Committee (Legal)

As well as by the following two committees:

- General Committee – a supervisory committee consisting of the assembly's president, vice-president, and committee heads.

- Credentials Committee – responsible for determining the credentials of each member nation's UN representatives.

Security Council

Photo: Colin Powell, the US Secretary of State, demonstrates a vial with allegedIraqi chemical weapon probes to the UN Security Council on Iraq warhearings, 5 February 2003

The Security Council is charged with maintaining peace and security among countries. While other organs of the UN can only make "recommendations" to member states, the Security Council has the power to make binding decisions that member states have agreed to carry out, under the terms of Charter Article 25. The decisions of the Council are known as United Nations Security Council resolutions.

The Security Council is made up of fifteen member states, consisting of five permanent members—China, France, Russia, the United Kingdom, and the United States—and ten non-permanent members elected for two-year terms by the General Assembly (with end of term date)—Bolivia (term ends 2018), Egypt (2017), Ethiopia (2018), Italy (2018), Japan (2017), Kazakhstan (2018), Senegal (2017), Sweden (2018), Ukraine (2017), Uruguay (2017). The five permanent members hold veto power over UN resolutions, allowing a permanent member to block adoption of a resolution, though not debate. The ten temporary seats are held for two-year terms, with five member states per year voted in by the General Assembly on a regional basis. The presidency of the Security Council rotates alphabetically each month.

Secretariat

The UN Secretariat is headed by the Secretary-General, assisted by the Deputy Secretary-General and a staff of international civil servants worldwide. It provides studies, information, and facilities needed by UN bodies for their meetings. It also carries out tasks as directed by the Security Council, the General Assembly, the Economic and Social Council, and other UN bodies.

Photo: The current Secretary-General, António Guterres

The Secretary-General acts as the *de facto* spokesperson and leader of the UN. The position is defined in the UN Charter as the organization's "chief administrative officer". Article 99 of the charter states that the Secretary-General can bring to the Security Council's attention "any matter which in his opinion may threaten the maintenance of international peace and security", a phrase that Secretaries-General since Trygve Lie have interpreted as giving the position broad scope for action on the world stage. The office has evolved into a dual role of an administrator of the UN organization and a diplomat and mediator addressing disputes between member states and finding consensus to global issues.

The Secretary-General is appointed by the General Assembly, after being recommended by the Security Council, where the permanent members have veto power. There are no specific criteria for the post, but over the years it has become accepted that the post shall be held for one or two terms of five years. The current Secretary-General is António Guterres, who replaced Ban Ki-moon in 2017.

International Court of Justice

The court had ruled that Kosovo's unilateral declaration of independencefrom Serbia in 2008 did not violate international law

The International Court of Justice (ICJ), located in The Hague, in the Netherlands, is the primary judicial organ of the UN. Established in 1945 by the UN Charter, the Court began work in 1946 as the successor to the Permanent Court of International Justice. The ICJ is composed of 15 judges who serve 9-year terms and are appointed by the General Assembly; every sitting judge must be from a different nation.

It is based in the Peace Palace in The Hague, sharing the building with the Hague Academy of International Law, a private centre for the study of international law. The ICJ's primary purpose is to adjudicate disputes among states. The court has heard cases related to war crimes, illegal state interference, ethnic cleansing, and other issues. The ICJ can also be called upon by other UN organs to provide advisory opinions.

FUNDING

Top 25 contributors to the United Nations budget for 2016

Member state	Contribution(% of UN budget)
United States	22.000
Japan	9.680
China	7.921
Germany	6.389
France	4.859
United Kingdom	4.463
Brazil	3.823
Italy	3.748
Russia	3.088
Canada	2.921
Spain	2.443
Australia	2.337
South Korea	2.039
Netherlands	1.482
Mexico	1.435
Saudi Arabia	1.146
Switzerland	1.140
Turkey	1.018
Sweden	0.956
Argentina	0.892
Belgium	0.885
Norway	0.849
Poland	0.841
India	0.737
Other member states	12.908

The UN is financed from assessed and voluntary contributions from member states. The General Assembly approves the regular budget and determines the assessment for each member. This is broadly based on the relative capacity of each country to pay, as measured by its gross national income (GNI), with adjustments for external debt and low per capita income. The two-year budget for 2012–13 was $5.512 billion in total.

The Assembly has established the principle that the UN should not be unduly dependent on any one member to finance its operations. Thus, there is a "ceiling" rate, setting the maximum amount that any member can be assessed for the regular budget. In December 2000, the Assembly revised the scale of assessments in response to pressure from the United States. As part of that revision, the regular budget ceiling was reduced from 25% to 22%. For the least developed countries (LDCs), a ceiling rate of 0.01% is applied. In addition to the ceiling rates, the minimum amount assessed to any member nation (or "floor" rate) is set at 0.001% of the UN budget ($55,120 for the two year budget 2013–2014).

A large share of the UN's expenditure addresses its core mission of peace and security, and this budget is assessed separately from the main organizational budget. The peacekeeping budget for the 2015–16 fiscal year was $8.27 billion, supporting 82,318 troops deployed in 15 missions around the world. UN peace operations are funded by assessments, using a formula derived from the regular funding scale that includes a weighted surcharge for the five permanent Security Council members, who must approve all peacekeeping operations. This surcharge serves to offset discounted peacekeeping assessment rates for less developed countries. In 2017, the top 8 providers of assessed financial contributions to UN peacekeeping operations were the United States (28.47%), China (10.25%), Japan (9.68%), Germany (6.39%), France (6.28%), United Kingdom (5.77%), Russian Federation (3.99%) and Italy (3.75%).

Special UN programmes not included in the regular budget, such as UNICEF and the World Food Programme, are financed by voluntary contributions from member governments, corporations, and private individuals.

EVALUATIONS, AWARDS, AND CRITICISM

A number of agencies and individuals associated with the UN have won the Nobel Peace Prize in recognition of their work. Two Secretaries-General, Dag Hammarskjöld and Kofi Annan, were each awarded the prize (in 1961 and 2001, respectively), as were Ralph Bunche (1950), a UN negotiator, René Cassin (1968), a contributor to the Universal Declaration of Human Rights, and the US Secretary of State Cordell Hull (1945), the latter for his role in the organization's founding. Lester B. Pearson, the Canadian Secretary of State for External Affairs, was awarded the prize in 1957 for his role in organizing the UN's first peacekeeping force to resolve the Suez Crisis. UNICEF won the prize in 1965, the International Labour Organization in 1969, the UN Peace-Keeping Forces in 1988, the International Atomic Energy Agency (which reports to the UN) in 2005, and the UN-supported Organization for the Prohibition of Chemical Weapons in 2013. The UN High Commissioner for Refugees was awarded in 1954 and 1981, becoming one of only two recipients to win the prize twice. The UN as a whole was awarded the prize in 2001, sharing it with Annan.

Since its founding, there have been many calls for reform of the UN but little consensus on how to do so. Some want the UN to play a greater or more effective role in world affairs, while others want its role reduced to humanitarian work. There have also been numerous calls for the UN Security Council's membership to be increased, for different ways of electing the UN's Secretary-General, and for a UN Parliamentary Assembly. Jacques Fomerand states the most enduring divide in views of the UN is "the North–South split" between richer Northern nations and developing Southern nations. Southern nations tend to favour a more empowered UN with a stronger General Assembly, allowing them a greater voice in world affairs, while Northern nations prefer an economically laissez-faire UN that focuses on transnational threats such as terrorism.

After World War II, the French Committee of National Liberation was late to be recognized by the US as the government of France, and so the country was initially excluded from the conferences that created the new organization. The future French president Charles de Gaullecriticized the UN, famously calling it a *machin* ("contraption"), and was not convinced that a global security alliance would help maintain world peace, preferring direct defence treaties between countries. Throughout the Cold War, both the US and USSR repeatedly accused the UN of favouring the other. In 1953, the USSR effectively forced the resignation of Trygve Lie, the Secretary-General, through its refusal to deal with him, while in the 1950s and 1960s, a popular US bumper sticker read, "You can't spell communism without U.N." In a sometimes-misquoted statement, President George W. Bush stated in February 2003 (referring to UN uncertainty towards Iraqi provocations under the Saddam Hussein regime) that "free nations will not allow the UN to fade into history as an ineffective, irrelevant debating society." In contrast, the French President, François Hollande, stated in 2012 that "France trusts the United Nations. She knows that no state, no matter how powerful, can solve urgent problems, fight for development and bring an end to all crises... France wants the UN to be the centre of global governance." Critics such as Dore Gold, an Israeli diplomat, Robert S. Wistrich, a British scholar, Alan Dershowitz, an American legal scholar, Mark Dreyfus, an Australian politician, and the Anti-Defamation Leagueconsider UN attention to Israel's treatment of Palestinians to be excessive. In September 2015, Saudi Arabia's Faisal bin Hassan Trad has been elected Chair of the UN Human Rights Council panel that appoints independent experts, a move criticized by human rights groups.

Since 1971, the Republic of China (Taiwan) has been excluded from the UN and since then has always been rejected in new applications. Citizens of this country are also not allowed to enter the buildings of the United Nations with the passport of Taiwan. In this way, critics agree that the UN is failing its own development goals and guidelines. This criticism also brought pressure from the People's Republic of China, which regards the territories administered by Taiwan as their own territory.

Critics have also accused the UN of bureaucratic inefficiency, waste, and corruption. In 1976, the General Assembly established the Joint Inspection Unit to seek out inefficiencies within the UN system. During the 1990s, the US withheld dues citing inefficiency and only started repayment on the condition that a major reforms initiative was introduced. In 1994, the Office of Internal Oversight Services (OIOS) was established by the General Assembly to serve as an efficiency watchdog. In 1994, former Special Representative of the Secretary-General of the UN to Somalia Mohamed Sahnoun published "Somalia: The Missed Opportunities", a book in which he analyses the reasons for the failure of the 1992 UN intervention in Somalia, showing that, between the start of the Somali civil war in 1988 and the fall of the Siad Barre regime in January 1991, the UN missed at least three opportunities to prevent major human tragedies; when the UN tried to provide humanitarian assistance, they were totally outperformed by NGOs, whose competence and dedication sharply contrasted with the UN's excessive caution and bureaucratic inefficiencies.

If radical reform was not undertaken, warned Mohamed Sahnoun, then the UN would continue to respond to such crisis with inept improvization. In 2004, the UN faced accusations that its recently ended Oil-for-Food Programme—in which Iraq had been allowed to trade oil for basic needs to relieve the pressure of sanctions—had suffered from widespread corruption, including billions of dollars of kickbacks.

An independent inquiry created by the UN found that many of its officials had been involved, as well as raising "significant" questions about the role of Kojo Annan, the son of Kofi Annan.

In evaluating the UN as a whole, Jacques Fomerand writes that the "accomplishments of the United Nations in the last 60 years are impressive in their own terms. Progress in human development during the 20th century has been dramatic and the UN and its agencies have certainly helped the world become a more hospitable and livable place for millions."Evaluating the first 50 years of the UN's history, the author Stanley Meisler writes that *"the United Nations never fulfilled the hopes of its founders, but it accomplished a great deal nevertheless"*, citing its role in decolonization and its many successful peacekeeping efforts. The British historian Paul Kennedy states that while the organization has suffered some major setbacks, "when all its aspects are considered, the UN has brought great benefits to our generation and ... will bring benefits to our children's and grandchildren's generations as well."

2

World Health Organization (WHO)

The World Health Organization (WHO) is a specialized agency of the United Nations that is concerned with international public health. It was established on 7 April 1948, and is headquartered in Geneva, Switzerland. The WHO is a member of the United Nations Development Group. Its predecessor, the Health Organization, was an agency of the League of Nations.

The constitution of the World Health Organization had been signed by 63 countries on 7 April 1948, with the first meeting of the World Health Assembly finishing on 24 July 1948. It incorporated the Office International d'Hygiène Publique and the League of Nations Health Organization. Since its establishment, it has played a leading role in the eradication of smallpox. Its current priorities include communicable diseases, in particular HIV/AIDS, Ebola, malaria and tuberculosis; the mitigation of the effects of non-communicable diseases such as sexual and reproductive health, development, and aging; nutrition, food security and healthy eating; occupational health; substance abuse; and driving the development of reporting, publications, and networking.

The WHO is responsible for the World Health Report, the worldwide World Health Survey, and World Health Day. The current Director-General of WHO is Tedros Adhanom, who started his five-year term on 1 July 2017.

HISTORY

Origins

The International Sanitary Conferences, originally held on 23 June 1851, were the first predecessors of the WHO. A series of 14 conferences that lasted from 1851 to 1938, the International Sanitary Conferences worked to combat many diseases, chief among them cholera, yellow fever, and the bubonic plague. The conferences were largely ineffective until the seventh, in 1892; when an International Sanitary Convention that dealt with cholera was passed. Five years later, a convention for the plague was signed. In part as a result of the successes of the Conferences, the Pan-American Sanitary Bureau, and the Office International d'Hygiène Publique were soon founded in 1902 and 1907, respectively. When the League of Nations was formed in 1920, they established the Health Organization of the League of Nations. After World War II, the United Nations absorbed all the other health organizations, to form the WHO.

Establishment

During the 1945 United Nations Conference on International Organization, Szeming Sze, a delegate from China, conferred with Norwegian and Brazilian delegates on creating an international health organization under the auspices of the new United Nations. After failing to get a resolution passed on the subject, Alger Hiss, the Secretary General of the conference, recommended using a declaration to establish such an organization. Sze and other delegates lobbied and a declaration passed calling for an international conference on health. The use of the word "world", rather than "international", emphasized the truly global nature of what the organization was seeking to achieve. The constitution of the World Health Organization was signed by all 51 countries of the United Nations, and by 10 other countries, on 22 July 1946. It thus became the first specialized agency of the United Nations to which every member subscribed. Its constitution formally came into force on the first World Health Day on 7 April 1948, when it was ratified by the

26th member state.The first meeting of the World Health Assembly finished on 24 July 1948, having secured a budget of US$5 million (then GB£1,250,000) for the 1949 year. Andrija Stampar was the Assembly's first president, and G. Brock Chisholm was appointed Director-General of WHO, having served as Executive Secretary during the planning stages. Its first priorities were to control the spread of malaria, tuberculosis and sexually transmitted infections, and to improve maternal and child health, nutrition and environmental hygiene. Its first legislative act was concerning the compilation of accurate statistics on the spread and morbidity of disease. The logo of the World Health Organization features the Rod of Asclepius as a symbol for healing.

STRUCTURE

The World Health Organization is a member of the United Nations Development Group.

Membership

As of 2016, the WHO has 194 member states: all of them Member States of the United Nations except for the Cook Islands and Niue. (A state becomes a full member of WHO by ratifying the treaty known as the Constitution of the World Health Organization.) As of 2013, it also had two associate members, Puerto Rico and Tokelau. Several other countries have been granted observer status. Palestine is an observer as a "national liberation movement" recognized by the League of Arab States under United Nations Resolution 3118. The Holy Seealso attends as an observer, as does the Order of Malta. In 2010, Taiwan was invited under the name of "Chinese Taipei".

WHO Member States appoint delegations to the World Health Assembly, WHO's supreme decision-making body. All UN Member States are eligible for WHO membership, and, according to the WHO website, "other countries may be admitted as members when their application has been approved by a simple majority vote of the World Health Assembly".

Liechtenstein is currently the only UN member not in the WHO membership.

In addition, the UN observer organizations International Committee of the Red Cross and International Federation of Red Cross and Red Crescent Societies have entered into "official relations" with WHO and are invited as observers. In the World Health Assembly they are seated alongside the other NGOs.

World Health Assembly and Executive Board

The World Health Assembly (WHA) is the legislative and supreme body of WHO. Based in Geneva, it typically meets yearly in May. It appoints the Director-General every five years and votes on matters of policy and finance of WHO, including the proposed budget. It also reviews reports of the Executive Board and decides whether there are areas of work requiring further examination. The Assembly elects 34 members, technically qualified in the field of health, to the Executive Board for three-year terms. The main functions of the Board are to carry out the decisions and policies of the Assembly, to advise it and to facilitate its work. The World Health Assembly's President is . The current chairman of the executive board is Dr. Assad Hafeez.

Regional offices

- Africa; HQ: Brazzaville, Republic of Congo
- Western Pacific; HQ: Manila, Philippines
- Eastern Mediterranean; HQ: Cairo, Egypt
- South East Asia; HQ: New Delhi, India
- Europe; HQ: Copenhagen, Denmark
- Americas; HQ: Washington D.C., USA

The regional divisions of WHO were created between 1949 and 1952, and are based on article 44 of the WHO's constitution, which allowed the WHO to "establish a [single] regional organization to meet the special needs of [each defined] area". Many decisions are made at regional level, including important discussions over WHO's budget, and in deciding the members of the next assembly, which are designated by the regions.

Each region has a Regional Committee, which generally meets once a year, normally in the autumn. Representatives attend from each member or associative member in each region, including those states that are not fully recognized. For example, Palestine attends meetings of the Eastern Mediterranean Regional office. Each region also has a regional office. Each Regional Office is headed by a Regional Director, who is elected by the Regional Committee. The Board must approve such appointments, although as of 2004, it had never over-ruled the preference of a regional committee. The exact role of the board in the process has been a subject of debate, but the practical effect has always been small. Since 1999, Regional Directors serve for a once-renewable five-year term, and typically take their position on 1 February.

Each Regional Committee of the WHO consists of all the Health Department heads, in all the governments of the countries that constitute the Region. Aside from electing the Regional Director, the Regional Committee is also in charge of setting the guidelines for the implementation, within the region, of the health and other policies adopted by the World Health Assembly. The Regional Committee also serves as a progress review board for the actions of WHO within the Region.

The Regional Director is effectively the head of WHO for his or her Region. The RD manages and/or supervises a staff of health and other experts at the regional offices and in specialized centres. The RD is also the direct supervising authority—concomitantly with the WHO Director-General—of all the heads of WHO country offices, known as WHO Representatives, within the Region.

Director-General

Directors-General of the WHO

Name and Nationality	Years of tenure
Tedros Adhanom	2017 – present
Margaret Chan	2007–2017
Anders Nordström*	2006–2007

Lee Jong-wook	2003–2006
Gro Harlem Brundtland	1998–2003
Hiroshi Nakajima	1988–1998
Halfdan T. Mahler	1973–1988
Marcolino Gomes Candau	1953–1973
Brock Chisholm	1948–1953

*Appointed acting Director-General following the death of Lee Jong-wook while in office

The head of the organization is the Director-General, elected by the World Health Assembly. The term lasts for 5 years, and Director-Generals are typically appointed in May, when the Assembly meets. The current Director-General is Dr. Tedros Adhanom Ghebreyesus, who was appointed on 1 July 2017.

Employees

The WHO employs 8,500 people in 147 countries. In support of the principle of a tobacco-free work environment, the WHO does not recruit cigarette smokers. The organization has previously instigated the Framework Convention on Tobacco Control in 2003.

Goodwill Ambassadors

The WHO operates "Goodwill Ambassadors"; members of the arts, sports, or other fields of public life aimed at drawing attention to WHO's initiatives and projects. There are currently five Goodwill Ambassadors (Jet Li, Nancy Brinker, Peng Liyuan, Yohei Sasakawa and the Vienna Philharmonic Orchestra) and a further ambassador associated with a partnership project (Craig David).

Country and liaison offices

The World Health Organization operates 147 country offices in all its regions. It also operates several liaison offices, including those with the European Union, United Nations and a single office covering the World Bank and International Monetary Fund. It also operates the International Agency for Research on Cancer in Lyon, France, and the WHO Centre for Health Development in Kobe, Japan. Additional offices include those in Pristina; the West Bank and Gaza; the US-Mexico Border Field Office in El Paso; the Office of the Caribbean Program Coordination in Barbados; and the Northern Micronesia office. There will generally be one WHO country office in the capital, occasionally accompanied by satellite-offices in the provinces or sub-regions of the country in question.

The country office is headed by a WHO Representative (WR). As of 2010, the only WHO Representative outside Europe to be a national of that country was for the Libyan Arab Jamahiriya ("Libya"); all other staff were international. WHO Representatives in the Region termed the Americas are referred to as PAHO/WHO Representatives. In Europe, WHO Representatives also serve as Head of Country Office, and are nationals with the exception of Serbia; there are also Heads of Country Office in Albania, the Russian Federation, Tajikistan, Turkey, and Uzbekistan. The WR is member of the UN system country team which is coordinated by the UN System Resident Coordinator.

The country office consists of the WR, and several health and other experts, both foreign and local, as well as the necessary support staff. The main functions of WHO country offices include being the primary adviser of that country's government in matters of health and pharmaceutical policies.

Financing and partnerships

The WHO is financed by contributions from member states and outside donors. As of 2012, the largest annual assessed contributions from member states came from the United States ($110 million), Japan ($58 million), Germany ($37 million), United Kingdom ($31 million) and France ($31 million). The combined 2012–2013 budget has proposed a total expenditure of $3,959 million, of which $944 million (24%) will come from assessed contributions. This represented a significant fall in outlay compared to the previous 2009–2010 budget, adjusting to take account of previous underspends. Assessed contributions were kept the same. Voluntary contributions will account for $3,015 million (76%), of which $800 million is regarded as highly or moderately flexible funding, with the remainder tied to particular programmes or objectives.

In recent years, the WHO's work has involved increasing collaboration with external bodies. As of 2002, a total of 473 non-governmental organizations (NGO) had some form of partnership with WHO. There were 189 partnerships with international NGOs in formal "official relations" – the rest being considered informal in character. Partners include the Bill and Melinda Gates Foundation and the Rockefeller Foundation.

CONTROVERSIES

IAEA - Agreement WHA 12-40

In 1959, the WHO signed Agreement WHA 12–40 with the International Atomic Energy Agency (IAEA). A reading of this document can result in the understanding that the IAEA is able to prevent the WHO from conducting research or work on some areas, as seen hereafter.

The agreement states that the WHO recognizes the IAEA as having responsibility for peaceful nuclear energy without prejudice to the roles of the WHO of promoting health. However, the following paragraph adds that "whenever either organization proposes to initiate a programme or activity on a subject in which the other organization has or may have a substantial interest, the first party shall consult the other with a view to adjusting the matter by mutual agreement".

The nature of this statement has led some pressure groups and activists (including Women in Europe for a Common Future) to claim that the WHO is restricted in its ability to investigate the effects on human health of radiation caused by the use of nuclear power and the continuing effects of nuclear disasters in Chernobyl and Fukushima. They believe WHO must regain what they see as "independence".

Roman Catholic Church and AIDS

In 2003, the WHO denounced the Roman Curia's health department's opposition to the use of condoms, saying: "These incorrect statements about condoms and HIV are dangerous when we are facing a global pandemic which has already killed more than 20 million people, and currently affects at least 42 million."

As of 2009, the Catholic Church remains opposed to increasing the use of contraception to combat HIV/AIDS. At the time, the World Health Assembly President, Guyana's Health Minister Leslie Ramsammy, has condemned Pope Benedict's opposition to contraception, saying he was trying to "create confusion" and "impede" proven strategies in the battle against the disease.

Intermittent preventive therapy

The aggressive support of the Bill & Melinda Gates Foundation for intermittent preventive therapy of malaria triggered a memo from the former WHO malaria chief Akira Kochi.

Diet and sugar intake

Some of the research undertaken or supported by WHO to determine how people's lifestyles and environments are influencing whether they live in better or worse health can be controversial, as illustrated by a 2003 joint WHO/FAO report on nutrition and the prevention of chronic non-communicable disease, which recommended that sugar should form no more than 10% of a healthy diet. The report led to lobbying by the sugar industry against the recommendation, to which the WHO/FAO responded by including in the report this statement: "The Consultation recognized that a population goal for free sugars of less than 10% of total energy is controversial". It also stood by its recommendation based upon its own analysis of scientific studies. In 2014, WHO reduced recommended sugar levels by half and said that sugar should make up no more than 5% of a healthy diet.

2009 swine flu pandemic

In 2007, the WHO organized work on pandemic influenza vaccine development through clinical trials in collaboration with many experts and health officials. A pandemic involving the H1N1 influenza virus was declared by the then Director-General Margaret Chan in April 2009. Margret Chan declared in 2010 that the H1N1 has moved into the post-pandemic period.

By the post-pandemic period critics claimed the WHO had exaggerated the danger, spreading "fear and confusion" rather than "immediate information". Industry experts countered that the 2009 pandemic had led to "unprecedented collaboration between global health authorities, scientists and manufacturers, resulting in the most comprehensive pandemic response ever undertaken, with a number of vaccines approved for use three months after the pandemic declaration. This response was only possible because of the extensive preparations undertaken during the last decade".

2013–2016 Ebola outbreak and reform efforts

Following the 2014 Ebola outbreak in West Africa, the organization was heavily criticized for its bureaucracy, insufficient financing, regional structure, and staffing profile.

An internal WHO report on the Ebola response pointed to underfunding and the lack of "core capacity" in health systems in developing countries as the primary weaknesses of the existing system. At the annual World Health Assembly in 2015, Director-General Margaret Chan announced a $100 million Contingency Fund for rapid response to future emergencies, of which it had received $26.9 million by April 2016 (for 2017 disbursement). WHO has budgeted an additional $494 million for its Health Emergencies Programme in 2016–17, for which it had received $140 million by April 2016.

The program was aimed at rebuilding WHO capacity for direct action, which critics said had been lost due to budget cuts in the previous decade that had left the organization in an advisory role dependent on member states for on-the-ground activities. In comparison, billions of dollars have been spent by developed countries on the 2013–2016 Ebola epidemic and 2015–16 Zika epidemic.

FCTC implementation database

The WHO has a Framework Convention on Tobacco implementation database which is one of the only mechanisms to help enforce compliance with the FCTC. However, there have been reports of numerous discrepancies between it and national implementation reports on which it was built. As researchers Hoffman and Rizvi report "As of July 4, 2012, 361 (32·7%) of 1104 countries' responses were misreported: 33 (3·0%) were clear errors (eg, database indicated "yes" when report indicated "no"), 270 (24·5%) were missing despite countries having submitted responses, and 58 (5·3%) were, in our opinion, misinterpreted by WHO staff".

IARC controversies

The World Health Organization sub-department, the International Agency for Research on Cancer (IARC), has been criticized for the way it analyses the tendency of certain substances and activities to cause cancer and for having a politically motivated bias when it selects studies for its analysis. Ed Yong, a British science journalist, has criticized the agency and its "confusing" category system for misleading the public. Marcel Kuntz, a French director of research at the French National Centre for Scientific Research, criticized the agency for its classification of potentially carcinogenic substances. He claimed that this classification did not take into account the extent of exposure: for example, red meat is qualified as probably carcinogenic, but the quantity of consumed red meat at which it could become dangerous is not specified.

Controversies have erupted multiple times when the IARC has classified many things as Class 2a (probable carcinogens), including cell phone signals, glyphosate, drinking hot beverages, and working as a barber.

Block of Taiwanese participation

Political pressure from China has led to Taiwan being barred from membership of the WHO and other UN-affiliated organizations, and in both 2017 and 2018 the WHO refused to allow Taiwanese delegates to attend the WHO annual assembly. On multiple occasions Taiwanese journalists have been denied access to report on the assembly. In May 2018, 172 members of the United States House of Representatives wrote to the Director General of the World Health Organization to argue for Taiwan's inclusion as an observer at the WHA.

Travel expenses

According to The Associated Press, the WHO routinely spends about $200 million a year on travel expenses, more than it spends to tackle mental health problems, HIV/AIDS, Tuberculosis and Malaria combined. In 2016, Margaret Chan, Director-General of WHO from November 2006 to June 2017, stayed in a $1000 per night hotel room while visiting West Africa.

Robert Mugabe's role as a goodwill ambassador

In 21 October 2017, the Director General Tedros Adhanom Ghebreyesus appointed former Zimbabwean president Robert Mugabe as a WHO Goodwill Ambassador to help promote the fight against non-communicable diseases. The appointment address praised Mugabe for his commitment to public health in Zimbabwe. The appointment attracted widespread condemnation and criticism in WHO member states and international organizations due to Robert Mugabe's poor record on human rights and presiding over a decline in Zimbabwe's public health.

WORLD HEADQUARTERS

The seat of the organization is in Geneva, Switzerland. It was designed by Swiss architect Jean Tschumi and inaugurated in 1966. In 2017, the organization launched an international competition to redesign and extend its headquarters.

3

European Union (EU)

The European Union (EU) is a political and economic union of 28 member states that are located primarily in Europe. It has an area of 4,475,757 km (1,728,099 sq mi) and an estimated population of over 510 million. The EU has developed an internal single market through a standardised system of laws that apply in all member states. EU policies aim to ensure the free movement of people, goods, services and capital within the internal market, enact legislation in justice and home affairs and maintain common policies on trade, agriculture, fisheries and regional development. For travel within the Schengen Area, passport controls have been abolished. A monetary union was established in 1999 and came into full force in 2002 and is composed of 19 EU member states which use the euro currency.

The EU traces its origins to the European Coal and Steel Community (ECSC) and the European Economic Community (EEC), established, respectively, by the 1951 Treaty of Paris and 1957 Treaty of Rome. The original members of what came to be known as the European Communities were the Inner Six: Belgium, France, Italy, Luxembourg, the Netherlands, and West Germany. The Communities and its successors have grown in size by the accession of new member states and in power by the addition of policy areas to its remit. While no member state has left the EU or its predecessors, the United Kingdom signified an intention to leave after a membership referendum in June 2016 and is negotiating its withdrawal. The Maastricht

Treatyestablished the European Union in 1993 and introduced European citizenship. The latest major amendment to the constitutional basis of the EU, the Treaty of Lisbon, came into force in 2009.

The European Union provides more foreign aid than any other economic union. Covering 7.3% of the world population,the EU in 2017 generated a nominal gross domestic product (GDP) of 19.670 trillion US dollars, constituting approximately 24.6% of global nominal GDP and 16.5% when measured in terms of purchasing power parity. Additionally, 27 out of 28 EU countries have a very high Human Development Index, according to the United Nations Development Programme. In 2012, the EU was awarded the Nobel Peace Prize. Through the Common Foreign and Security Policy, the EU has developed a role in external relations and defence. The union maintains permanent diplomatic missions throughout the world and represents itself at the United Nations, the World Trade Organization, the G7 and the G20. Because of its global influence, the European Union has been described as an emerging superpower.

HISTORY

Background

During the centuries following the fall of Rome in 476, several European States viewed themselves as *translatio imperii* of the defunct Roman Empire: the Frankish Empire(481–843) and the Holy Roman Empire (962–1806) were attempts to resurrect Rome in the West. The Russian Tsardom, and ultimately the Empire (1547–1917), declared Moscow to be Third Rome and inheritor of the Eastern tradition after the fall of Constantinople in 1453. The gap between Greek East and Latin West had already been widened by the political scission of the Roman Empire in the 4th century and the Great Schism of 1054; and would be eventually widened again by the Iron Curtain (1945–91).

Medieval Christendom and the political power of the Papacy are also often cited as premisses to European integration and unity. Pan-European political thought truly emerged during the 19th century, inspired by the liberal ideas of the French and American Revolutions after the demise of Napoléon's Empire (1804–15). In the decades following the outcomes of the Congress of Vienna, ideals of European unity flourished across the continent, especially in the writings of Wojciech Jastrzêbowski,Giuseppe Mazzini or Theodore de Korwin Szymanowski. The term *United States of Europe* (French: *États-Unis d'Europe*) was used at that time by Victor Hugo during a speech at the International Peace Congress held in Paris in 1849:

A day will come when all nations on our continent will form a European brotherhood ... A day will come when we shall see ... the United States of America and the United States of Europe face to face, reaching out for each other across the seas.

During the interwar period, the consciousness that national markets in Europe were interdependent though confrontational, along with the observation of a larger and growing US market on the other side of the ocean, nourished the urge for the economic integration of the continent. In 1920, advocating the creation of a European economic union, British economist John Maynard Keynes wrote that "a Free Trade Union should be established ... to impose no protectionist tariffs whatever against the produce of other members of the Union."During the same decade, Richard von Coudenhove-Kalergi, one of the first to imagine of a modern political union of Europe, founded the Pan-Europa Movement. His ideas influenced his contemporaries, among which then Prime Minister of France Aristide Briand. In 1929, the latter gave a speech in favour of a European Union before the assembly of the League of Nations, precursor of the United Nations.

Preliminary (1945–57)

After World War II, European integration was seen as an antidote to the extreme nationalism which had devastated the continent. In a speech delivered on 19 September 1946 at the University of Zürich, Switzerland, Winston Churchill postulated the emerging of a United States of Europe during the 20th century. The 1948 Hague Congress was a pivotal moment in European federal history, as it led to the creation of the European Movement International and of the College of Europe, where Europe's future leaders would live and study together. 1952 saw the creation of the European Coal and Steel Community, which was declared to be "a first step in the federation of Europe." The supporters of the Community included Alcide De Gasperi, Jean Monnet, Robert Schuman, and Paul-Henri Spaak. These men and others are officially credited as the Founding fathers of the European Union.

Treaty of Rome (1957–92)

In 1957, Belgium, France, Italy, Luxembourg, the Netherlands, and West Germany signed the Treaty of Rome, which created the European Economic Community (EEC) and established a customs union. They also signed another pact creating the European Atomic Energy Community (Euratom) for co-operation in developing nuclear energy. Both treaties came into force in 1958.

The EEC and Euratom were created separately from the ECSC, although they shared the same courts and the Common Assembly. The EEC was headed by Walter Hallstein (Hallstein Commission) and Euratom was headed by Louis Armand (Armand Commission) and then Étienne Hirsch. Euratom was to integrate sectors in nuclear energy while the EEC would develop a customs union among members.

During the 1960s, tensions began to show, with France seeking to limit supranational power. Nevertheless, in 1965 an agreement was reached and on 1 July 1967 the Merger Treaty created a single set of institutions for the three communities, which were collectively referred to as the *European Communities.* Jean Rey presided over the first merged Commission (Rey Commission).

In 1973, the Communities were enlarged to include Denmark (including Greenland, which later left the Communities in 1985, following a dispute over fishing rights), Ireland, and the

United Kingdom. Norway had negotiated to join at the same time, but Norwegian voters rejected membership in a referendum. In 1979, the first direct elections to the European Parliament were held.

Greece joined in 1981, Portugal and Spain following in 1986. In 1985, the Schengen Agreement paved the way for the creation of open borders without passport controls between most member states and some non-member states. In 1986, the European flag began to be used by the EEC and the Single European Act was signed.

In 1990, after the fall of the Eastern Bloc, the former East Germany became part of the Communities as part of a reunified Germany. A close fiscal integration with the introduction of the euro was not matched by institutional oversight making things more troubling. Attempts to solve the problems and to make the EU more efficient and coherent had limited success. With further enlargement planned to include the former communist states of Central and Eastern Europe, as well as Cyprus and Malta, the Copenhagen criteria for candidate members to join the EU were agreed upon in June 1993. The expansion of the EU introduced a new level of complexity and discord.

Maastricht Treaty (1992–2007)

The European Union was formally established when the Maastricht Treaty—whose main architects were Helmut Kohl and François Mitterrand—came into force on 1 November 1993. The treaty also gave the name European Community to the EEC, even if it was referred as such before the treaty. In 1995, Austria, Finland, and Sweden joined the EU.

In 2002, euro banknotes and coins replaced national currencies in 12 of the member states. Since then, the eurozone has increased to encompass 19 countries. The euro currency became the second largest reserve currency in the world. In 2004, the EU saw its biggest enlargement to date when Cyprus, the Czech Republic, Estonia, Hungary, Latvia, Lithuania, Malta, Poland, Slovakia, and Slovenia joined the Union.

Lisbon Treaty (2007–present)

In 2007, Bulgaria and Romania became EU members. The same year, Slovenia adopted the euro, followed in 2008 by Cyprus and Malta, by Slovakia in 2009, by Estonia in 2011, by Latvia in 2014, and by Lithuania in 2015.

On 1 December 2009, the Lisbon Treaty entered into force and reformed many aspects of the EU. In particular, it changed the legal structure of the European Union, merging the EU three pillars system into a single legal entity provisioned with a legal personality, created a permanent President of the European Council, the first of which was Herman Van Rompuy, and strengthened the position of the High Representative of the Union for Foreign Affairs and Security Policy.

In 2012, the EU received the Nobel Peace Prize for having "contributed to the advancement of peace and reconciliation, democracy, and human rights in Europe." In 2013, Croatia became the 28th EU member.

From the beginning of the 2010s, the cohesion of the European Union has been tested by several issues, including a debt crisis in some of the Eurozone countries, increasing migration from the Middle East, and the United Kingdom's withdrawal from the EU. A referendum in the UK on its membership of the European Union was held in 2016, with 51.9% of participants voting to leave. The UK formally notified the European Council of its decision to leave on 29 March 2017 initiating the formal withdrawal procedure for leaving the EU, committing the UK to leave the EU on 29 March 2019.

POLITICS

The European Union operates according to the principles of conferral (which says that it should act only within the limits of the competences conferred on it by the treaties) and of subsidiarity (which says that it should act only where an objective cannot be sufficiently achieved by the member states acting alone). Laws made by the EU institutions are passed in a variety of forms. Generally speaking, they can be classified into two groups: those which come into force without the necessity for national implementation measures (regulations) and those which specifically require national implementation measures (directives).

Member states

Through successive enlargements, the European Union has grown from the six founding states (Belgium, France, West Germany, Italy, Luxembourg, and the Netherlands) to the current 28. Countries accede to the union by becoming party to the founding treaties, thereby subjecting themselves to the privileges and obligations of EU membership. This entails a partial delegation of sovereignty to the institutions in return for representation within those institutions, a practice often referred to as "pooling of sovereignty".

To become a member, a country must meet the Copenhagen criteria, defined at the 1993 meeting of the European Council in Copenhagen. These require a stable democracy that respects human rights and the rule of law; a functioning market economy; and the acceptance of the obligations of membership, including EU law. Evaluation of a country's fulfilment of the criteria is the responsibility of the European Council. No member state has yet left the Union, although Greenland (an autonomous province of Denmark) withdrew in 1985. The Lisbon Treaty now contains a clause under Article 50, providing for a member to leave the EU.

There are six countries that are recognised as candidates for membership: Albania, Iceland, Macedonia, Montenegro, Serbia, and Turkey, though Iceland suspended negotiations in 2013. Bosnia and Herzegovina and Kosovo are officially recognised as potential candidates, with Bosnia and Herzegovina having submitted a membership application.

The four countries forming the European Free Trade Association (EFTA) are not EU members, but have partly committed to the EU's economy and regulations: Iceland,

Liechtensteinand Norway, which are a part of the single market through the European Economic Area, and Switzerland, which has similar ties through bilateral treaties. The relationships of the European microstates, Andorra, Monaco, San Marino, and the Vatican include the use of the euro and other areas of co-operation. The following 28 sovereign states (of which the map only shows territories situated in and around Europe) constitute the European Union:

Institutions

The EU operates through a hybrid system of supranational and intergovernmental decision-making.

EU policy is in general promulgated by EU directives, which are then implemented in the domestic legislation of its member states, and EU regulations, which are immediately enforceable in all member states. The EU's seven principal decision making bodies—known as the Institutions of the European Union are:

- the European Council, which sets the *general political directions* and *priorities* of the Union by gathering together its member states' heads of state/government (elected chief executives). The conclusions of its summits (held at least quarterly) are adopted by consensus.
- the European Commission, the "Guardian of the Treaties" consists of an executive cabinet of public officials, led by an indirectly elected President. This *College of Commissioners* manages and directs the Commission's permanent civil service. It turns the consensus objectives of the European Council into legislative proposals.
- the Council of the European Union is an executive meeting of ministers of member states governments' departments, which meets to amend, approve or reject proposed legislation from the Commission. It forms the *upper house* of the EU's essentially bicameral legislature. Its approval is required for any proposal to enter into law.

- the European Parliament consists of 751 directly elected representatives, forming the EU's *lower house* of its bicameral legislature. It shares with the Council of the EU equal legislative powers to amend, approve or reject Commission proposals for most areas of EU legislation. Its powers are limited in areas where member states' view sovereignty to be of primary concern (i.e. defence). It elects the Commission's President, must approve the College of Commissioners, and may vote to remove them collectively from office.
- the Court of Justice of the European Union ensures the uniform application of EU law and resolves disputes between EU institutions and member states, and against EU institutions on behalf of individuals.
- the European Central Bank is responsible for monetary stability within member states.
- the European Court of Auditors investigates the proper management of finances within both the EU entities and EU funding provided to its member states. As well as providing oversight and advice, it can refer unresolved issues to the European Court of Justice to arbitrate on any alleged irregularities.

LEGAL SYSTEM

The EU is based on a series of treaties. These first established the European Community and the EU, and then made amendments to those founding treaties. These are power-giving treaties which set broad policy goals and establish institutions with the necessary legal powers to implement those goals. These legal powers include the ability to enact legislation which can directly affect all member states and their inhabitants. The EU has legal personality, with the right to sign agreements and international treaties.

Under the principle of supremacy, national courts are required to enforce the treaties that their member states have ratified, and thus the laws enacted under them, even if doing so requires them to ignore conflicting national law, and (within limits) even constitutional provisions.

Courts of Justice

The judicial branch of the EU—formally called the Court of Justice of the European Union—consists of two courts: the Court of Justice and the General Court

The Court of Justice primarily deals with cases taken by member states, the institutions, and cases referred to it by the courts of member states. The General Court mainly deals with cases taken by individuals and companies directly before the EU's courts, and the European Union Civil Service Tribunal adjudicates in disputes between the European Union and its civil service. Decisions from the General Court can be appealed to the Court of Justice but only on a point of law.

Fundamental rights

The treaties declare that the EU itself is "founded on the values of respect for human dignity, freedom, democracy, equality, the rule of law and respect for human rights, including the rights of persons belonging to minorities ... in a society in which pluralism, non-discrimination, tolerance, justice, solidarity and equality between women and men prevail."

In 2009, the Lisbon Treaty gave legal effect to the Charter of Fundamental Rights of the European Union. The charter is a codified catalogue of fundamental rights against which the EU's legal acts can be judged. It consolidates many rights which were previously recognised by the Court of Justice and derived from the "constitutional traditions common to the member states." The Court of Justice has long recognised fundamental rights and has, on occasion, invalidated EU legislation based on its failure to adhere to those fundamental rights.

Although signing the European Convention on Human Rights (ECHR) is a condition for EU membership, previously, the EU itself could not accede to the Convention as it is neither a state nor had the competence to accede. The Lisbon Treaty and Protocol 14 to the ECHR have changed this: the former binds the EU to accede to the Convention while the latter formally permits it.

Although, the EU is independent from Council of Europe, they share purpose and ideas especially on rule of law, human rights and democracy. Further European Convention on Human Rights and European Social Charter, the source of law of Charter of Fundamental Rights are created by Council of Europe. The EU also promoted human rights issues in the wider world. The EU opposes the death penalty and has proposed its worldwide abolition. Abolition of the death penalty is a condition for EU membership.

Acts

The main legal acts of the EU come in three forms: regulations, directives, and decisions. Regulations become law in all member states the moment they come into force, without the requirement for any implementing measures, and automatically override conflicting domestic provisions. Directives require member states to achieve a certain result while leaving them discretion as to how to achieve the result. The details of how they are to be implemented are left to member states. When the time limit for implementing directives passes, they may, under certain conditions, have direct effect in national law against member states.

Decisions offer an alternative to the two above modes of legislation. They are legal acts which only apply to specified individuals, companies or a particular member state. They are most often used in competition law, or on rulings on State Aid, but are also frequently used for procedural or administrative matters within the institutions. Regulations, directives, and decisions are of equal legal value and apply without any formal hierarchy.

Area of freedom, security and justice

Since the creation of the EU in 1993, it has developed its competencies in the area of freedom, security and justice, initially at an intergovernmental level and later by supranationalism. To this end, agencies have been established that co-ordinate associated actions: Europol for co-operation of police forces, Eurojust for co-operation between prosecutors, and Frontex for co-operation between border control authorities. The EU also operates the Schengen Information System which provides a common database for police and immigration authorities. This co-operation had to particularly be developed with the advent of open borders through the Schengen Agreement and the associated cross border crime. Furthermore, the Union has legislated in areas such as extradition, family law, asylum law, and criminal justice. Prohibitions against sexual and nationality discrimination have a long standing in the treaties. In more recent years, these have been supplemented by powers to legislate against discrimination based on race, religion, disability, age, and sexual orientation. By virtue of these powers, the EU has enacted legislation on sexual discrimination in the work-place, age discrimination, and racial discrimination.

FOREIGN RELATIONS

Foreign policy co-operation between member states dates from the establishment of the Community in 1957, when member states negotiated as a bloc in international trade negotiations under the EU's common commercial policy. Steps for a more wide-ranging co-ordination in foreign relations began in 1970 with the establishment of European Political Cooperation which created an informal consultation process between member states with the aim of forming common foreign policies. It was not, however, until 1987 when European Political Cooperation was introduced on a formal basis by the Single European Act. EPC was renamed as the Common Foreign and Security Policy (CFSP) by the Maastricht Treaty.

The aims of the CFSP are to promote both the EU's own interests and those of the international community as a whole, including the furtherance of international co-operation, respect for human rights, democracy, and the rule of law. The CFSP requires unanimity among the member states on the appropriate policy to follow on any particular issue. The unanimity and difficult issues treated under the CFSP sometimes lead to disagreements, such as those which occurred over the war in Iraq.

The coordinator and representative of the CFSP within the EU is the High Representative of the Union for Foreign Affairs and Security Policy who speaks on behalf of the EU in foreign policy and defence matters, and has the task of articulating the positions expressed by the member states on these fields of policy into a common alignment. The High Representative heads up the European External Action Service (EEAS), a unique EU department that has been officially implemented and operational since 1 December 2010 on the occasion of the first anniversary of the entry into force of the Treaty of Lisbon. The EEAS will serve as a foreign ministry and diplomatic corps for the European Union.

Donald Tusk and Jean-Claude Juncker with U.S. President Donald Trump, 2017

Besides the emerging international policy of the European Union, the international influence of the EU is also felt through enlargement. The perceived benefits of becoming a member of the EU act as an incentive for both political and economic reform in states wishing to fulfil the EU's accession criteria, and are considered an important factor contributing to the reform of European formerly Communist countries. This influence on the internal affairs of other countries is generally referred to as "soft power", as opposed to military "hard power".

The European Union has concluded free trade agreements (FTAs) and other agreements with a trade component with many countries worldwide and is negotiating with many others.

Defence

The predecessors of the European Union were not devised as a military alliance because NATO was largely seen as appropriate and sufficient for defence purposes. 22 EU members are members of NATO while the remaining member states follow policies of neutrality. The Western European Union, a military alliance with a mutual defence clause, was disbanded in 2010 as its role had been transferred to the EU.

According to the Stockholm International Peace Research Institute (SIPRI), the United Kingdom spent $61 billion on defence in 2014, placing it fifth in the world, while France spent $53 billion, the sixth largest. Together, the UK and France account for approximately 40 per cent of European countries' defence budget and 50 per cent of their military capacity. Both are officially recognised nuclear weapon statesholding permanent seats on the United Nations Security Council.

Following the Kosovo War in 1999, the European Council agreed that "the Union must have the capacity for autonomous action, backed by credible military forces, the means to decide to use them, and the readiness to do so, in order to respond to international crises without prejudice to actions by NATO". To that end, a number of efforts were made to increase the EU's military capability, notably the Helsinki Headline Goal process. After much discussion, the most concrete result was the EU Battlegroups initiative, each of which is planned to be able to deploy quickly about 1500 personnel.

EU forces have been deployed on peacekeeping missions from middle and northern Africa to the western Balkans and western Asia. EU military operations are supported by a number of bodies, including the European Defence Agency, European

Union Satellite Centre and the European Union Military Staff. Frontex is an agency of the EU established to manage the cooperation between national border guards securing its external borders. It aims to detect and stop illegal immigration, human trafficking and terrorist infiltration. In 2015 the European Commission presented its proposal for a new European Border and Coast Guard Agency having a stronger role and mandate along with national authorities for border management. In an EU consisting of 28 members, substantial security and defence co-operation is increasingly relying on collaboration among all member states.

Humanitarian aid

The European Commission's Humanitarian Aid and Civil Protection department, or "ECHO", provides humanitarian aid from the EU to developing countries. In 2012, its budget amounted to €874 million, 51% of the budget went to Africa and 20% to Asia, Latin America, the Caribbean and Pacific, and 20% to the Middle East and Mediterranean.

Humanitarian aid is financed directly by the budget (70%) as part of the financial instruments for external action and also by the European Development Fund (30%). The EU's external action financing is divided into 'geographic' instruments and 'thematic' instruments. The 'geographic' instruments provide aid through the Development Cooperation Instrument (DCI, €16.9 billion, 2007–2013), which must spend 95% of its budget on official development assistance (ODA), and from the European Neighbourhood and Partnership Instrument (ENPI), which contains some relevant programmes. The European Development Fund (EDF, €22.7 bn, 2008–2013) is made up of voluntary contributions by member states, but there is pressure to merge the EDF into the budget-financed instruments to encourage increased contributions to match the 0.7% target and allow the European Parliament greater oversight.

In 2016, the average among EU countries was 0.4% and five had met or exceeded the 0.7% target: Denmark, Germany, Luxembourg, Sweden and the United Kingdom.

4

Shanghai Cooperation Organisation (SCO)

The Shanghai Cooperation Organisation (SCO), or Shanghai Pact, is a Eurasian political, economic, and security alliance, the creation of which was announced on 15 June 2001 in Shanghai, China by the leaders of China, Kazakhstan, Kyrgyzstan, Russia, Tajikistan, and Uzbekistan; the Shanghai Cooperation Organisation Charter, formally establishing the organisation, was signed in June 2002 and entered into force on 19 September 2003. The Heads of State Council (HSC) is the supreme decision-making body in the SCO, it meets once a year and adopts decisions and guidelines on all important matters of the organisation. Military exercises among members are also regularly conducted to promote coordination against terrorism, and to maintain regional peace and stability. The original six nations, with the exception of Uzbekistan, were previously members of the Shanghai Five group, founded on 26 April 1996. India and Pakistan joined SCO as full members on 9 June 2017 at a summit in Astana, Kazakhstan. The SCO is often dubbed as the "alliance of Asia", due to its growing centrality in the Asian continent, and has been the primary security pillar of the region. Being the world's forefront regional organisation in economic power and political influence, and one of the world's strongest military alliances, it is also the largest regional organisation in the world in terms of geographical coverage and population, covering three-fifths of the Eurasian continent and nearly half of the human population. At present, the SCO is one of the world's most powerful and influential organisations.

With the growing power and enlargement of the organisation, its scope of unity and cooperation has expanded to many other areas, including education, science, technology, health care, environmental protection, tourism, media, sports, humanitarian and culture.The organisation has also expanded its principle to include global governance and fostering of international relationships, in relation to its vast influence on the global stage. It has been a major partner of ASEAN, with both of the organisations establishing cooperation model in the field of security, economy, finance, tourism, culture, environmental protection, development and sustainability.

ORIGINS

The Shanghai Five grouping was created 26 April 1996 with the signing of the *Treaty on Deepening Military Trust in Border Regions* in Shanghai, China by the heads of states of China, Kazakhstan, Kyrgyzstan, Russia and Tajikistan.

Russian President Vladimir Putin, Kazakh President Nursultan Nazarbayev, Chinese President Jiang Zemin, Kyrgyz President Askar Akayev, and Tajik President Emomali Rahmon, at one time the leaders of the Shanghai Five.

On 24 April 1997, the same countries signed the *Treaty on Reduction of Military Forces in Border Regions* in a meeting in Moscow, Russia. On 20 May 1997, President of Russia Boris Yeltsin and prime minister of China Jiang Zemin signed a declaration on a "multipolar world".

Subsequent annual summits of the Shanghai Five group occurred in Almaty, Kazakhstan in 1998, in Bishkek, Kyrgyzstan in 1999, and in Dushanbe, Tajikistan in 2000. At the Dushanbe summit, members agreed to "oppose intervention in other countries' internal affairs on the pretexts of 'humanitarianism' and 'protecting human rights;' and support the efforts of one another in safeguarding the five countries' national independence, sovereignty, territorial integrity, and social stability."

In 2001, the annual summit returned to Shanghai. There the five member nations first admitted Uzbekistan in the Shanghai Five mechanism (thus transforming it into the Shanghai Six). Then all six heads of state signed on 15 June 2001 the *Declaration of Shanghai Cooperation Organisation*, praising the role played thus far by the Shanghai Five mechanism and aiming to transform it to a higher level of cooperation.

In June 2002, the heads of the SCO member states met in Saint Petersburg, Russia. There they signed the *SCO Charter* which expounded on the organisation's purposes, principles, structures and forms of operation, and established it in international law.

In July 2005, at the summit in Astana, Kazakhstan, with representatives of India, Iran, Mongolia and Pakistan attending a SCO summit for the first time, the president of the host country, Nursultan Nazarbayev, greeted the guests in words that had never been used before in any context: "The leaders of the states sitting at this negotiation table are representatives of half of humanity".

By 2007 the SCO had initiated over twenty large-scale projects related to transportation, energy and telecommunications and held regular meetings of security, military, defence, foreign affairs, economic, cultural, banking and other officials from its member states.

In July 2015 in Ufa, Russia, the SCO decided to admit India and Pakistan as full members. Both signed the memorandum of obligations in June 2016 in Tashkent, Uzbekistan, thereby starting the formal process of joining the SCO as full members. On 9 June 2017, at a summit in Astana, India and Pakistan officially joined SCO as full-fledged members.

The SCO has established relations with the United Nations in 2004 (where it is an observer in the General Assembly), Commonwealth of Independent States in 2005, Association of Southeast Asian Nations (ASEAN) in 2005, the Collective Security Treaty Organization in 2007, the Economic Cooperation Organization in 2007, the United Nations Office on Drugs and Crime in 2011, the Conference on Interaction and Confidence-Building Measures in Asia (CICA) in 2014, and the United Nations Economic and Social Commission for Asia and the Pacific in 2015.

In 2017, SCO's eight full members account for approximately half of the world's population, a quarter of the world's GDP, and about 80% of Eurasia's landmass.

ORGANISATIONAL STRUCTURE

- Almazbek Atambayev (Kyrgyzstan)
- Emomalii Rahmon (Tajikistan)
- Shavkat Mirziyoyev (Uzbekistan)
- Xi Jinping (China)
- Nursultan Nazarbayev (Kazakhstan)
- Vladimir Putin (Russia)
- Ram Nath Kovind (India)
- Mamnoon Hussain (Pakistan)

The Council of Heads of Government is the second-highest council in the organisation. This council also holds annual summits, at which time members discuss issues of multilateral cooperation. The council also approves the organisation's budget. The current Council of Heads of Government consists of:

- Sooronbay Jeenbekov (Kyrgyzstan)
- Kokhir Rasulzoda (Tajikistan)
- Abdulla Aripov (Uzbekistan)
- Li Keqiang (China)
- Bakhytzhan Sagintayev (Kazakhstan)
- Dmitry Medvedev (Russia)
- Narendra Modi (India)
- Nasirul Mulk (Pakistan)

The Council of Foreign Ministers also hold regular meetings, where they discuss the current international situation and the SCO's interaction with other international organisations.

The Council of National Coordinators coordinates the multilateral cooperation of member states within the framework of the SCO's charter.

The Secretariat of the SCO is the primary executive body of the organisation.

It serves to implement organisational decisions and decrees, drafts proposed documents (such as declarations and agendas), function as a document depository for the organisation, arranges specific activities within the SCO framework, and promotes and disseminates information about the SCO. It is located in Beijing.

The current SCO Secretary-General is Rashid Alimov of Tajikistan, appointed to the office of Shanghai Cooperation Organisation Secretary-General on January 2016.

The Regional Anti-Terrorist Structure (RATS), headquartered in Tashkent, Uzbekistan, is a permanent organ of the SCO which serves to promote cooperation of member states against the three evils of terrorism, separatism and extremism. The Head of RATS is elected to a three-year term. Each member state also sends a permanent representative to RATS.

The official working languages of the Shanghai Cooperation Organisation are Chinese and Russian.

MEMBERSHIP

Member states

Date	Country
26 April 1996	China
	Kazakhstan
	Kyrgyzstan
	Russia
	Tajikistan
15 June 2001	Uzbekistan
9 June 2017	India
	Pakistan

Observer states

Putin with representatives from Iran and Mongolia, observers in the SCO, at a meeting of the Council of Heads of Government in 2005.

- Afghanistan: Afghanistan received observer status at the 2012 SCO summit in Beijing, China on 6 June 2012.
- Belarus: In 2008, Belarus applied for partner status in the organisation and was promised Kazakhstan's support towards that goal. However, Russian Defence Minister Sergei Ivanov voiced doubt on the probability of Belarus' membership, saying that Belarus was a purely European country. Despite this, Belarus was accepted as a Dialogue Partner at the 2009 SCO Summit in Yekaterinburg, and

after applying in 2012, was granted observer status in 2015.

- Iran: Iran has observer status in the organisation, and applied for full membership on 24 March 2008. However, because it was under sanctions levied by the United Nations at the time, it was blocked from admission as a new member. The SCO stated that any country under UN sanctions could not be admitted. After the UN sanctions were lifted, Chinese president Xi Jinping announced its support for Iran's full membership in SCO during a state visit to Iran in January 2016.
- Mongolia: Mongolia became the first country to receive observer status at the 2004 Tashkent Summit. Pakistan, India and Iran received observer status at the 2005 SCO summit in Astana, Kazakhstan on 5 July 2005.

Dialogue partners

The position of Dialogue Partner was created in 2008.

- Armenia
- Azerbaijan
- Cambodia
- Nepal

Nepal was granted dialogue partner status in the Shanghai Cooperation Organisation (SCO) at the group's 2015 summit in Ufa, Russia.

- Sri LankaL Sri Lanka was granted dialogue partner status in the Shanghai Cooperation Organisation (SCO) at the group's 2009 summit in Yekaterinburg.
- Turkey: Turkey, a member of NATO, was granted dialogue partner status in the Shanghai Cooperation Organisation (SCO) at the group's 2012 summit in Beijing. Turkish Prime Minister Recep Tayyip Erdoðan has stated that he has discussed the possibility of abandoning Turkey's European Union membership candidacy in return for full membership in the Shanghai Cooperation Organization. This was reinforced again on

21 November 2016, after the European Parliament voted unanimously to suspend accession negotiations with Turkey.Two days later, on 23 November 2016, Turkey was granted the chairmanship of the energy club of SCO for the 2017 period. That made Turkey the first country to chair a club in the organisation without full membership status.

Future membership possibilities

In June 2010, the SCO approved the procedure of admitting new members, though new members have yet to be admitted. Several states, however, participate as observers, some of whom have expressed interest in becoming full members in the future. The implications of Iran joining the organization has been given much thought academically. In early September 2013 Armenian Prime Minister Tigran Sargsyan said during his meeting with his Chinese counterpart that Armenia would like to obtain an observer status in the SCO.

Meanwhile, in 2012 Armenia, Azerbaijan, Bangladesh, Nepal and Sri Lanka applied for observer status within the organization. Egypt and Syria have also submitted applications for observer status, while Israel, Maldives and Ukraine have applied for dialogue partner status. Iraq also signaled its interest in becoming a Dialogue Partner of the SCO in 2017 during the visit to SCO headquarters in Beijing of Mr. Ahmed Tahseen Birwari, the Iraqi ambassador. Bahrain and Qatar have also expressed interest in joining SCO.

ACTIVITIES

Cooperation on security

The SCO is primarily centered on its member nations' Central Asian security-related concerns, often describing the main threats it confronts as being terrorism, separatism and extremism. However evidence is growing that its activities in the area of social development of its member states is increasing fast.

At 16–17 June 2004 SCO summit, held in Tashkent, Uzbekistan, the Regional Antiterrorism Structure (RATS) was established. On 21 April 2006, the SCO announced plans to fight cross-border drug crimes under the counter-terrorism rubric.

In October 2007, the SCO signed an agreement with the Collective Security Treaty Organization (CSTO), in the Tajik capital Dushanbe, to broaden cooperation on issues such as security, crime, and drug trafficking. Joint action plans between the two organisations are planned to be signed by early 2008 in Beijing.

The organisation is also redefining cyberwarfare, saying that the dissemination of information "harmful to the spiritual, moral and cultural spheres of other states" should be considered a "security threat". An accord adopted in 2009 defined "information war", in part, as an effort by a state to undermine another's "political, economic, and social systems". *The Diplomat* reported in 2017 that SCO has foiled 600 terror plots and extradited 500 terrorists through RATS.

Military activities

Over the past few years, the organisation's activities have expanded to include increased military cooperation, intelligence sharing, and counterterrorism.

There have been a number of SCO joint military exercises. The first of these was held in 2003, with the first phase taking place in Kazakhstan and the second in China. Since then China and Russia have teamed up for large-scale war games in 2005 (Peace Mission 2005), 2007 and 2009, under the auspices of the Shanghai Cooperation Organisation. More than 4,000 soldiers participated at the joint military exercises in 2007 (known as "Peace Mission 2007") which took place in Chelyabinsk Russia near the Ural Mountains, as was agreed upon in April 2006 at a meeting of SCO Defence Ministers. Russian Defence Minister Sergei Ivanov said that the exercises would be transparent and open to media and the public. Following the war games' successful completion, Russian officials began speaking of India joining such exercises in the future and the SCO taking on a military role. Peace Mission 2010, conducted 9–25 September at Kazakhstan's Matybulak training area, saw over 5,000 personnel from China, Russia, Kazakhstan, Kyrgyzstan and Tajikistan conduct joint planning and operational maneuvers.

The SCO has served as a platform for larger military announcements by members. During the 2007 war games in Russia, with leaders of SCO member states in attendance including Chinese President Hu Jintao, Russia's President Vladimir Putin used the occasion to take advantage of a captive audience: Russian strategic bombers, he said, would resume regular long-range patrols for the first time since the Cold War. "Starting today, such tours of duty will be conducted regularly and on the strategic scale", Putin said. "Our pilots have been grounded for too long. They are happy to start a new life".

On 4 June 2014, in the Tajik capital Dushanbe, the idea was brought up to merge the SCO with the Collective Security Treaty Organization. It is still being debated.

Economic cooperation

Russia, Kazakhstan and Kyrgyzstan are also members of the Eurasian Economic Union. A Framework Agreement to enhance economic cooperation was signed by the SCO member states on 23 September 2003. At the same meeting the PRC's Premier, Wen Jiabao, proposed a long-term objective to establish a free trade area in the SCO, while other more immediate measures would be taken to improve the flow of goods in the region. A follow up plan with 100 specific actions was signed one year later, on 23 September 2004.

On 26 October 2005, during the Moscow Summit of the SCO, the Secretary General of the Organisation said that the SCO will prioritise joint energy projects; such will include the oil and gas sector, the exploration of new hydrocarbon reserves, and joint use of water resources. The creation of an Inter-bank

SCO Council was also agreed upon at that summit in order to fund future joint projects. The first meeting of the SCO Interbank Association was held in Beijing on 21–22 February 2006. On 30 November 2006, at *The SCO: Results and Perspectives*, an international conference held in Almaty, the representative of the Russian Foreign Ministry announced that Russia is developing plans for an SCO "Energy Club". The need for this "club" was reiterated by Moscow at an SCO summit in November 2007. Other SCO members, however, have not committed themselves to the idea. However, on 28 August 2008 summit it was stated that "Against the backdrop of a slowdown in the growth of world economy pursuing a responsible currency and financial policy, control over the capital flowing, ensuring food and energy security have been gaining special significance".

At the 2007 SCO summit Iranian Vice President Parviz Davudi addressed an initiative that has been garnering greater interest and assuming a heightened sense of urgency when he said, "The Shanghai Cooperation Organisation is a good venue for designing a new banking system which is independent from international banking systems".

The address by Putin also included these comments:

We now clearly see the defectiveness of the monopoly in world finance and the policy of economic selfishness. To solve the current problem Russia will take part in changing the global financial structure so that it will be able to guarantee stability and prosperity in the world and to ensure progress.

The world is seeing the emergence of a qualitatively different geo-political situation, with the emergence of new centers of economic growth and political influence.

We will witness and take part in the transformation of the global and regional security and development architectures adapted to new realities of the 21st century, when stability and prosperity are becoming inseparable notions.

On 16 June 2009, at the Yekaterinburg Summit, China announced plans to provide a US$10 billion loan to SCO member states to shore up the struggling economies of its members amid the global financial crisis. The summit was held together with the first BRIC summit, and the China-Russia joint statement said that they want a bigger quota in the International Monetary Fund.

Cultural cooperation

Cultural cooperation also occurs in the SCO framework. Culture ministers of the SCO met for the first time in Beijing on 12 April 2002, signing a joint statement for continued cooperation. The third meeting of the Culture Ministers took place in Tashkent, Uzbekistan, on 27–28 April 2006. An SCO Arts Festival and Exhibition was held for the first time during the Astana Summit in 2005. Kazakhstan has also suggested an SCO folk dance festival to take place in 2008, in Astana.

SUMMITS

According to the Charter of the SCO, summits of the Council of Heads of State shall be held annually at alternating venues. The locations of these summits follow the alphabetical order of the member state's name in Russian. The charter also dictates that the Council of Heads of Government (that is, the Prime Ministers) shall meet annually in a place decided upon by the council members. The Council of Foreign Ministers is supposed to hold a summit one month before the annual summit of Heads of State. Extraordinary meetings of the Council of Foreign Ministers can be called by any two member states.

List of summits

Heads of State

Date	Country	Location
14 June 2001	China	Shanghai
7 June 2002	Russia	Saint Petersburg
29 May 2003	Russia	Moscow
17 June 2004	Uzbekistan	Tashkent
5 July 2005	Kazakhstan	Astana
15 June 2006	China	Shanghai

16 August 2007	Kyrgyzstan	Bishkek
28 August 2008	Tajikistan	Dushanbe
15–16 June 2009	Russia	Yekaterinburg
10–11 June 2010	Uzbekistan	Tashkent
14–15 June 2011	Kazakhstan	Astana
6–7 June 2012	China	Beijing
13 September 2013	Kyrgyzstan	Bishkek
11–12 September 2014	Tajikistan	Dushanbe
9–10 July 2015	Russia	Ufa
23–24 June 2016	Uzbekistan	Tashkent
8–9 June 2017	Kazakhstan	Astana
9–10 June 2018 (zh)	China	Qingdao
TBD 2019	Kyrgyzstan	
TBD 2020	Russia	Chelyabinsk

Heads of Government

Date	Country	Location
14 September 2001	Kazakhstan	Almaty
—	—	—
23 September 2003	China	Beijing
23 September 2004	Kyrgyzstan	Bishkek
26 October 2005	Russia	Moscow
15 September 2006	Tajikistan	Dushanbe
2 November 2007	Uzbekistan	Tashkent
30 October 2008	Kazakhstan	Astana
14 October 2009	China	Beijing
25 November 2010	Tajikistan	Dushanbe
7 November 2011	Russia	Saint Petersburg
5 December 2012	Kyrgyzstan	Bishkek
29 November 2013	Uzbekistan	Tashkent
14–15 December 2014	Kazakhstan	Astana
14–15 December 2015	China	Zhengzhou
2–3 November 2016	Kyrgyzstan	Bishkek
30 November 2017	Russia	Sochi

ANALYSIS

Relations with the West

While not a member state, the President of Iran Mahmoud Ahmadinejad used his speeches at the SCO to make verbal remarks towards the United States. The United States applied for observer status in the SCO, but was rejected in 2005.

At the Astana summit in July 2005, with the wars in Afghanistan and Iraq foreshadowing an indefinite presence of U.S. forces in Uzbekistan and Kyrgyzstan, the SCO requested the U.S. to set a clear timetable for withdrawing its troops from SCO member states. Shortly afterwards, Uzbekistan requested the U.S. to leave the K2 air base. The SCO has made no direct comments against the U.S. or its military presence in the region; however, some indirect statements at the past summits have been viewed by Western media outlets as "thinly veiled swipes at Washington". A European Parliament researcher expressed her view that "institutional weaknesses, a lack of common financial funds for the implementation of joint projects and conflicting national interests have prevented the SCO from achieving a higher level of regional cooperation".

Geopolitical aspects of the SCO

There have been many discussions and commentaries about the geopolitical nature of the Shanghai Cooperation Organisation. Matthew Brummer, in the Journal of International Affairs, tracks the implications of SCO expansion into the Persian Gulf. Also, according to political scientist Thomas Ambrosio, one aim of SCO was to ensure that liberal democracy could not gain ground in these countries.

Iranian writer Hamid Golpira had this to say on the topic: "According to Zbigniew Brzezinski's theory, control of the Eurasian landmass is the key to global domination and control of Central Asia is the key to control of the Eurasian landmass....Russia and China have been paying attention to Brzezinski's theory, since they formed the Shanghai Cooperation

Organisation in 2001, ostensibly to curb extremism in the region and enhance border security, but most probably with the real objective of counterbalancing the activities of the United States and NATO in Central Asia".

At a 2005 summit in Kazakhstan the SCO issued a Declaration of Heads of Member States of the Shanghai Cooperation Organisation which addressed their "concerns" and contained an elaboration of the organisation's principles. It included: "The heads of the member states point out that, against the backdrop of a contradictory process of globalisation, multilateral cooperation, which is based on the principles of equal right and mutual respect, non-intervention in internal affairs of sovereign states, non-confrontational way of thinking and consecutive movement towards democratisation of international relations, contributes to overall peace and security, and call upon the international community, irrespective of its differences in ideology and social structure, to form a new concept of security based on mutual trust, mutual benefit, equality and interaction."

In November 2005 Russian Foreign Minister Sergey Lavrov reiterated that the "Shanghai Cooperation Organisation (SCO) is working to establish a rational and just world order" and that "The Shanghai Cooperation Organisation provides us with a unique opportunity to take part in the process of forming a fundamentally new model of geopolitical integration".

The People's Daily expressed the matter in these terms: "The Declaration points out that the SCO member countries have the ability and responsibility to safeguard the security of the Central Asian region, and calls on Western countries to leave Central Asia. That is the most noticeable signal given by the Summit to the world".

A 2010 analysis in *American Legion Magazine* said that 'Chinese Prime Minister Wen Jiabao... has concluded that the United States is maneuvering "to preserve its status as the world's sole superpower and will not allow any country the chance to pose a challenge to it."'

5

Association of Southeast Asian Nations (ASEAN)

The Association of Southeast Asian Nations (ASEAN) is a regional intergovernmental organization comprising ten Southeast Asian countries that promotes intergovernmental cooperation and facilitates economic, political, security, military, educational, and sociocultural integration amongst its members and other Asian states. It also regularly engages other states in the Asia-Pacific region and beyond. Being a global powerhouse, the central platform for cooperation in Asia-Pacific, and one of the world's most prominent and influential organisations, ASEAN maintains a global network of alliances and is involved in numerous international affairs. It is a major partner of the Shanghai Cooperation Organisation (SCO), developing cooperation model with the organisation for the peace, stability, development and sustainability of the Asian continent. It also serves as an international role model in seeking harmony and strength among diversity and differences, as well as a leading figure in international diplomacy.

HISTORY

Founding

ASEAN was preceded by an organization formed in 31 July 1961 called the Association of Southeast Asia (ASA), a group consisting of the Philippines, Federation of Malaya, and Thailand. ASEAN itself was created on 8 August 1967, when the foreign ministers of five countries: Indonesia, Malaysia, the Philippines, Singapore, and Thailand, signed the ASEAN Declaration. As set out in the Declaration, the aims and purposes of ASEAN are to accelerate economic growth, social progress, and cultural development in the region, to promote regional peace, collaboration and mutual assistance on matters of common interest, to provide assistance to each other in the form of training and research facilities, to collaborate for better utilisation of agriculture and industry to raise the living standards of the people, to promote Southeast Asian studies and to maintain close, beneficial co-operation with existing international organisations with similar aims and purposes.

The creation of ASEAN was motivated by a common fear of communism,ASEAN achieved greater cohesion in the mid-1970s following a change in balance of power after the end of the Vietnam War. The region's dynamic economic growth during the 1970s strengthened the organization, enabling ASEAN to adopt a unified response to Vietnam's invasion of Cambodia in 1979. ASEAN's first summit meeting, held in Bali, Indonesia in 1976, resulted in an agreement on several industrial projects and the signing of a Treaty of Amity and Cooperation, and a Declaration of Concord. The end of the Cold War between the United States and the Soviet Union at the end of the 1980s allowed ASEAN countries to exercise greater political independence in the region, and in the 1990s ASEAN emerged as a leading voice on regional trade and security issues.

Expansion

In 1984, Brunei became ASEAN's sixth member and on 28 July 1995, Vietnam joined as the seventh member. Laos and Myanmar (Burma) joined two years later on 23 July 1997. Cambodia was to have joined at the same time as Laos and Burma, but its entry was delayed due to the country's internal political struggle. It later joined on 30 April 1999, following the stabilization of its government.

Nascent Economic Cooperation

In 1990, Malaysia proposed the creation of an East Asia Economic Caucus composed of the members of ASEAN as well as China, Japan, and South Korea, with the intention of counterbalancing the growing US influence in Asia-Pacific Economic Cooperation (APEC) and in Asia as a whole. However, the proposal failed because of heavy opposition from the US and Japan. Work for further integration continued, and the ASEAN Plus Three, consisting of ASEAN, China, Japan and South Korea, was created in 1997. In 1992, the Common Effective Preferential Tariff (CEPT) scheme was adopted as a schedule for phasing out tariffs with the goal to increase the "region's competitive advantage as a production base geared for the world market". This law would act as the framework for the ASEAN Free Trade Area (AFTA), which is an agreement by member states concerning local manufacturing in ASEAN. It was signed on 28 January 1992 in Singapore. After the 1997 Asian financial crisis, a revival of the Malaysian proposal, known as the Chiang Mai Initiative, was put forward in Chiang Mai, Thailand. It called for better integration of the economies of ASEAN as well as the ASEAN Plus Three

Nuclear Free ASEAN

The bloc also focused on peace and stability in the region. On 15 December 1995, the Southeast Asian Nuclear-Weapon-Free Zone Treaty was signed with the intention of turning Southeast Asia into a nuclear-weapon-free zone. The treaty took effect on 28 March 1997 after all but one of the member states had ratified it. It became fully effective on 21 June 2001 after the Philippines ratified it, effectively banning all nuclear weapons in the region.

The ASEAN Charter

On 15 December 2008, member states met in Jakarta to launch a charter, signed in November 2007, with the aim of moving closer to "an EU-style community". The charter turned ASEAN into a legal entity and aimed to create a single free-trade area for the region encompassing 500 million people. President of Indonesia Susilo Bambang Yudhoyono stated: "This is a momentous development when ASEAN is consolidating, integrating, and transforming itself into a community. It is achieved while ASEAN seeks a more vigorous role in Asian and global affairs at a time when the international system is experiencing a seismic shift". Referring to climate change and economic upheaval, he concluded: "Southeast Asia is no longer the bitterly divided, war-torn region it was in the 1960s and 1970s".

The financial crisis of 2007–2008 was seen as a threat to the goals envisioned by the charter, and also set forth the idea of a proposed human rights body to be discussed at a future summit in February 2009. This proposition caused controversy, as the body would not have the power to impose sanctions or punish countries which violated citizens' rights and would therefore be limited in effectiveness. The body was established later in 2009 as the ASEAN Intergovernmental Commission on Human Rights (AICHR). In November 2012, the commission adopted the ASEAN Human Rights Declaration.

THE ASEAN WAY

The 'ASEAN Way' refers to a methodology or approach to solving issues that respects the cultural norms of Southeast Asia. Masilamani and Peterson summarise it as "a working process or style that is informal and personal. Policymakers constantly utilize compromise, consensus, and consultation in the informal decision-making process... it above all prioritizes a consensus-based, non-conflictual way of addressing problems. Quiet diplomacy allows ASEAN leaders to communicate without bringing the discussions into the public view. Members avoid embarrassment that may lead to further conflict." It has been said that the merits of the ASEAN Way might "be usefully applied to global conflict management". However, critics have argued that such an approach can be only applied to Asian countries to specific cultural norms and understandings notably due to a difference in mindset and level of tension. Critics object claiming that the ASEAN Way's emphasis on consultation, consensus, and non-interference, forces the organisation to adopt only those policies which satisfy the lowest common denominator. Decision making by consensus requires members to see eye-to-eye before ASEAN can move forward on an issue. Members may not have a common conception of the meaning of the ASEAN Way. Myanmar, Cambodia, and Laos emphasise non-interference while older member countries focus on co-operation and co-ordination. These differences hinder efforts to find common solutions to particular issues, but also make it difficult to determine when collective action is appropriate in a given situation.

East Asian Summit

ASEAN Plus Three was the first of attempts for further integration to improve existing ties with China, Japan, and South Korea. This was followed by the even larger East Asia Summit (EAS), which included ASEAN Plus Three as well as India, Australia, and New Zealand. This group acted as a prerequisite for the planned East Asia Community which was supposedly patterned after the now-defunct European Community.

The ASEAN Eminent Persons Group was created to study the possible successes and failures of this policy. In 2006, ASEAN was given observer status at the United Nations General Assembly. In response, the organisation awarded the status of "dialogue partner" to the UN.

The group became ASEAN Plus Six with Australia, New Zealand and India. Codification of the relations between these countries has seen progress through the development of the Regional Comprehensive Economic Partnership, a proposed free-trade agreement involving the 16 countries of ASEAN Plus Six. RCEP would, in part, allow the members to protect local sectors and give more time to comply with the aim for developed country members.

STRUCTURE

ASEAN Community 2015

Beginning in 1997, heads of each member state adopted the ASEAN Vision 2020 during ASEAN's 30th anniversary meeting held in Kuala Lumpur. This vision, as a means for the realisation of a single ASEAN community, sees Southeast Asia becoming a group of countries which are: "outward looking, living in peace, stability and prosperity". Included in ASEAN Vision 2020 were provisions on: peace and stability, being nuclear-free, closer economic integration, human development, sustainable development, cultural heritage, being drug-free, environment, among others. The Vision also aimed to: "see an outward-looking ASEAN playing a pivotal role in the international fora, and advancing ASEAN's common interests". Such vision was formalised and made comprehensive through the Bali Concord II in 2003. Three major pillars of a single ASEAN community were originally established: Security Community, Economic Community and Socio-Cultural Community. The ASEAN Community, initially planned to commence by 2020, was accelerated to begin by 31 December 2015. This was decided during the 12th ASEAN Summit in Cebu in 2007. To fully embody the three Bali Concord II pillars as part of the 2015 integration, blueprints for ASEAN Political-Security Community (APSC) and ASEAN Socio-Cultural Community (ASCC) were subsequently adopted in 2009 in Cha-am, Thailand.

At the 23rd ASEAN Summit in November 2013, ASEAN leaders made the decision to develop a post-2015 Vision and thus created the High-Level Task Force (HLTF), which consists of ten high-level representatives from all member states. The Vision was adopted at the 27th ASEAN Summit in November 2015 in Kuala Lumpur, Malaysia. The ASEAN community revises and renews its vision every ten years to provide a framework for continuous development and further integration of the community. The terms in the Vision are divided into mainly four subcategories: ASEAN Political-Security

Community, ASEAN Economic Community, ASEAN Socio-Cultural Community, and Moving Forward. ASEAN Political-Security issues are covered under article 7 and 8 of the Vision. Article 7 generally states the overall aspiration of the community aiming to achieve a united, inclusive and resilient community. It also puts human and environmental security at the center of its aspirations. Deepening engagement with both internal Members and eternal parties are also stressed to contribute the international peace, security and stability. The final part of the Vision, under "oving Forward" subcategory, implies the acknowledgement of the weakness of the institution capacity to process and coordinate ASEAN work. Strengthening ASEAN Secretariat and other ASEAN Organs and Bodies is desired. There is also a call for greater level of ASEAN institutional presence at the national, regional and international levels.

Economic Community Blueprint

The ASEAN Economic Community (AEC) aims to "implement economic integration initiatives" to create a single market across ASEAN member states. On 20 November 2007, during the 13th ASEAN Summit in Singapore, its blueprint, which serves as a master plan guiding the establishment of the community, was adopted. Its characteristics include a single market and production base, a highly competitive economic region, a region of fair economic development, and a region fully integrated into the global economy. The areas of co-operation include human resources development; recognition of professional qualifications; closer consultation on macroeconomic and financial policies; trade financing measures; enhanced infrastructure and communications connectivity; development of electronic transactions through e-ASEAN; integrating industries across the region to promote regional sourcing; and enhancing private sector involvement. Through the free movement of skilled labour, goods, services and investment, ASEAN will rise globally as one market with each member gaining from each other's strengths, thus increasing its competitiveness and opportunities for development.

The AEC is the embodiment of the ASEAN's vision of "a stable, prosperous and highly competitive ASEAN economic region in which there is a free flow of goods, services, investment and a freer flow of capital, equitable economic development and reduced poverty and socio-economic disparities". The formulation the blueprint established the member states' commitment to a common goal as well as ensuring compliance with stated objectives and timelines. The blueprint also lays out the overall vision as well as the goals, implementing plans and strategies (actions), as well as the strategic schedule (timeline) for achieving the establishment of the AEC by end-2015.

2020 ASEAN Banking Integration Framework

As trade is liberalised with the ASEAN Economic Integration in 2015, the need arises for ASEAN banking institutions to accommodate and expand their services to a greater intra-ASEAN market. While the financial integration is not going to take effect until 2020, experts from the financial services industry have already forecast a shaky economic transition, especially for smaller players in the banking and financial services industry. Two separate reports by Standard & Poor's, *ASEAN Financial Integration: The Long Road to Bank Consolidation* and *The Philippines' Banking System: The Good, the Bad and the Ambivalent*, outline the challenges ASEAN financial institutions are facing as they prepare for the 2020 banking integration. The Philippines, with its overcrowded banking sector, for example, is among the ASEAN-member countries who are forecast to feel the most pressure as the integration welcomes tighter competition with the entry of bigger, more established foreign banks. To lessen the impact of this consolidation, countries with banking sectors considered smaller by global standards must expand regionally. S&P in a follow up report recently cited the Philippines for "shoring up its network bases and building up capital ahead of the banking integration – playing defence and strengthening their domestic networks".

Socio-Cultural Community Blueprint

It was also during the 14th ASEAN Summit that the member governments of ASEAN adopted the *ASEAN Socio-Cultural Community Blueprint* (ASCC). The ASCC envisions an: "ASEAN Community that is people-centered and socially responsible with a view to achieving enduring solidarity and unity among the countries and peoples of ASEAN by forging a common identity and building a caring and sharing society which is inclusive and harmonious where the well-being, livelihood, and welfare of the peoples are enhanced". Among its focus areas are: human development, social welfare and protection, social justice and rights, ensuring environmental sustainability, building the ASEAN identity, and narrowing the development gap.

To track the progress of the AEC, the AEC Scorecard, a compliance tool was developed based on the EU Internal Market Scorecard. This scorecard is the only one in effectand is expected to serve as an unbiased assessment tool to measure the extent of integration among member statess, and the economic health of the region. It is expected to provide relevant information about regional priorities, and thus foster productive, inclusive, and sustainable growth. Moreover, scores create incentives for improvement by highlighting what is working and what is not. It is also a compliance tool that makes it possible to monitor the implementation of ASEAN agreements, and the achievement of milestones indicated in the AEC Strategic Schedule. The Scorecard outlines specific actions that must be undertaken by ASEAN collectively, and by its member states individually, to establish AEC by 2015. To date, two official scorecards have been published, one in 2010, and the other in 2012. According to the *AEC Scorecard 2012*, the implementation rates of AEC's four primary objectives: (a) single market and production base; (b) competitive economic region; (c) equitable economic development; and (d) integration into the global economy were 65.9%, 67.9%, 66.7%, and 85.7%, respectively, with 187 out of 277 measures being fully implemented by 2011. The scorecard is purely quantitative. It only examines whether a member state has performed the AEC task or not. The more "yes" answers, the higher the score.

While Brunei, Indonesia, Malaysia, the Philippines, Singapore, and Thailand have eliminated 99.65% of their tariff lines, Cambodia, Laos, Myanmar, and Vietnam have decreased tariffs on 98.86% of their lines to the 0-5% tariff range in 2010, and are projected to eliminate tariffs on these goods by 2015, with the ability to do so for a few import duty lines until 2018. According to Lim Hng Kiang, Singapore's Minister for Trade and Industry, ASEAN was already the seventh largest economy in the world, and the third largest in Asia in 2013, estimated at US$2.3 trillion. A recent study by Deloitte Touche Tohmatsu Limited has projected that five of the top fifteen manufacturing locations in the world will be in ASEAN by 2018. Furthermore, by 2050, ASEAN is also expected to be the fourth-largest economy in the world (after the European Union, the US, and China).

The AEC envisions the free flow of overseas labour. However, receiving countries may require would-be workers to take licensing examinations in those countries regardless of whether or not the worker has a professional license from their home country. Singapore is a major destination for skilled migrants from other ASEAN countries, mostly from Malaysia and the Philippines. Total employment in Singapore doubled between 1992 and 2008 from 1.5 million to three million, and the number of foreign workers almost tripled, from fewer than 400,000 to almost 1.1 million. High-skilled foreign talents (customer service, nursing, engineering, IT) earn at least US$2,000 a month and with a credential (usually a college degree) receive S Passes, employment passes, including an EP-1 for those earning more than US$7,000 a month; EP-2 for those earning US$3,500—7,000 a month; and EP-3 for those earning US$2,500–3,500 a month. In recent years, Singapore has been slowly cutting down the number of foreign workers to challenge companies to upgrade their hiring criteria and offer more jobs to local residents. The International Monetary Fund (IMF) has warned that the Singapore policy of reducing the number of foreign workers could retard the country's economic growth and lower its competitiveness.

ASEAN members by

Human Development Index

Country	HDI (2016)	
Singapore	0.925	very high
Brunei	0.865	very high
Malaysia	0.789	high
Thailand	0.740	high
Indonesia	0.689	medium
ASEAN	0.684	medium
Vietnam	0.683	medium
Philippines	0.682	medium
Laos	0.568	medium
Cambodia	0.563	medium
Myanmar	0.556	medium

Narrowing the Development Gap (NDG) is the framework for addressing disparities among, and within, member states where pockets of underdevelopment exist. Under NDG, ASEAN has continued co-ordinating closely with other sub-regional co-operation frameworks (e.g., BIMP-EAGA, IMT-GT, GMS, Mekong programs), viewing them as "equal partners in the development of regional production and distribution networks" in the AEC, and as a platform to "mainstream social development issues in developing and implementing projects," in the context of the ASCC. The six-year Initiative for ASEAN Integration (IAI) Work Plans have been developed to assist Cambodia, Laos, Myanmar, Vietnam as well as ASEAN's other sub-regions to ensure that the wheels of their economies move at an accelerated pace. The First IAI Work Plan was implemented from 2002 to 2008, prior to the development of the Roadmap for an ASEAN Community (2009-2015). The second plan (2009-2015) supports the goals of the ASEAN Community and is composed of 182 prescribed actions, which includes studies, training programs, and policy implementation support, conducted through projects supported by older ASEAN member states, and ASEAN's Dialogue partners and external parties. The IAI Work Plan is patterned after and supports the key program areas in the three ASEAN Community Blueprints: Political-Security Community, Economic Community, and Socio-Cultural Community. The IAI Task Force, composed of representatives of the Committee of Permanent Representatives and its working group from all member states, is in charge of providing general advice and policy guidelines and directions in the design and implementation of the lan. All member states are represented in the IAI Task Force, with the task force chaired by representatives of Cambodia, Laos, Myanmar, Vietnam. Chairmanship is rotated annually in alphabetical order by country name.

The ASEAN Secretariat, in particular through the IAI and NDG Division, supports the implementation and management of the IAI Work Plan and coordinates activities related to sub-regional frameworks. This includes servicing meetings, assisting in the formulation, implementation, monitoring and reporting of projects, resource mobilisation, and overall operational co-ordination among various IAI&NDG-related stakeholders. The Division works closely with the Dialogue Partners, and international agencies, to develop strategies and programs to assist in promoting and implementing IAI and NDG activities in ASEAN.

ASEAN's planned integration has challenged its citizens to embrace a regional identity. The call for ASEAN identity delivers a challenge to construct dynamic institutions and foster sufficient amounts of social capital. The underlying assumption is that the creation of a regional identity is of special interest to ASEAN and the intent of the 2020 Vision policy document was to reassert the belief in a regional framework designed as an action plan related to human development and civic empowerment. Accordingly, these assumptions will be the basis for recommendations and strategies in developing a participatory regional identity.

ECONOMY

The group sought economic integration by creating the AEC by the end of 2015 that established a single market. The average economic growth of member states from 1989 to 2009 was between 3.8% and 7%. This was greater than the average growth of APEC, which was 2.8%. The ASEAN Free Trade Area (AFTA), established on 28 January 1992, includes a Common Effective Preferential Tariff (CEPT) to promote the free flow of goods between member states. ASEAN had only six members when it was signed. The new member states (Vietnam, Laos, Burma and Cambodia) have not fully met AFTA's obligations, but are officially considered part of the agreement as they were required to sign it upon entry into ASEAN, and were given longer time frames to meet AFTA's tariff reduction obligations. The next steps are to create a single market and production base, a competitive economic region, a region of equitable economic development, and a region that is fully integrated into the global economy. Since 2007, ASEAN countries have gradually lowered their import duties to member states, with a target of zero import duties by 2016.

ASEAN countries have many economic zones (industrial parks, eco-industrial parks, special economic zones, technology parks, and innovation districts). In 2015, UNIDO Viet Nam (United Nations Industrial Development Organization) has compiled a list of economic zones in the ASEAN Economic Community in a report titled "Economic Zones in the ASEAN", written by Arnault Morisson.

Internal market

By the end of 2015, ASEAN plans to establish a single market based upon the four freedoms. It will ensure free flow of goods, services, skilled labour, and capital. Until the end of 2010, intra-ASEAN trade was still low as trade involved mainly exports to countries outside the region, with the exception of Laos and Myanmar, whose foreign trade was ASEAN-oriented. In 2009, realised foreign direct investment (FDI) was US$37.9

billion and increased two-fold in 2010 to US$75.8 billion. 22% of FDI came from the European Union, followed by ASEAN countries (16%), and by Japan and the United States. The ASEAN Framework Agreement on Trade in Services (AFAS) was adopted at the ASEAN Summit in Bangkok in December 1995. Under the agreement, member states enter into successive rounds of negotiations to liberalise trade in services with the aim of submitting increasingly higher levels of commitment. At present, ASEAN has concluded seven packages of commitments under AFAS. Mutual Recognition Agreements (MRAs) have been agreed upon by ASEAN for eight professions: physicians, dentists, nurses, architects, engineers, accountants, surveyors, and tourism professionals. Individuals in these professions will be free to work in any ASEAN states after the AEC goes into effect on 31 December 2015. In addition, six member states (Malaysia, Vietnam (2 exchanges), Indonesia, Philippines, Thailand, and Singapore) has collaborated on integrating their stock exchanges, which includes 70% of its transaction values with the goal to compete with international exchanges.

Single market will also include the ASEAN Single Aviation Market (ASEAN-SAM), the region's aviation policy geared towards the development of a unified and single aviation marketin Southeast Asia. It was proposed by the ASEAN Air Transport Working Group, supported by the ASEAN Senior Transport Officials Meeting, and endorsed by the ASEAN Transport Ministers. It is expected to liberalise air travel between member states allowing ASEAN airlines to benefit directly from the growth in air travel, and also free up tourism, trade, investment, and service flows. Since 1 December 2008, restrictions on the third and fourth freedoms of the air between capital cities of member states for air passenger services have been removed, while from 1 January 2009, full liberalisation of air freight services in the region took effect. On 1 January 2011, full liberalisation on fifth freedom traffic rights between all capital cities took effect. This policy supersedes existing unilateral, bilateral, and multilateral air services agreements among member states which are inconsistent with its provisions.

FOREIGN RELATIONS

ASEAN maintains a global network of alliances, and is involved in numerous international affairs. The organisation holds ASEAN Summits, where heads of government of each member states meet to discuss and resolve regional issues, as well as to conduct other meetings with countries outside the bloc to promote external relations and deal with international affairs. The first summit was held in Bali in 1976. The third summit was in Manila in 1987, and during this meeting, it was decided that the leaders would meet every five years. The fourth meeting was held in Singapore in 1992 where the leaders decided to meet more frequently, every three years. In 2001, it was decided to meet annually to address urgent issues affecting the region. Member states were assigned to be the summit host in alphabetical order except in the case of Burma which dropped its 2006 hosting rights in 2004 due to pressure from the United States and the European Union. In December 2008, the ASEAN Charter came into force and with it, the ASEAN Summit will be held twice a year. The formal summit meets for three days, and usually includes internal organisation meeting, a conference with foreign ministers of the ASEAN Regional Forum, an ASEAN Plus Three meeting and ASEAN-CER, a meeting of member states with Australia and New Zealand.

ASEAN also participates in the East Asia Summit (EAS), a pan-Asian forum held annually by the leaders of eighteen countries in the East Asian region, with ASEAN in a leadership position. Initially, membership included all member states of ASEAN plus China, Japan, South Korea, India, Australia, and New Zealand, but was expanded to include the United States and Russia at the Sixth EAS in 2011. The first summit was held in Kuala Lumpur on 14 December 2005, and subsequent meetings have been held after the annual ASEAN Leaders' Meeting. The summit has discussed issues including trade, energy, and security and the summit has a role in regional community building. It is a major partner of the Shanghai Cooperation Organisation (SCO), developing cooperation model with the organisation in the field of security, economy, finance, tourism, culture, environmental protection, development and sustainability.

Other meetings include the ASEAN Ministerial Meeting that focus mostly on specific topics, such as defence or the environment, and are attended by ministers. The ASEAN Regional Forum (ARF), which met for the first time in 1994, fosters dialogue and consultation, and to promote confidence-building and preventive diplomacy in the region. As of July 2007, it consists of twenty-seven participants that include all ASEAN member states, Australia, Bangladesh, Canada, China, the EU, India, Japan, North and South Korea, Mongolia, New Zealand, Pakistan, Papua New Guinea, Russia, East Timor, the United States, and Sri Lanka.Taiwan has been excluded since the establishment of the ARF, and issues regarding the Taiwan Strait are neither discussed at ARF meetings nor stated in the ARF Chairman's Statements.

ASEAN also holds meetings with Europe during the Asia–Europe Meeting (ASEM), an informal dialogue process initiated in 1996 with the intention of strengthening co-operation between the countries of Europe and Asia, especially members of the European Union and ASEAN in particular. ASEAN, represented by its Secretariat, is one of the forty-five ASEM partners. It also appoints a representative to sit on the governing board of Asia-Europe Foundation (ASEF), a socio-cultural organisation associated with the meeting. Annual bilateral meetings between ASEAN and India, Russia and the United States are also held.

6

South Asian Association for Regional Cooperation (SAARC)

The South Asian Association for Regional Cooperation (SAARC) is the regional intergovernmental organization and geopoliticalunion of nations in South Asia. Its member states include Afghanistan, Bangladesh, Bhutan, India, Nepal, the Maldives, Pakistan and Sri Lanka. SAARC comprises 3% of the world's area, 21% of the world's population and 3.8% (US$2.9 trillion) of the global economy, as of 2015.

SAARC was founded in Dhaka on 8 December 1985. Its secretariat is based in Kathmandu, Nepal. The organization promotes development of economic and regional integration. It launched the South Asian Free Trade Area in 2006. SAARC maintains permanent diplomatic relations at the United Nations as an observer and has developed links with multilateral entities, including the European Union.

HISTORICAL BACKGROUND

The idea of co-operation in South Asia was discussed in at least three conferences: the Asian Relations Conference held in New Delhion April 1947; the Baguio Conference in the Philippines on May 1950; and the Colombo Powers Conference held in Sri Lanka in April 1954.

In the ending years of the 1970s, the seven inner South Asian nations that included Bangladesh, Bhutan, India, Maldives, Nepal, Pakistan, and Sri Lanka agreed upon the creation of a trade bloc and to provide a platform for the people of South Asia to work together in a spirit of friendship, trust, and understanding. President Ziaur Rahman later addressed official letters to the leaders of the countries of the South Asia, presenting his vision for the future of the region and the compelling arguments for region. During his visit to India in December 1977, Rahman discussed the issue of regional cooperation with the Indian Prime Minister, Morarji Desai. In the inaugural speech to the Colombo Plan Consultative Committee which met in Kathmandu also in 1977, King Birendra of Nepal gave a call for close regional cooperation among South Asian countries in sharing river waters. After the USSR's intervention in Afghanistan, the efforts to establish the union was accelerated in 1979 and the resulting rapid deterioration of South Asian security situation.Responding to Rahman and Birendra's convention, the officials of the foreign ministries of the seven countries met for the first time in Colombo in April 1981. The Bangladeshi proposal was promptly endorsed by Nepal, Sri Lanka, Bhutan, and the Maldives but India and Pakistan were sceptical initially. The Indian concern was the proposal's reference to the security matters in South Asia and feared that Rahman's proposal for a regional organisation might provide an opportunity for new smaller neighbours to renationalise all bilateral issues and to join with each other to form an opposition against India. Pakistan assumed that it might be an Indian strategy to organise the other South Asian countries against Pakistan and ensure a regional market for Indian products, thereby consolidating and further strengthening India's economic dominance in the region.

However, after a series of diplomatic consultations headed by Bangladesh between South Asian U.N. representatives at the UN headquarters in New York, from September 1979 to 1980, it was agreed that Bangladesh would prepare the draft of a working paper for discussion among the foreign secretaries of South Asian countries.The foreign secretaries of the inner seven countries again delegated a Committee of the Whole in Colombo on September 1981, which identified five broad areas for regional cooperation. New areas of co-operation were added in the following years.

In 1983, the international conference held in Dhaka by its Ministry of Foreign Affairs, the foreign ministers of the inner seven countries adopted the Declaration on South Asian Association Regional Cooperation (SAARC) and formally launched the Integrated Programme of Action (IPA) initially in five agreed areas of cooperation namely, Agriculture; Rural Development; Telecommunications; Meteorology; and Health and Population Activities.

Officially, the union was established in Dhaka with Kathmandu being union's secretariat-general. The first SAARC summit was held in Dhaka on 7–8 December 1985 and hosted by the President of Bangladesh Hussain Ershad. The declaration signed by King of Bhutan Jigme Singye Wangchuk, President of Pakistan Zia-ul-Haq, Prime Minister of India Rajiv Gandhi, King of Nepal Birendra Shah, President of Sri Lanka JR Jayewardene, and President of Maldives Maumoon Gayoom.

MEMBERS AND OBSERVERS

Economic data is sourced from the International Monetary Fund, current as of April 2015, and is given in US dollars.

Members

The member states are Afghanistan, Bangladesh, Bhutan, India, Maldives, Nepal, Pakistan, and Sri Lanka.

SAARC was founded by seven states in 1985. In 2005, Afghanistan began negotiating their accession to SAARC and formally applied for membership on the same year. The issue of Afghanistan joining SAARC generated a great deal of debate in each member state, including concerns about the definition of South Asian identity because Afghanistan is a Central Asian country.

The SAARC member states imposed a stipulation for Afghanistan to hold a general election; the non-partisan elections were held in late 2005. Despite initial reluctance and internal debates, Afghanistan joined SAARC as its eighth member state in April 2007.

Observers

States with observer status include Australia, China, the European Union, Iran, Japan, Mauritius, Myanmar, South Korea and the United States.

On 2 August 2006, the foreign ministers of the SAARC countries agreed in principle to grant observer status to three applicants; the US and South Korea (both made requests in April 2006), as well as the European Union (requested in July 2006). On 4 March 2007, Iran requested observer status, followed shortly by Mauritius.

Potential future members

Myanmar has expressed interest in upgrading its status from an observer to a full member of SAARC. Russia has applied for observer status membership of SAARC.Turkey applied for observer status membership of SAARC in 2012. South Africa has participated in meetings.

SECRETARIAT

The SAARC Secretariat was established in Kathmandu on 16 January 1987 and was inaugurated by Late King Birendra Bir Bikram Shah of Nepal.

Regional Centres

The SAARC Secretariat is supported by following Regional Centres established in the Member States to promote regional co-operation. These Centres are managed by Governing Boards comprising representatives from all the Member States, SAARC Secretary-General and the Ministry of Foreign/External Affairs of the Host Government. The Director of the Centre acts as Member Secretary to the Governing Board which reports to the

Programming Committee. After 31 December 2015, there 6 regional centers were stopped by unanimous decision. These are SMRC, SFC, SDC, SCZMC, SIC, SHRDC.

Regional Centre	Location	Country
SAARC Agricultural Centre (SAC)	Dhaka	Bangladesh
SAARC Meteorological Research Centre (SMRC)	Dhaka	Bangladesh
SAARC Forestry Centre (SFC)	Thimphu	Bhutan
SAARC Development Fund (SDF)	Thimphu	Bhutan
SAARC Documentation Centre (SDC)	New Delhi	India
SAARC Disaster Management Centre (SDMC)	Gandhinagar	India
SAARC Coastal Zone Management Centre (SCZMC)	Malé	Maldives
SAARC Information Centre (SIC)	Kathmandu	Nepal
SAARC Tuberculosis and HIV/AIDS Centre (STAC)	Kathmandu	Nepal
SAARC Human Resources Development Centre (SHRDC)	Islamabad	Pakistan
SAARC Energy Centre (SEC)	Islamabad	Pakistan
SAARC Cultural Centre (SCC)	Colombo	Sri Lanka

APEX AND RECOGNISED BODIES

SAARC has six Apex Bodies, they are-

- SAARC Chamber of Commerce & Industry (SCCI),
- South Asian Association for Regional Cooperation (SAARCLAW),
- South Asian Federation of Accountants (SAFA),
- South Asia Foundation (SAF),
- South Asia Initiative to End Violence Against Children (SAIEVAC),
- Foundation of SAARC Writers and Literature (FOSWAL)

Amjad Hussain B Sial is the current Secretary General of SAARC. SAARC also has about 17 recognised bodies.

POLITICAL ISSUES

Lasting peace and prosperity in South Asia has been elusive because of the various ongoing conflicts in the region. Political dialogue is often conducted on the margins of SAARC meetings which have refrained from interfering in the internal matters of its member states. During the 12th and 13th SAARC summits, extreme emphasis was laid upon greater cooperation between the SAARC members to fight terrorism.

The 19th SAARC summit scheduled to be held in Pakistan was called off as India, Bangladesh, Bhutan and Afghanistan decided to boycott it. It was for the first time that four countries boycotted a SAARC summit, leading to its cancellation.

SOUTH ASIAN FREE TRADE AREA

SAFTA was envisaged primarily as the first step towards the transition to a South Asian Free Trade Area (SAFTA) leading subsequently towards a Customs Union, Common Market and the Economic Union. In 1995, Sixteenth session of the Council of Ministers (New Delhi, 18–19 December 1995) agreed on the need to strive for the realisation of SAFTA and to this end an Inter-Governmental Expert Group (IGEG) was set up in 1996 to identify the necessary steps for progressing to a free trade area. The Tenth SAARC Summit (Colombo, 29–31 July 1998) decided to set up a Committee of Experts (COE) to draft a comprehensive treaty framework for creating a free trade area within the region, taking into consideration the asymmetries in development within the region and bearing in mind the need to fix realistic and achievable targets.

The SAFTA Agreement was signed on 6 January 2004 during Twelfth SAARC Summit held in Islamabad, Pakistan. The Agreement entered into force on 1 January 2006, and the Trade Liberalisation Programme commenced from 1 July 2006. Under this agreement, SAARC members will bring their duties down to 20 percent by 2009. Following the Agreement coming into force the SAFTA Ministerial Council (SMC) has been established comprising the Commerce Ministers of the Member

States. In 2012 the SAARC exports increased substantially to US$354.6 billion from US$206.7 billion in 2009. Imports too increased from US$330 billion to US$602 billion over the same period. But the intra-SAARC trade amounts to just a little over 1% of SAARC's GDP. In contrast, in ASEAN (which is actually smaller than SAARC in terms of the size of the economy) the intra-bloc trade stands at 10% of its GDP.

SAFTA was envisaged to gradually move towards South Asian Economic Union, but the current intra-regional trade and investment relation are not encouraging and it may be difficult to achieve this target. The SAARC intra-regional trade stands at just five per cent on the share of intra-regional trade in overall trade in South Asia. Similarly, foreign direct investment is also dismal. The intra-regional FDI flow stands at around four per cent of the total foreign investment.

The Asian Development Bank has estimated that inter-regional trade in SAARC region possessed potential of shooting up agricultural exports by $14 billion per year from existing level of $8 billion to $22 billion.The study by Asian Development Bank states that against the potential average SAARC intra-regional trade of $22 billion per year, the actual trade in South Asia has been only around $8 billion. The uncaptured potential for intra-regional trade is therefore $14 billion per year, i.e. 68%.

SAARC VISA EXEMPTION SCHEME

The SAARC Visa Exemption Scheme was launched in 1992. The leaders at the Fourth Summit (Islamabad, 29–31 December 1988), realizing the importance of people-to-people contact among SAARC countries, decided that certain categories of dignitaries should be entitled to a Special Travel document. The document would exempt them from visas within the region. As directed by the Summit, the Council of Ministers regularly kept under review the list of entitled categories.

Currently, the list included 24 categories of entitled persons, which include dignitaries, judges of higher courts, parliamentarians, senior officials, entrepreneurs, journalists, and athletes.

The Visa Stickers are issued by the respective Member States to the entitled categories of that particular country. The validity of the Visa Sticker is generally for one year. The implementation is reviewed regularly by the Immigration Authorities of SAARC Member States.

AWARDS

SAARC Award

The Twelfth Summit approved the SAARC Award to support individuals and organisations within the region. The main aims of the SAARC Award are:

- To encourage individuals and organisations based in South Asia to undertake programmes and activities that complement the efforts of SAARC
- To encourage individuals and organisations in South Asia contributing to bettering the conditions of women and children
- To honour outstanding contributions and achievements of individuals and organisations within the region in the fields of peace, development, poverty alleviation, environment protection and regional cooperation
- To honour any other contributions and achievement not covered above of individuals and organisations in the region.

The SAARC Award consists of a gold medal, a letter of citation, and cash prize of US $25,000 (15 lakhs). Since the institution of the SAARC Award in 2004, it has been awarded only once and the Award was posthumously conferred upon the late President Ziaur Rahman of Bangladesh.

SAARC Literary Award

The SAARC Literary Award is an annual award conferred by the Foundation of SAARC Writers and Literature (FOSWAL) since 2001which is an apex SAARC body. Shamshur Rahman,

Mahasweta Devi, Jayanta Mahapatra, Abhi Subedi, Mark Tully, Sitakant Mahapatra, Uday Prakash, Suman Pokhrel and Abhay K are some of the prominent recipients of this award.

Nepali poet, lyricist and translator Suman Pokhrel is the only poet/writer to get this award twice.

SAARC Youth Award

The SAARC Youth Award is awarded to outstanding individuals from the SAARC region. The award is notable because of the recognition it gives to the Award winner in the SAARC region. The award is based on specific themes which apply to each year. The award recognises and promotes the commitment and talent of the youth who give back to the world at large through various initiatives such as Inventions, Protection of the Environment and Disaster relief. The recipients who receive this award are ones who have dedicated their lives to their individual causes to improve situations in their own countries as well as paving a path for the SAARC region to follow. The Committee for the SAARC Youth Award selects the best candidate based on his/her merits and their decision is final.

Previous Winners:

- 1997: Outstanding Social Service in Community Welfare – Mohammed Sukur Salek (Bangladesh)
- 1998: New Inventions and Shanu — Najmul Hasnain Shah (Pakistan)
- 2001: Creative Photography: South Asian Diversity – Mushfiqul Alam (Bangladesh)
- 2002: Outstanding contribution to protect the Environment – Masil Khan (Pakistan)
- 2003: Invention in the Field of Traditional Medicine – Hassan Sher (Pakistan)
- 2004: Outstanding contribution to raising awareness of TB and/or HIV/AIDS – Ajij Prasad Poudyal (Nepal)
- 2006: Promotion of Tourism in South Asia – Syed Zafar Abbas Naqvi (Pakistan)

- 2008: Protecting the Environment in South Asia – Uswatta Liyanage Deepani Jayantha (Sri Lanka)
- 2009: Outstanding contribution to humanitarian works in the aftermath of Natural Disasters – Ravikant Singh (India)
- 2010: Outstanding contribution for the Protection of Environment and mitigation of Climate Change – Anoka Primrose Abeyrathne (Sri Lanka)

ANTHEM

SAARC does not have an official anthem like some other regional organisations (e.g. ASEAN). A poem by poet-diplomat Abhay Kumar spurred a search for a better SAARC anthem. Nepal's foreign minister has expressed the need for an SAARC anthem to connect SAARC nations. Nepal at the 18th summit in Kathmandu in November 2014 planned to introduce proposal for an SAARC Anthem in the agenda of summit when heads of all member states meet here.

7

Gulf Cooperation Council

The Cooperation Council for the Arab States of the Gulf , originally (and still colloquially) known as the Gulf Cooperation Council (GCC), is a regional intergovernmental political and economic union consisting of all Arab states of the Persian Gulf except Iraq. Its member states are Bahrain, Kuwait, Oman, Qatar, Saudi Arabia, and the United Arab Emirates. The Charter of the Gulf Cooperation Council was signed on 25 May 1981, formally establishing the institution.

All current member states are monarchies, including three constitutional monarchies (Qatar, Kuwait, and Bahrain), two absolute monarchies (Saudi Arabia and Oman), and one federal monarchy (the United Arab Emirates, which is composed of seven member states, each of which is an absolute monarchy with its own emir). There have been discussions regarding the future membership of Jordan, Morocco, and Yemen.

A 2011 proposal to transform the GCC into a "Gulf Union" with tighter economic, political and military coordination has been advanced by Saudi Arabia, a move meant to counterbalance the Iranian influence in the region. Objections have been raised against the proposal by other countries. In 2014, Bahrain prime minister Khalifa bin Salman Al Khalifa said that current events in the region highlighted the importance of the proposal.

In order to reduce their dependence on oil in the future, the GCC states are pursuing unprecedented structural reform initiatives.

FOUNDING

Heads of states of the GCC in Abu Dhabi on 25 May 1981.

The original union comprised the 1,032,093-square-mile (2,673,110 km) Bahrain, Kuwait, Oman, Qatar, Saudi Arabia and the United Arab Emirates. The unified economic agreement between the countries of the Gulf Cooperation Council was signed on 11 November 1981 in Abu Dhabi. These countries are often referred to as "the GCC states" or "Gulf countries".

Objectives

In 2001, the Supreme Council set the following goals:

- Customs union in January 2003
- Common market by 2007
- Common currency by 2010

Oman announced in December 2006 it would not be able to meet the 2010 target date for a common currency. Following the announcement that the central bank for the monetary union would be located in Riyadh and not in the UAE, the UAE announced their withdrawal from the monetary union project in May 2009.

The name Khaleeji has been proposed as a name for this currency. If realised, the GCC monetary union would be the second largest supranational monetary union in the world, measured by GDP of the common-currency area.

Other stated objectives include:

- Formulating similar regulations in various fields such as religion, finance, trade, customs, tourism, legislation, and administration
- Fostering scientific and technical progress in industry, mining, agriculture, water and animal resources
- Establishing scientific research centers
- Setting up joint ventures
- Unified military (Peninsula Shield Force)
- Encouraging cooperation of the private sector
- Strengthening ties between their people

This area has some of the fastest growing economies in the world, mostly due to a boom in oil and natural gas revenues coupled with a building and investment boom backed by decades of saved petroleum revenues. In an effort to build a tax base and economic foundation before the reserves run out, the UAE's investment arms, including Abu Dhabi Investment Authority, retain over $900 billion in assets. Other regional funds also have several hundreds of billions of dollars of assets under management.

The region is also an emerging hotspot for events, including the 2006 Asian Games in Doha, Qatar. Doha also submitted an unsuccessful application for the 2016 Summer Olympic Games. Qatar was later chosen to host the 2022 FIFA World Cup, but it is possible that Qatar might lose the right to host the game because of its poor human rights record.

Recovery plans have been criticized for crowding out the private sector, failing to set clear priorities for growth, failing to restore weak consumer and investor confidence, and undermining long-term stability.

Logo

The logo of the GCC consists of two concentric circles. On the upper part of the larger circle, the Bismillah phrase is written in Arabic, which means "In the name of God", and on the lower part the Council's full name, in Arabic. The inner circle contains an embossed hexagonal shape that represents the Council's six member countries. The inside of the hexagon is filled by a map encompassing the Arabian Peninsula, on which the areas of the member countries are borderless and colored in brown. On the edge of the hexagon are colors representing the flags of the six member countries.

ECONOMY

Internal market

A common market was launched on 1 January 2008 with plans to realise a fully integrated single market. It eased the movement of goods and services. However, implementation lagged behind after the 2009 financial crisis. The creation of a customs union began in 2003 and was completed and fully operational on 1 January 2015. In January 2015, the common market was also further integrated, allowing full equality among GCC citizens to work in the government and private sectors, social insurance and retirement coverage, real estate ownership, capital movement, access to education, health and other social services in all member states. However, some barriers remained in the free movement of goods and services. The coordination of taxation systems, accounting standards and civil legislation is currently in progress. The interoperability of professional qualifications, insurance certificates and identity documents is also underway.

Monetary union

In 2014, Bahrain, Kuwait, Qatar, and Saudi Arabia took major steps to ensure the creation of a single currency. Kuwait's finance minister said the four members are pushing ahead with the monetary union but said some "technical points" need to be cleared. "A common market and common central bank would also position the GCC as one entity that would have great "influence on the international financial system" he added. The implementation of a single currency and the creation of a central bank is overseen by the Monetary Council.

There is currently a degree to which a nominal GCC single currency already exists. Businesses trade using a basket of GCC currencies, just as before the euro was introduced, the European Currency Unit (ECU) was long used beforehand as a nominal medium of exchange. Plans to introduce a single currency had been drawn up as far back as 2009, however due to the financial crisis and political differences, the UAE and Oman withdrew their membership.

Mergers and acquisitions

Companies and investors from GCC countries are active in mergers and acquisitions (M&A). Since 1999, more than 5,200 transactions with a known value of US$573 billion have been announced. They are not only active in national deals or within GCC, but also as important investors in cross-border M&A abroad. The investor group includes in particular a number of Sovereign Wealth Funds.

Infrastructure

The Gulf Cooperation Council launched common economic projects to promote and facilitate integration. The member states have cooperated in order to connect their power grids. A water connection project was launched and plans to be partly in use by 2020. A project to create common air transport was also unveiled.

The GCC also launched major rail projects in order to connect the peninsula. The railways are expected to fuel intra-regional trade while helping reduce fuel consumption. Over $200 billion will be invested to develop about 40,000 kilometres of rail network across the GCC, according to Oman's Minister of Transport and Communications. The project, estimated to be worth $15.5 billion, is scheduled to be completed by 2021. "It will link the six member states as a regional transport corridor, further integrating with the national railway projects, deepening economic social and political integration, and it is developed from a sustainable perspective." stated, Ramiz Al Assar, Resident World Bank advisor for the GCC.

Saudi Arabian Railways, Etihad Rail, and national governments have poured billions into railway infrastructure to create rail networks for transporting freight, connecting cities, and reducing transport times.

POLITICS AND GOVERNANCE

Supreme council

The supreme council is the highest authority of the organization. It is composed of the heads of the member states. It is the highest decision-making entity of the GCC. The supreme council sets the vision and the goals of the Gulf Cooperation Council. Decisions on substantive issues require unanimous approval, while issues on procedural matters require a majority. Every member state has one vote.

Ministerial Council

The Ministerial Council is composed of the Foreign Ministers of all the Member States. It convenes every 3 months. It primarily formulates policies and makes recommendations to promote cooperation and achieve coordination among the member states when implementing ongoing projects. Its decisions are submitted in the form of recommendations to the Supreme Council for its approval.

The Ministerial Council is also responsible for preparations of meetings of the Supreme Council and its agenda. The voting procedure in the Ministerial Council is the same as in the Supreme Council.

Secretariat General

The Secretariat is the executive arm of the Gulf Cooperation Council. It takes decisions within its authority and implements decisions approved by the Supreme or Ministerial Council. The Secretariat also compiles studies relating to cooperation, coordination, and planning for common action. It prepares periodical reports regarding the work done by the GCC as a whole and regarding the implementation of its own decisions.

Monetary Council

On 15 December 2009, Bahrain, Kuwait, Qatar, and Saudi Arabia announced the creation of a Monetary Council to introduce a single currency for the union. The board of the council, which set a timetable and action plan for establishing a central bank and choose a currency regime, met for the first time on 30 March 2010. Kuwaiti foreign ministerMohammad Sabah Al-Sabah said on 8 December 2009 that a single currency may take up to ten years to establish. The original target was in 2010. Oman and the UAE later announced their withdrawal of the proposed currency.

In 2014, major moves were taken to ensure the launch of a single currency. Kuwait's finance minister stated that a currency should be implemented without delay. Negotiations with the UAE and Oman to expand the monetary union were renewed.

Patent Office

The GCC Patent Office was approved in 1992 and established soon after in Riyadh, Saudi Arabia. Applications are filed and prosecuted in the Arabic language before the GCC Patent Office in Riyadh, Saudi Arabia, which is a separate office from the Saudi Arabian Patent Office.

Peninsula Shield Force

Amidst the Bahraini uprising, Saudi Arabia and the UAE sent ground troops to Bahrain in order to protect vital infrastructure such as the airport and highway system.Kuwait and Oman refrained from sending troops. Instead, Kuwait sent a navy unit.

In September 2014 GCC members Saudi Arabia, Bahrain, UAE, and Qatar, plus pending member Jordan, commenced air operations against ISIL in Syria.

Saudi Arabia and the UAE however are among the nations that oppose the Muslim Brotherhood in Syria, whereas Qatar has historically supported it. They also pledged other support including operating training facilities for Syrian rebels (Saudi Arabia) and allowing the use of their airbases by other countries fighting ISIL.

GCC Standardization Organization (GSO)

This is the standardization organization of the GCC, and Yemen also belongs to this organization.

Gulf Organization for Industrial Consulting (GOIC)

The Gulf Organization for Industrial Consulting (GOIC) was founded in 1976 by the Gulf Cooperation Council (GCC) member states: The United Arab Emirates, Bahrain, Saudi Arabia, Oman, Qatar and Kuwait, and in 2009, Yemen joined the Organization, which is headquartered at Doha, Qatar. The organization chart of GOIC includes the Board members and the General Secretariat. The Board is formed by member state representatives appointed by their governments.

Macro-economic trend

Year	GDP	
(millions)	GDP per capita	
(as % of USA's GDP per capita)		
1980	$250,675	152.00
1985	$183,069	60.19
1990	$207,735	41.28
1995	$261,072	37.10
2000	$375,483	36.26
2005	$664,582	45.19
2010	$1,084,647	56.56

SPORTS

The union has served as a grouping for sports co-operation and competition. The GCC states have an annual Meeting of the Youth and Sports ministers to boost youth and sports initiatives in the region; in 2015, this gathering was held for the 29th time. The promotion of the hosting of international sports events has also served an economic purpose for the union's countries, leading to investment and development in the region.

The GCC Games, a quadrennial multi-sport event, was established by the union and first held in 2011. There are numerous long-running GCC Championships for individual sports, including: the Gulf Cooperation Council Athletics Championships (first held in 1986; youth section from 2000) sailing, basketball, swimming, tennis, gymnastics (senior and youth levels), weightlifting, futsal, snooker, and table tennis.

2014 SAUDI–QATARI RIFT

Qatar's support for the Muslim Brotherhood across the MENA area, Hamas and radical Islamists in Libya has led to increasing tensions with other Arab states of the Persian Gulf. These tensions came to a head during a March 2014 meeting of the Gulf Cooperation Council, after which the UAE, Saudi Arabia and Bahrain announced the recall of their ambassadors to Qatar.

Some financial economists have interpreted the 2014 Saudi–Qatari rift as the tangible political sign of a growing economic rivalry between oil and natural gas producers, which could "have deep and long-lasting consequences" beyond the MENA area.

2017 RIFT WITH QATAR

On June 5, 2017, Saudi Arabia, UAE, Bahrain and Egypt had officially cut diplomatic ties with Qatar. Saudi Arabia said it took the decision to cut diplomatic ties due to Qatar's "embrace of various terrorist and sectarian groups aimed at destabilising the region", including the Muslim Brotherhood, al-Qaida, Islamic State of Iraq and the Levant and groups supported by Iran in the kingdom's eastern province of Qatif. Islam Hassan argues "Starting from 2000 and ahead, Qatar has been pursuing an independent foreign policy that at times clash with the Saudi strategic interests in the region. The fact that Qatar has not been toeing the Saudi foreign policy, and dealing with states and non-state actors that the Saudis do not approve of have caused this tension in relations over the past couple of years, mainly after the Arab uprisings. This tension was revived by the hacking saga of Qatar News Agency and the statement that was attributed to Sheikh Tamim bin Hamad. This happened at a time Mohamed bin Salman is facing competition from Mohamed bin Nayef over the Saudi throne. Mohamed bin Salman tried to have the US blessing during Trump's visit to Saudi to force Qatar to its knees and go back home with a win that would give him more popularity in Saudi Arabia, easing his journey to power. With regards to UAE, there has been always competition between al-Nahyans of Abu Dhabi and al-Thanis of Qatar. This competition goes back to the 1800s. The Arab uprisings ushered a new chapter in the Qatari-Emirati competition. The competition led to the Emiratis playing a major role in the withdrawal of ambassadors from Qatar in 2014. At the beginning of the current diplomatic crisis, particularly after the hacking saga, UAE was trying to maintain the problem. Yet, Aljazeera's publishing of Yousuf al-Otaiba's leaked emails got the UAE on board with Saudi Arabia. Insofar as Bahrain is concerned, the small Kingdom has been toeing the Saudi foreign policy for the past couple of years. It seems that their severing of ties with Qatar was mainly an answer to a Saudi call."

In June, various members put a ban on Qataris and their businesses. Qataris are not allowed to enter or live in the country unless they have a spouse living there or they need to carry a visa in order to enter these countries. Flights from Qatar are also not allowed to land there and vice versa.

RELATED STATES

Since the creation of the council in 1981 its membership has not expanded, with all members being Arab monarchies.

Some GCC countries have land borders with Iraq, Jordan and Yemen, and sea borders with Iran, Egypt, Sudan, Eritrea and Somalia.

Egypt

Only the Sinai peninsula lies in the Arabian peninsula, Bahrain has been vocal about its stance on Egypt joining the GCC, in 2011, Bahraini Foreign Minister has called for Egypt to be admitted as a member of the GCC.

Iraq

Iraq is the only Arab country bordering the Persian Gulf that is not a member of the Gulf Cooperation Council. In 2012, Iraqi Defence Minister Saadoun al-Dulaimi stated that Iraq wants to join the GCC. Kuwait supports Iraq joining the GCC. The lack of membership of Iraq is widely believed to be due to the low-income economy, its substantial Shia population, its republican political system, and its invasion of member state Kuwait during the Gulf War.

Iran

At the December 2012 Manama summit, the GCC states called for an end to Iranian interference in their internal affairs.

Jordan and Morocco

In May 2011, Jordan's request to join the GCC, which had been first submitted 15 years earlier, was accepted and Morocco was invited to join the union. In September 2011 a five-year economic plan for both countries was put forward after a meeting between the foreign ministers of both countries and those of the GCC States, the first GCC meeting since May which included the Jordanian and Moroccan ministers. Although a plan for accession was being looked into, it was noted that there was no timetable for either's accession, and that discussions would continue.

As Jordan and Morocco are the only two Arab monarchies not currently in the council, the current members see them as strong potential allies. Jordan borders member Saudi Arabia and is economically connected to the Persian Gulf States. Although Morocco is not near the Persian Gulf, the Moroccan foreign minister Taieb Fassi Fihri notes that "geographical distance is no obstacle to a strong relationship".

Yemen

Yemen was in negotiations for GCC membership, and hoped to join by 2015. Although it has no coastline on the Persian Gulf, Yemen lies in the Arabian Peninsula and shares a common culture and history with other members of the GCC. The GCC has already approved Yemen's accession to the GCC Standardization Authority, Gulf Organization for Industrial Consulting (GOIC), GCC Auditing and Accounting Authority, Gulf Radio and TV Authority, GCC Council of Health Ministers, GCC Education and Training Bureau, GCC Council of Labour and Social Affairs Ministers, and Gulf Cup Football Tournament. The Council issued directives that all the necessary legal measures be taken so that Yemen would have the same rights and obligations of GCC member states in those institutions.

In May 2017, the Gulf Cooperation Council rejected the formation of a transitional political council in southern Yemen, which called for the separation of Southern Yemen, siding with Yemen President Abd-Rabbu Mansour Hadi in doing so.

RELATED ORGANIZATIONS

The GCC members and Yemen are also members of the Greater Arab Free Trade Area (GAFTA). However, this is unlikely to affect the agenda of the GCC significantly as it has a more aggressive timetable than GAFTA and is seeking greater integration.

8

The North Atlantic Treaty Organization (NATO)

The North Atlantic Treaty Organization (NATO), also called the North Atlantic Alliance, is an intergovernmental military alliance between 29 North American and European countries.

The organization implements the North Atlantic Treaty that was signed on 4 April 1949. NATO constitutes a system of collective defencewhereby its independent member states agree to mutual defence in response to an attack by any external party.

NATO Headquarters are located in Haren, Brussels, Belgium, while the headquarters of Allied Command Operations is near Mons, Belgium.

Since its founding, the admission of new member states has increased the alliance from the original 12 countries to 29. The most recent member state to be added to NATO is Montenegro on 5 June 2017. NATO currently recognizes Bosnia and Herzegovina, Georgia, Macedonia and Ukraine as aspiring members. An additional 21 countries participate in NATO's Partnership for Peace program, with 15 other countries involved in institutionalized dialogue programs. The combined military spending of all NATO members constitutes over 70% of the global total. Members have committed to reach or maintain defense spending of at least 2% of GDP by 2024.

HISTORY

On 4 March 1947 the Treaty of Dunkirk was signed by France and the United Kingdom as a *Treaty of Alliance and Mutual Assistance* in the event of a possible attack by Germany or the Soviet Union in the aftermath of World War II. In 1948, this alliance was expanded to include the Benelux countries, in the form of the Western Union, also referred to as the Brussels Treaty Organization (BTO), established by the Treaty of Brussels. Talks for a new military alliance which could also include North America resulted in the signature of the North Atlantic Treaty on 4 April 1949 by the member states of the Western Union plus the United States, Canada, Portugal, Italy, Norway, Denmark and Iceland.

The North Atlantic Treaty was largely dormant until the Korean War initiated the establishment of NATO to implement it, by means of an integrated military structure: This included the formation of Supreme Headquarters Allied Powers Europe (SHAPE) in 1951, which adopted the Western Union's military structures and plans. In 1952 the post of Secretary General of NATO was established as the organization's chief civilian, the first major NATO maritime exercises began; Exercise Mainbrace, and Greece and Turkey acceded. In 1955 West Germany was also incorporated into NATO, which resulted in the creation of the Soviet-dominated Warsaw Pact, delineating the two opposing sides of the Cold War.

Doubts over the strength of the relationship between the European states and the United States ebbed and flowed, along with doubts over the credibility of the NATO defense against a prospective Soviet invasion – doubts that led to the development of the independent French nuclear deterrent and the withdrawal of France from NATO's military structure in 1966. In 1982 the newly democratic Spain joined the alliance.

The collapse of the Warsaw Pact in 1989-1991 removed the *de facto* main adversary of NATO and caused a strategic re-evaluation of NATO's purpose, nature, tasks, and their focus on the continent of Europe. This shift started with the 1990 signing in Paris of the Treaty on Conventional Armed Forces in Europe between NATO and the Soviet Union, which mandated specific military reductions across the continent that continued after the dissolution of the Soviet Union in December 1991. At that time, European countries accounted for 34 percent of NATO's military spending; by 2012, this had fallen to 21 percent. NATO also began a gradual expansion to include newly autonomous Central and Eastern European nations, and extended its activities into political and humanitarian situations that had not formerly been NATO concerns.

After the fall of the Berlin Wall in Germany in 1989, the organization conducted its first military interventions in Bosnia from 1992 to 1995 and later Yugoslavia in 1999 during the breakup of Yugoslavia.

Politically, the organization sought better relations with former Warsaw Pact countries, most of which joined the alliance in 1999 and 2004. Article 5 of the North Atlantic treaty, requiring member states to come to the aid of any member state subject to an armed attack, was invoked for the first and only time after the September 11 attacks, after which troops were deployed to Afghanistan under the NATO-led ISAF.

The organization has operated a range of additional roles since then, including sending trainers to Iraq, assisting in counter-piracy operations and in 2011 enforcing a no-fly zone over Libya in accordance with UN Security Council Resolution 1973. The less potent Article 4, which merely invokes consultation among NATO members, has been invoked five times following incidents in the Iraq War, Syrian Civil War, and annexation of Crimea.

The first post-Cold War expansion of NATO came with German reunification on 3 October 1990, when the former East Germany became part of the Federal Republic of Germany and the alliance. As part of post-Cold War restructuring, NATO's military structure was cut back and reorganized, with new forces such as the Headquarters Allied Command Europe Rapid Reaction Corps established. The changes brought about by the collapse of the Soviet Union on the military balance in Europe were recognized in the Adapted Conventional Armed Forces in Europe Treaty, which was signed in 1999. The policies of French President Nicolas Sarkozy resulted in a major reform of France's military position, culminating with the return to full membership on 4 April 2009, which also included France rejoining the NATO Military Command Structure, while maintaining an independent nuclear deterrent.

Between 1994 and 1997, wider forums for regional cooperation between NATO and its neighbors were set up, like the Partnership for Peace, the Mediterranean Dialogue initiative and the Euro-Atlantic Partnership Council. In 1998, the NATO–Russia Permanent Joint Council was established. Between 1999 and 2017 NATO incorporated the following Central and Eastern European countries, including several former communist states: the Czech Republic, Hungary, Poland, Bulgaria, Estonia, Latvia, Lithuania, Romania, Slovakia, Slovenia, Albania, Croatia and Montenegro.

The Russian intervention in Crimea in 2014 lead to strong condemnation by NATO nations and the creation of a new "spearhead" force of 5,000 troops at bases in Estonia, Lithuania, Latvia, Poland, Romania, and Bulgaria. At the subsequent 2014 Wales summit, the leaders of NATO's member states formally committed for the first time spend the equivalent of at least 2% of their gross domestic products on defence by 2024, which had previously been only an informal guideline.

MILITARY OPERATIONS

Early operations

No military operations were conducted by NATO during the Cold War. Following the end of the Cold War, the first operations, *Anchor Guard* in 1990 and *Ace Guard* in 1991, were prompted by the Iraqi invasion of Kuwait. Airborne early warning aircraft were sent to provide coverage of southeastern Turkey, and later a quick-reaction force was deployed to the area.

Bosnia and Herzegovina intervention

The Bosnian War began in 1992, as a result of the breakup of Yugoslavia. The deteriorating situation led to United Nations Security Council Resolution 816 on 9 October 1992, ordering a no-fly zone over central Bosnia and Herzegovina, which NATO began enforcing on 12 April 1993 with Operation *Deny Flight.* From June 1993 until October 1996, Operation *Sharp Guard* added maritime enforcement of the arms embargo and economic sanctions against the Federal Republic of Yugoslavia. On 28 February 1994, NATO took its first wartime action by shooting down four Bosnian Serb aircraft violating the no-fly zone.

On 10 and 11 April 1994, during the Bosnian War, the United Nations Protection Force called in air strikes to protect the Gora•de safe area, resulting in the bombing of a Bosnian Serb military command outpost near Gora•de by two US F-16 jets acting under NATO direction.This resulted in the taking of 150 U.N. personnel hostage on 14 April. On 16 April a British Sea Harrier was shot down over Gora•de by Serb forces. A two-week NATO bombing campaign, Operation *Deliberate Force,* began in August 1995 against the Army of the Republika Srpska, after the Srebrenica massacre.

NATO air strikes that year helped bring the Yugoslav wars to an end, resulting in the Dayton Agreement in November 1995. As part of this agreement, NATO deployed a UN-mandated peacekeeping force, under Operation *Joint Endeavor,* named IFOR. Almost 60,000 NATO troops were joined by forces from non-NATO nations in this peacekeeping mission. This transitioned into the smaller SFOR, which started with 32,000 troops initially and ran from December 1996 until December 2004, when operations were then passed onto European Union Force Althea. Following the lead of its member nations, NATO began to award a service medal, the NATO Medal, for these operations.

Kosovo intervention

In an effort to stop Slobodan Miloševiæ's Serbian-led crackdown on KLA separatists and Albanian civilians in Kosovo, the United Nations Security Council passed Resolution 1199 on 23 September 1998 to demand a ceasefire. Negotiations under US Special Envoy Richard Holbrooke broke down on 23 March 1999, and he handed the matter to NATO, which started a 78-day bombing campaign on 24 March 1999. Operation *Allied Force* targeted the military capabilities of what was then the Federal Republic of Yugoslavia. During the crisis, NATO also deployed one of its international reaction forces, the ACE Mobile Force (Land), to Albania as the Albania Force (AFOR), to deliver humanitarian aid to refugees from Kosovo.

Though the campaign was criticized for high civilian casualties, including bombing of the Chinese embassy in Belgrade, Miloševiæ finally accepted the terms of an international peace plan on 3 June 1999, ending the Kosovo War.

On 11 June, Miloševiæ further accepted UN resolution 1244, under the mandate of which NATO then helped establish the KFOR peacekeeping force. Nearly one million refugees had fled Kosovo, and part of KFOR's mandate was to protect the humanitarian missions, in addition to deterring violence. In August–September 2001, the alliance also mounted Operation *Essential Harvest*, a mission disarming ethnic Albanian militias in the Republic of Macedonia. As of 1 December 2013, 4,882 KFOR soldiers, representing 31 countries, continue to operate in the area.

The US, the UK, and most other NATO countries opposed efforts to require the UN Security Council to approve NATO military strikes, such as the action against Serbia in 1999, while France and some others claimed that the alliance needed UN approval. The US/UK side claimed that this would undermine the authority of the alliance, and they noted that Russia and China would have exercised their Security Council vetoes to block the strike on Yugoslavia, and could do the same in future conflicts where NATO intervention was required, thus nullifying the entire potency and purpose of the organization. Recognizing the post-Cold War military environment, NATO adopted the Alliance Strategic Concept during its Washington summit in April 1999 that emphasized conflict prevention and crisis management.

War in Afghanistan

The September 11 attacks in the United States caused NATO to invoke Article 5 of the NATO Charter for the first time in the organization's history. The Article says that an attack on any member shall be considered to be an attack on all. The invocation was confirmed on 4 October 2001 when NATO determined that the attacks were indeed eligible under the terms of the North Atlantic Treaty. The eight official actions taken by NATO in response to the attacks included Operation *Eagle Assist* and Operation *Active Endeavour*, a naval operation in the Mediterranean Sea which is designed to prevent the movement of terrorists or weapons of mass destruction, as well as enhancing the security of shipping in general which began on 4 October 2001.

The alliance showed unity: On 16 April 2003, NATO agreed to take command of the International Security Assistance Force (ISAF), which includes troops from 42 countries. The decision came at the request of Germany and the Netherlands, the two nations leading ISAF at the time of the agreement, and all nineteen NATO ambassadors approved it unanimously. The handover of control to NATO took place on 11 August, and marked the first time in NATO's history that it took charge of a mission outside the north Atlantic area.

ISAF was initially charged with securing Kabul and surrounding areas from the Taliban, al Qaedaand factional warlords, so as to allow for the establishment of the Afghan Transitional Administrationheaded by Hamid Karzai. In October 2003, the UN Security Council authorized the expansion of the ISAF mission throughout Afghanistan, and ISAF subsequently expanded the mission in four main stages over the whole of the country.

On 31 July 2006, the ISAF additionally took over military operations in the south of Afghanistan from a US-led anti-terrorism coalition. Due to the intensity of the fighting in the south, in 2011 France allowed a squadron of Mirage 2000 fighter/attack aircraft to be moved into the area, to Kandahar, in order to reinforce the alliance's efforts. During its 2012 Chicago Summit, NATO endorsed a plan to end the Afghanistan war and to remove the NATO-led ISAF Forces by the end of December 2014. ISAF was disestablished in December 2014 and replaced by the follow-on training Resolute Support Mission

Iraq training mission

In August 2004, during the Iraq War, NATO formed the NATO Training Mission – Iraq, a training mission to assist the Iraqi security forces in conjunction with the US led MNF-I.The NATO Training Mission-Iraq (NTM-I) was established at the request of the Iraqi Interim Government under the provisions of United Nations Security Council Resolution 1546. The aim of NTM-I was to assist in the development of Iraqi security forces training structures and institutions so that Iraq can build an effective and sustainable capability that addresses the needs of the nation. NTM-I was not a combat mission but is a distinct mission, under the political control of NATO's North Atlantic Council. Its operational emphasis was on training and mentoring. The activities of the mission were coordinated with Iraqi authorities and the US-led Deputy Commanding General Advising and Training, who was also dual-hatted as the Commander of NTM-I. The mission officially concluded on 17 December 2011.

Turkey invoked the first Article 4 meetings in 2003 at the start of the Iraq War. Turkey also invoked this article twice in 2012 during the Syrian Civil War, after the downing of an unarmed Turkish F-4 reconnaissance jet, and after a mortar was fired at Turkey from Syria, and again in 2015 after threats by Islamic State of Iraq and the Levant to its territorial integrity.

Gulf of Aden anti-piracy

Beginning on 17 August 2009, NATO deployed warships in an operation to protect maritime traffic in the Gulf of Aden and the Indian Ocean from Somali pirates, and help strengthen the navies and coast guards of regional states. The operation was approved by the North Atlantic Council and involves warships primarily from the United States though vessels from many other nations are also included. Operation *Ocean Shield* focuses on protecting the ships of Operation *Allied Provider* which are distributing aid as part of the World Food Programme mission in Somalia. Russia, China and South Korea have sent warships to participate in the activities as well. The operation seeks to dissuade and interrupt pirate attacks, protect vessels, and abetting to increase the general level of security in the region.

Libya intervention

During the Libyan Civil War, violence between protestors and the Libyan government under Colonel Muammar Gaddafi escalated, and on 17 March 2011 led to the passage of United Nations Security Council Resolution 1973, which called for a ceasefire, and authorized military action to protect civilians. A coalition that included several NATO members began enforcing a no-fly zone over Libya shortly afterwards, beginning with Opération Harmattan by the French Air Force on March 19.

On 20 March 2011, NATO states agreed on enforcing an arms embargo against Libya with Operation *Unified Protector* using ships from NATO Standing Maritime Group 1 and Standing Mine Countermeasures Group 1, and additional ships and submarines from NATO members. They would "monitor, report and, if needed, interdict vessels suspected of carrying illegal arms or mercenaries".

On 24 March, NATO agreed to take control of the no-fly zone from the initial coalition, while command of targeting ground units remained with the coalition's forces. NATO began officially enforcing the UN resolution on 27 March 2011 with assistance from Qatar and the United Arab Emirates. By June, reports of divisions within the alliance surfaced as only eight of the 28 member nations were participating in combat operations, resulting in a confrontation between US Defense Secretary Robert Gates and countries such as Poland, Spain, the Netherlands, Turkey, and Germany to contribute more, the latter believing the organization has overstepped its mandate in the conflict. In his final policy speech in Brussels on 10 June, Gates further criticized allied countries in suggesting their actions could cause the demise of NATO. The German foreign ministry pointed to "a considerable [German] contribution to NATO and NATO-led operations" and to the fact that this engagement was highly valued by President Obama.

While the mission was extended into September, Norway that day announced it would begin scaling down contributions and complete withdrawal by 1 August. Earlier that week it was reported Danish air fighters were running out of bombs. The following week, the head of the Royal Navy said the country's operations in the conflict were not sustainable. By the end of the mission in October 2011, after the death of Colonel Gaddafi, NATO planes had flown about 9,500 strike sorties against pro-Gaddafi targets. A report from the organization Human Rights Watch in May 2012 identified at least 72 civilians killed in the campaign. Following a coup d'état attempt in October 2013, Libyan Prime Minister Ali Zeidan requested technical advice and trainers from NATO to assist with ongoing security issues.

PARTICIPATING COUNTRIES

Members

NATO has twenty-nine members, mainly in Europe and North America. Some of these countries also have territory on multiple continents, which can be covered only as far south as the Tropic of Cancer in the Atlantic Ocean, which defines NATO's "area of responsibility" under Article 6 of the North Atlantic Treaty. During the original treaty negotiations, the United States insisted that colonies such as the Belgian Congo be excluded from the treaty. French Algeria was however covered until their independence on 3 July 1962. Twelve of these twenty-nine are original members who joined in 1949, while the other seventeen joined in one of seven enlargement rounds.

From the mid-1960s to the mid-1990s, France pursued a military strategy of independence from NATO under a policy dubbed "Gaullo-Mitterrandism". Nicolas Sarkozy negotiated the return of France to the integrated military command and the Defence Planning Committee in 2009, the latter being disbanded the following year. France remains the only NATO member outside the Nuclear Planning Group and unlike the United States and the United Kingdom, will not commit its nuclear-armed submarines to the alliance. Few members spend more than two percent of their gross domestic product on defence, with the United States accounting for three quarters of NATO defense spending.

Enlargement

New membership in the alliance has been largely from Central and Eastern Europe, including former members of the Warsaw Pact. Accession to the alliance is governed with individual Membership Action Plans, and requires approval by each current member. NATO currently has two candidate countries that are in the process of joining the alliance: Bosnia and Herzegovina and the Republic of Macedonia. In NATO official statements, the Republic of Macedonia is always referred to as the "former Yugoslav Republic of Macedonia", with a footnote stating that "Turkey recognizes the Republic of Macedonia under its constitutional name". Though Macedonia completed its requirements for membership at the same time as Croatia and Albania, who joined NATO in 2009, its accession was blocked by Greece pending a resolution of the Macedonia naming dispute. In order to support each other in the process, new and potential members in the region formed the Adriatic Charter in 2003. Georgia was also named as an aspiring member, and was promised "future membership" during the 2008 summit in Bucharest, though in 2014, US President Barack Obama said the country was not "currently on a path" to membership.

Russia continues to oppose further expansion, seeing it as inconsistent with understandings between Soviet leader Mikhail Gorbachev and European and American negotiators that allowed for a peaceful German reunification. NATO's expansion efforts are often seen by Moscow leaders as a continuation of a Cold War attempt to surround and isolate Russia, though they have also been criticised in the West. A June 2016 Levada poll found that 68% of Russians think that deploying NATO troops in the Baltic states and Poland – former Eastern bloc countries bordering Russia – is a threat to Russia. Ukraine's relationship with NATO and Europe has been politically divisive, and contributed to "Euromaidan" protests that saw the ousting of pro-Russian President Viktor Yanukovych in 2014. In March 2014, Prime Minister Arseniy Yatsenyuk reiterated the government's stance that Ukraine is not seeking NATO membership.Ukraine's president subsequently signed a bill dropping his nation's nonaligned status in order to pursue NATO membership, but signaled that it would hold a referendum before seeking to join. Ukraine is one of eight countries in Eastern Europe with an Individual Partnership Action Plan. IPAPs began in 2002, and are open to countries that have the political will and ability to deepen their relationship with NATO.

A 2006 study in the journal *Security Studies* argued that NATO enlargement contributed to democratic consolidation in Central and Eastern Europe.

Partnerships

The Partnership for Peace (PfP) programme was established in 1994 and is based on individual bilateral relations between each partner country and NATO: each country may choose the extent of its participation. Members include all current and former members of the Commonwealth of Independent States. The Euro-Atlantic Partnership Council (EAPC) was first established on 29 May 1997, and is a forum for regular coordination, consultation and dialogue between all fifty participants. The PfP programme is considered the operational wing of the Euro-Atlantic Partnership. Other third countries also have been contacted for participation in some activities of the PfP framework such as Afghanistan.

The European Union (EU) signed a comprehensive package of arrangements with NATO under the Berlin Plus agreement on 16 December 2002. With this agreement, the EU was given the possibility to use NATO assets in case it wanted to act independently in an international crisis, on the condition that NATO itself did not want to act – the so-called "right of first refusal". For example, Article 42(7) of the 1982 Treaty of Lisbon specifies that "If a Member State is the victim of armed aggression on its territory, the other Member States shall have towards it an obligation of aid and assistance by all the means in their power". The treaty applies globally to specified territories whereas NATO is restricted under its Article 6 to operations north of the Tropic of Cancer. It provides a "double framework" for the EU countries that are also linked with the PfP programme.

Additionally, NATO cooperates and discusses its activities with numerous other non-NATO members. The Mediterranean Dialogue was established in 1994 to coordinate in a similar way with Israel and countries in North Africa. The Istanbul Cooperation Initiative was announced in 2004 as a dialog forum for the Middle East along the same lines as the Mediterranean Dialogue. The four participants are also linked through the Gulf Cooperation Council.

Political dialogue with Japan began in 1990, and since then, the Alliance has gradually increased its contact with countries that do not form part of any of these cooperation initiatives. In 1998, NATO established a set of general guidelines that do not allow for a formal institutionalisation of relations, but reflect the Allies' desire to increase cooperation. Following extensive debate, the term "Contact Countries" was agreed by the Allies in 2000.

By 2012, the Alliance had broadened this group, which meets to discuss issues such as counter-piracy and technology exchange, under the names "partners across the globe" or "global partners". Australia and New Zealand, both contact countries, are also members of the AUSCANNZUKUS strategic alliance, and similar regional or bilateral agreements between contact countries and NATO members also aid cooperation. Colombia is the NATO's latest partner and Colombia has access to the full range of cooperative activities NATO offers to partners;

Colombia became the first and only Latin American country to cooperate with NATO.

STRUCTURE

All agencies and organizations of NATO integrated into either the civilian administrative or military executive roles. For the most part they perform roles and functions that directly or indirectly support the security role of the alliance as a whole.

The civilian structure includes:

- The North Atlantic Council (NAC) is the body which has effective governance authority and powers of decision in NATO, consisting of member states' permanent representatives or representatives at higher level (ministers of foreign affairs or defence, or heads of state or government). The NAC convenes at least once a week and takes major decisions regarding NATO's policies. The meetings of the North Atlantic Council are chaired by the Secretary General and, when decisions have to be made, action is agreed upon on the basis of unanimity and common accord. There is no voting or decision by majority. Each nation represented at the Council table or on any of its subordinate committees retains complete sovereignty and responsibility for its own decisions.
- NATO Headquarters, located on Boulevard Léopold III/ Leopold III-laan, B-1110 Brussels, which is in Haren, part of the City of Brusselsmunicipality. The staff at the Headquarters is composed of national delegations of member countries and includes civilian and military liaison offices and officers or diplomatic missions and diplomats of partner countries, as well as the International Staff and International Military Staff filled from serving members of the armed forces of member states. Non-governmental citizens' groups have also grown up in support of NATO, broadly under the banner of the Atlantic Council/Atlantic Treaty Association movement.

The military structure includes:

- The Military Committee (MC) is the body of NATO that is composed of member states' Chiefs of Defence (CHOD) and advises the North Atlantic Council (NAC) on military policy and strategy. The national CHODs are regularly represented in the MC by their permanent Military Representatives (MilRep), who often are two- or three-star flag officers. Like the Council, from time to time the Military Committee also meets at a higher level, namely at the level of Chiefs of Defence, the most senior military officer in each nation's armed forces. The MC is led by its chairman, who directs NATO's military operations. Like the Council, from time to time the Military Committee also meets at a higher level, namely at the level of Chiefs of Defence, the most senior military officer in each nation's armed forces. Until 2008 the Military Committee excluded France, due to that country's 1966 decision to remove itself from the NATO Military Command Structure, which it rejoined in 1995. Until France rejoined NATO, it was not represented on the Defence Planning Committee, and this led to conflicts between it and NATO members. Such was the case in the lead up to Operation *Iraqi Freedom*. The operational work of the Committee is supported by the International Military Staff
- Allied Command Operations (ACO) is the NATO command of responsible for NATO operations worldwide.
- Allied Command Transformation (ACT), responsible for transformation and training of NATO forces.
- The Rapid Deployable Corps include Eurocorps, I. German/Dutch Corps, Multinational Corps Northeast, and NATO Rapid Deployable Italian Corps among others, as well as naval High Readiness Forces (HRFs), which all report to Allied Command Operations.

The organizations and agencies of NATO include:

- Headquarters for the NATO Support Agency will be in

- Capellen Luxembourg (site of the current NATO Maintenance and Supply Agency – NAMSA).
- The NATO Communications and Information Agency Headquarters will be in Brussels, as will the very small staff which will design the new NATO Procurement Agency.
- A new NATO Science and Technology (S&T) Organization will be created before July 2012, consisting of Chief Scientist, a Programme Office for Collaborative S&T, and the NATO Undersea Research Centre (NURC).
- The current NATO Standardization Agency will continue and be subject to review by Spring 2014.

The NATO Parliamentary Assembly (NATO PA) is a body that sets broad strategic goals for NATO, which meets at two session per year. NATO PA interacts directly with the parliamentary structures of the national governments of the member states which appoint Permanent Members, or ambassadors to NATO. The NATO Parliamentary Assembly is made up of legislators from the member countries of the North Atlantic Alliance as well as thirteen associate members. It is however officially a different structure from NATO, and has as aim to join together deputies of NATO countries in order to discuss security policies on the NATO Council.

9

Union of South American Nations (USAN)

The Union of South American Nations (USAN; Spanish: *Unión de Naciones Suramericanas*, UNASUR; Portuguese: *União de Nações Sul-Americanas*, UNASUL; Dutch: *Unie van Zuid-Amerikaanse Naties*, UZAN; and sometimes referred to as the South American Union) is an intergovernmental regional organization comprising twelve South American countries.

The UNASUR Constitutive Treaty was signed on 23 May 2008, at the Third Summit of Heads of State, held in Brasília, Brazil.According to the Constitutive Treaty, the Union's headquarters will be located in Quito, Ecuador. On 1 December 2010, Uruguay became the ninth state to ratify the UNASUR treaty, thus giving the union full legality. As the Constitutive Treaty entered into force on 11 March 2011, UNASUR became a legal entity during a meeting of Foreign Ministers in Mitad del Mundo, Ecuador, where they had laid the foundation stone for the Secretariat Headquarters. The South American Parliament will be located in Cochabamba, Bolivia, while the headquarters of its bank, the Bank of the South are located in Caracas, Venezuela.

On 4 May 2010, at a heads of state summit held in Campana, 75 km (47 mi) north of Buenos Aires, former Argentine President Néstor Kirchner was unanimously elected the first Secretary General of UNASUR for a two-year term. The new post was conceived as a first step towards the creation of a permanent bureaucratic body for a supranational union, which will eventually replace the political bodies of Mercosur and CAN. The headquarters of the secretariat is located in Quito.

After Argentina, Bolivia, Chile, Ecuador, Guyana, Peru, Suriname and Venezuela, Uruguay became the ninth nation to ratify the constitutive treaty of the organization on 1 December 2010, thus completing the minimum number of ratifications Necessary for the entry into force of the Treaty, on 11 March 2011 With the entry into force of the Treaty, Unasur became a legal entity during the Summit Ministers of Foreign Affairs, in Mitad del Mundo, Ecuador, where the cornerstone was laid for the headquarters of the General Secretariat of the Union.

In April 2018, six countries suspended membership: Argentina, Brazil, Chile, Colombia, Paraguay and Peru.

Overview

At the Third South American Summit on 8 December 2004, presidents or representatives from 12 South American nations signed the *Cusco Declaration*, a two-page statement of intent announcing the foundation of the South American Community. Panama and Mexico attended the signing ceremony as observers.

The mechanics of the new entity came out of the First South American Community of Nations Heads of State Summit, which was held in Brasília on 29–30 September 2005. An important operating condition of UNASUR is that no new institutions will be created in the first phase, so as not to increase bureaucracy, and the community will use the existing institutions belonging to the previous trade blocs.

HISTORY

Background

Between the 15th and 19th centuries, the Spanish and Portuguese colonization brought about the establishment and development of colonial empires in the Americas that integrated politically, economically and culturally vast extensions of the continent each with their respective metropolis.

Since the Spanish American wars of independence a trend towards the political integration of the newly born republics of Hispanic Americabecame strong in the thinking of several independence leaders, influenced in turn by the Spanish Enlightenment and the French and American revolutions. A notable early exponent of this trend was Francisco de Miranda, who envisioned a federated republic encompassing all of Hispanic America, which he called "Colombia".

The independence war efforts saw the concurrence of integrated armies composed by Spanish Americans of diverse regions on both sides of the conflict (v.g. Patriots and Royalists), and fighting all over the territories of many future nations. For example, the Army of the Andeswhich was gathered in the United Provinces of the River Plate fought in Chile, Peru and Ecuador, and later integrated with Simón Bolívar's Army (which itself included troops of future Venezuela, Colombia and Ecuador) to further fight in Peru and the Upper Peru.

By the 1820s, the main proponent of a federation of the newly born republics was Simón Bolívar, although this idea was shared by many notable contemporaries, including José de San Martín and Bernardo de Monteagudo, under either republican or constitutional monarchical governments. In 1826, Bolívar summoned a conference to be held in Panama, which was to be known as the "Amphictyonic" Congress of Panama because of the parallelism with the Hellenic Amphictyonic League. The Congress was attended by Gran Colombia(including present-day Colombia, Venezuela, Panama and Ecuador), the Federal Republic of Central America (including present-day Costa Rica, Nicaragua, El Salvador, Honduras and Guatemala), the United Mexican States, and Peru. The ostensible intention was to form a defensive league that could prevent foreign expansionism and foster the interests of the Spanish American republics. The Congress' conclusions, however, were not ratified by the participants, except for Gran Colombia. Soon after, both Gran Colombia and the United Provinces of Central America fell apart and the whole of Hispanic America was balkanized by competing national governments.

By the 1990s, however, Brazil had consolidated as the most powerful country in South America (accounting for half of the regional GDP) and began to promote the notion of a united South America (a new regional framing) where Brasilia would be pivotal. The project did not take hold until the United States' foreign policy priorities turned to other regions in the 2000s.

Formation

South American presidents gathered during an extraordinary meeting for the signing of the UNASUR Constitutive Treaty in May 2008 in Brasilia.

The complete integration between the Andean Community and the Mercosur nations was formalized during the meeting of South American heads of state that took place on 23 May 2008 in Brasília.

In the 2004 South American Summit, representatives of twelve South American nations signed the Cuzco Declaration, a two-page letter of intent announcing the establishment of the then-named "South American Community of Nations". Panama and Mexico were present as observers. The leaders announced the intention of modeling the new community in the mold of the European Union, including a unified passport, a parliament and, eventually, a single currency. The then Secretary General of the Andean Community Allan Wagner speculated that an advanced union such as the EU should be possible within the next fifteen years.

Naming

On 28 December 2005, Chilean former foreign minister Ignacio Walker proposed that the Union's former designation, the South American Community of Nations, abbreviated as CSN, be changed to *South American Union*; nevertheless, many members responded that that proposal had already been rejected to prevent confusion since its acronym of U.S.A. (Spanish: *Unión Sudamericana*) would be easily confused for the United States of America. In the press, the phrase "United States of South America" was bandied about as an analogy to the United States to reflect the economic and political power that the union would have on the world stage.

The name was finally changed on 16 April 2007 to *Union of South American Nations*. The new name was jointly agreed by all member states during the first day of meeting at the First South American Energy Summit, held at Isla Margarita, Venezuela.

Leadership crisis

After Colombian Ernesto Samper completed his term as Secretary General in January 2017, the UNASUR governments have been unable to reach consensus on the organization's future leadership. Venezuela, with the support of Bolivia and Suriname, has blocked the nomination of Argentine diplomat José Octavio Bordón.

In August 2017, six members of UNASUR—Argentina, Brazil, Chile, Colombia, Paraguay and Peru—joined in forming the Lima Group, a coalition of Western Hemisphere nations that repudiates the Venezuela government of Nicolás Maduro as antidemocratic. In February 2018, Maduro was disinvited from the Summit of the Americas hosted by Peru (held in Lima in April 2018). In response, Bolivia's leftist president Evo Morales urged Unasur to defend Venezuela, stating "Unasur should call an emergency meeting and enforce the sovereignty of a brotherly people." Morales acceded to the rotating role of president pro tempore of UNASUR on 17 April 2018.

On 20 April 2018, six countries—Argentina, Brazil, Chile, Colombia, Paraguay and Peru—announced that they would suspend their own membership for a year until the regional group became more organized. Chilean Foreign Minister Roberto Ampuero stated that the organization "isn't getting anywhere, there is no integration" and that "We can't be throwing this money to an institution that doesn't work."

A briefing sent to the Brazilian cabinet stated that the countries share the view that Bolivia's leadership of the block has been ineffective. Paraguayan Foreign Minister stated that his country's objection concerned the failure to put a new Secretary General in place, and the need to make the organization less ideological, but did not reflect negatively on Bolivia's leadership. Bolivian Foreign Minister Fernando Huanacuni has called an emergency meeting for May 2018 to attempt to resolve the crisis.

STRUCTURE

The presidents of each member nation will have an annual meeting, which will be the top political mandate. The first meeting was held in Brasilia on 29 and 30 September 2005. The second meeting was held in Cochabamba, Bolivia, on 8 and 9 December 2006. The third meeting was held in Brasília – this meeting should have taken place in Indias (Colombia), but was postponed because of tension between Ecuador, Colombia and

Venezuela. It was at this meeting that UNASUR was formalized and in which the Constitutive Treaty of the organization was signed. The foreign ministers of each country will meet once every six months. They will make concrete proposals for action and executive decision. The Permanent Representative Committee of the President of Mercosur and the Director of the Mercosur Department, the Secretary General of the Andean Community, the Secretary General of ALADI and the Permanent Secretaries of any institution for regional cooperation and integration, Amazon Cooperation Treaty Organization, Among others, will also attend these meetings.

On 9 December 2005, the Strategic Reflection Commission on the South American Integration Process was created. It consists of 12 members, whose function is to elaborate proposals that will help in the process of integration among the South American nations. These proposals were to be made at the 2nd UNASUR Meeting (2006).

The Executive Committee, created at the 2nd UNASUR Meeting, was transformed into the Political Commission or Council of Deputies, in accordance with the Decisions of the Political Dialogue. The text prepared by heads of state to form UNASUR was approved at the 3rd UNASUR Meeting in Brasília on 23 May 2008. This meeting was scheduled to take place in Cartagena de Indias, Colombia, on 24–28 January 2008, but was postponed because of tensions between Ecuador, Colombia and Venezuela.

Secretary General

A Secretary General is the legal representative of the Secretariat in Quito, Ecuador. Former Ecuadorian president Rodrigo Borja was nominated to this position but resigned a few days before the formation of the USAN in May 2008.

On 4 May, Néstor Kirchner of Argentina was appointed as the first Secretary General, despite resistance from Colombia, Uruguay, and Peru. After the death of Néstor Kirchner in 2010, there was a period of time when the position went unfilled, which eventually ended when María Emma Mejía Vélez was elected in March 2011. After Ernesto Samper completed his term in January 2017, UNASUR members have been unable to come to consensus on a successor.

ECONOMY

In recent decades the economies of South America have been transformed into fully competitive and efficient markets. In recent years, one characteristic of the economy of UNASUR has been its excessive growth and high competitiveness, leading to world profits alongside China and India. This economic situation is marked by policies favoring market opening, aimed at the exploitation of natural resources, industrialization and a very attractive destination for investors. In spite of all this, the situation is marked by immense regional differences and by an irregularity in the distribution of the income that stands out at world level, although it is recognized as one of the regions of the world where poverty and inequality have been reduced more energetically in recent decades.

There are regions with very high industrialization, where the main economic flows move, while there are sectors where there are hardly any industries. Most of the possessions are concentrated in the hands of a minority of the population, whereas millions of individuals experience different levels of privations arriving, in extreme cases, to the absolute poverty. However, it is necessary to emphasize that poverty in South America has been reduced in a surprising way, especially in the Southern Cone and North of South America. Today, thanks to the development of many South American nations, it has allowed the world, their eyes on some governments, even forming part of economic blocs like G20 and BRICS. Although this reality is common to the entire South American group, the countries of the so-called Southern Cone (Argentina, southern Brazil, Chile, and Uruguay) present more positive socioeconomic data and high HDI rates.

The South American economy is divided between the mineral extractivism in the Amazon region and the agriculture present in practically all its States. Industrialization is of medium level to high in diverse regions, although very strong the presence of local industries of origin Foreign (multinational). The extraction and export of oil is notable in Venezuela, which owns some of the largest world reserves, in Argentina and in the Atlantic Ocean compared to the Brazilian states of Rio de Janeiro and São Paulo. Bolivia stands out for the production of natural gas, with important reserves of this matter that in recent years have led to what has been known as the "Gas War."

The richest and most industrialized regions of the continent are: São Paulo State in Brazil, where its main financial center (in its capital), the main technological centers in South America (São Carlos, São José dos Campos and Campinas) and its largest and most mobile port -; Followed by the Fluvial-Industrial axis of Paraná between Rosario and La Plata in Argentina centered in Buenos Aires (second most active port and city with higher GDP); And for the also Brazilian State of Rio de Janeiro.

Brazil and Argentina are considered the regional leaders of South America. They are the two largest nations and the two largest economies in South America. These are the only South American countries that are members of the G-20 and Brazil, specially, as member of the BRICS. They're also the largest producers and exporters of agricultural products of the continent.

The highest nominal GDP in 2017 is Brazil (8th worldwide) with 2,140,940 trillion dollars, followed by Argentina (21st worldwide) with 628,935 billion dollars, and Colombia (31st at the global level) with 306,439 billion dollars.

The highest GDP in 2017 is in Brazil (8th worldwide) with 3,216,031 trillion dollars, Argentina (27th worldwide) with 912,816 billion dollars, and Colombia (31st Worldwide) with 720,151 billion dollars.

The highest GDP per capita in 2017 is held by Chile with US$24,113, followed by Uruguay with 21,527 and Argentina with 20,047. In terms of nominal per capita GDP, the ranking is headed by Uruguay with US$15,679, Chile with US$13,576, and Argentina with US$12,503.

Common Market

One of the initiatives of Unasur is the creation of a common market, starting with the elimination of tariffs for products considered non-sensitive until 2014 and for sensitive products until 2019.

The Initiative for the Integration of the Regional Infrastructure of South America is currently underway, with investments estimated at US$38 billion from the Inter-American Development Bank, the Andean Development Corporation, the National Bank for Economic and Social Development and the Financial Fund for Development of the Plata Basin.

The initial integration plans through the infrastructure cooperation of UNASUR came with the construction of the Bioceanic Corridor and the Interoceanic Highway. Roads that will link more firmly the countries of the Pacific coast, especially Chile and Peru, with the countries of the Atlantic coast like Brazil and Argentina, extending highways through the continent, allowing better connections of the ports to Bolivia and more internal parts of Argentina, Peru And Brazil. The Pacific Highway, between Peru and Brazil, began to be built in September 2005, financed 60% by Brazil and 40% by Peru, and was completed in December 2010.

The South American Energy Ring will interconnect Argentina, Brazil, Chile, Paraguay and Uruguay with natural gas from various sources, such as the Camisea Gas project in Peru and the Tarija gas deposits in Bolivia. Although this proposal has been signed and ratified, political and economic difficulties in Argentina and Bolivia have delayed this initiative, and to this day, this agreement remains more a protocol than a current project, since Chile and Brazil are already building LNG terminals for Gas from external suppliers.

Economic development

Presidents of the seven founding countries (Argentina, Bolivia, Brazil, Ecuador, Paraguay, Venezuela and Uruguay) officially launched the South American Bank in Buenos Aires in December 2007. The heads of all the founding countries were at the ceremony, with the exception of President Tabaré Vázquez of Uruguay. The capital will be US$7b, with Venezuela responsible for US$3b and Brazil US$2b. The headquarters will be located in Caracas with offices in Buenos Aires and La Paz.

The Bank of the South will finance economic development projects to improve local competitiveness and to promote the scientific and technological development of the member states. Its founding charter affirms that the bank will promote projects in a "stable and equal" manner and priorities will be oriented towards reinforcing South American integration, reducing asymmetries, and promoting an egalitarian distribution of investments.

The Brazilian Minister, Guido Mantega, stated that the bank is not similar to the International Monetary Fund; it will be a credit institution similar to the World Bank.

Monetary policy

The Bank of the South (Portuguese: Banco do Sul, Spanish: Banco del Sur, Dutch: Bank van het Zuiden, English: Bank of the South) will establish monetary policy and finance development projects. One of the objectives of monetary union is to establish a Single South American currency. Support for the creation of this currency was provided in January 2007 by Peruvian President Alan García, and other South American authorities expressed themselves in favor, as Bolivian President Evo Morales in April of that year, who proposed that the currency Only one denominated "Pacha" ("earth" in Quechua language), however, except for the right of each country to suggest a name for the common currency.

The South American economy is divided between mineral industry in the Amazon region and agriculture, which is present in practically all member states. Industrialization is advanced in several regions, although there is a strong presence of local industries of foreign (multinational) origin. In Brazil and Argentina the level of industrialization is intense.

DEFENSE POLICY

The South American Defense Council (CDS) was proposed by Venezuela and Brazil to serve as a mechanism for regional security, promoting military co-operation. From the beginning Brazil, Argentina and Chile, the countries that took the leadership of the project, made clear that they did not intend to form a NATO-like alliance, but a cooperative security arrangement, enhancing multilateral military cooperation, promoting confidence and security building measures and fostering defense industry exchange. Colombia initially refused to join the defense council due to the strong military ties it has with the United States through the Plan Colombia. However, after reviewing the proposal they decided to join on 20 July 2008. Shortly following the signing by Colombia's President, President of Chile Michelle Bachelet appointed a working group to investigate and draft a plan for the new council. Finally, on 10 March 2009, the 12 nation members held, in Chile, the first meeting of the newly formed council.

In mid-2010, UNASUR played a key role in mediating the 2010 Colombia–Venezuela diplomatic crisis. On 1 September 2010, the agency "UnasurHaití" was created to provide US$100 million in help to Haiti.

DEMOCRACY

South American presidents in front of the Casa Rosada, Buenos Aires, during the bicentenary of the May Revolution.

On 26 November 2010, the Additional Protocol on Commitment to Democracy was signed in the city of Georgetown, Cooperative Republic of Guyana. The protocol derives from the mandate established in the Buenos Aires Declaration of 1 October 2010, which affirms that member states will not tolerate a challenge to institutional authority, nor attempt to strike a legitimately constituted civilian power, adopting concrete and immediate measures in case of breach of constitutional order. It is applicable "in the event of a breach or threat of a breach of the democratic order, of a violation of the constitutional order or in any situation that endangers the legitimate exercise of power and the observance of democratic values and principles."

In the event of such a situation, the Council of Heads of State and Government or the Council of Ministers of Foreign Affairs may be convened extraordinarily by the Pro-Tempore Presidency of the Union, ex officio or at the request of the affected State or another member of UNASUR, to deliberate on the application of sanctions to the affected state. Among the political and diplomatic sanctions envisaged by the Protocol, the following stand out:

- Suspension of the right to participate in the different organs and instances of Unasur
- Partial or total closure of land borders with the affected State, including suspension or limitation of trade, air and sea transportation, communications, energy supply, services and supply.

FREE MOVEMENT OF PEOPLE

Visits by South American citizens to any South American independent country of up to 90 days only require an identification document issued by the traveler's country. In November 2006, Argentina, Bolivia, Brazil, Chile, Colombia, Ecuador, Guyana, Paraguay, Peru, Suriname, and Uruguay agreed to abolish visa requirements for tourists between any of those nations.

Mercosur, along with its Associate members of Bolivia, Chile, Colombia and Ecuador established that their territories together form an "area of free residence with the right to work" to all its citizens, with no additional requirements other than nationality. The Free Movement and Residence Agreement was established in the Brasília summit based in a previous document signed on 6 December 2002.

Citizens of any Mercosur countries will have a simplified process in temporary residence visa of up to two years in any other member countries, with the requirements of a valid passport, birth certificate, and no criminal record. Temporary residence can become permanent if a licit means of living can be verified.

At a summit in Guayaquil, Ecuador on 4 December 2014, UNASUR general secretary Ernesto Samper announced, "We have approved the concept of South American citizenship," including the creation of a single passport.

ELECTORAL MONITORS

UNASUR has also initiated the creation of electoral monitor teams that could replace the monitors from the Organization of American States.

10

Arab League

The Arab League (formally the League of Arab States, is a regional organization of Arab states in and around North Africa, the Horn of Africa and Arabia. It was formed in Cairo on 22 March 1945 with six members: Kingdom of Egypt, Kingdom of Iraq, Transjordan (renamed Jordan in 1949), Lebanon, Saudi Arabia, and Syria. Yemen joined as a member on 5 May 1945. Currently, the League has 22 members, but Syria's participation has been suspended since November 2011, as a consequence of government repression during the Syrian Civil War.

The League's main goal is to "draw closer the relations between member States and co-ordinate collaboration between them, to safeguard their independence and sovereignty, and to consider in a general way the affairs and interests of the Arab countries".

Through institutions, such as the Arab League Educational, Cultural and Scientific Organization (ALECSO) and the Economic and Social Council of the Arab League's Council of Arab Economic Unity (CAEU), the Arab League facilitates political, economic, cultural, scientific, and social programmes designed to promote the interests of the Arab world. It has served as a forum for the member states to coordinate their policy positions, to deliberate on matters of common concern, to settle some Arab disputes and to limit conflicts such as the 1958 Lebanon crisis. The League has served as a platform for the drafting and conclusion of many landmark documents promoting economic integration. One example is the *Joint Arab Economic Action Charter*, which outlines the principles for economic activities in the region.

Each member state has one vote in the *League Council*, and decisions are binding only for those states that have voted for them. The aims of the league in 1945 were to strengthen and coordinate the political, cultural, economic and social programs of its members and to mediate disputes among them or between them and third parties. Furthermore, the signing of an agreement on *Joint Defence and Economic Cooperation* on 13 April 1950 committed the signatories to coordination of military defence measures. In March 2015, the Arab League General Secretary announced the establishment of a Joint Arab Force with the aim of counteracting extremism and other threats to the Arab States. The decision was reached while Operation Decisive Storm was intensifying in Yemen. Participation in the project is voluntary, and the army intervenes only at the request of one of the member states. The growing militarization of the region and the increase in violent civil wars as well as terrorist movements are the reason behind the creation of the JAF, financed by the rich Gulf countries.

In the early 1970s, the Economic Council of the League of Arab States put forward a proposal to create the Joint Arab Chambers of Commerce across the European states. That led, under the decree of the League of Arab States no. K1175/D52/G, to the decision by the Arab governments to set up the Arab British Chamber of Commerce which was mandated to "promote, encourage and facilitate bilateral trade" between the Arab world and its major trading partner, the United Kingdom.

HISTORY

Following adoption of the Alexandria Protocol in 1944, the Arab League was founded on 22 March 1945. It aimed to be a regional organisation of Arab states with a focus to developing the economy, resolving disputes and coordinating political aims. Other countries later joined the league. Each country was given one vote in the council. The first major action was the joint intervention, allegedly on behalf of the majority Arab population being uprooted as the state of Israel emerged in 1948 (and in response to popular protest in the Arab world), but a major participant in this intervention, Transjordan, had agreed with the Israelis to divide up the Arab Palestinian state proposed by the United Nations General Assembly, and Egypt intervened primarily to prevent its rival in Amman from accomplishing its objective. It was followed by the creation of a mutual defence treaty two years later. A common market was established in 1965.

GEOGRAPHY

The Arab League member states cover over 13,000,000 km (5,000,000 sq mi) and straddles two continents: Africa and Asia. The area largely consists of arid deserts, such as the Sahara. Nevertheless, it also contains several highly fertile lands like the Nile Valley, the Jubba Valley and Shebelle Valley in the Horn of Africa, the Atlas Mountains in the Maghreb, and the Fertile Crescent that stretches over Mesopotamia and the Levant. The area comprises deep forests in southern Arabia and parts of the world's longest river, the Nile.

MEMBERSHIP

The Charter of the Arab League, also known as the Pact of the League of Arab States, is the founding treaty of the Arab League. Adopted in 1945, it stipulates that "the League of Arab States shall be composed of the independent Arab States that have signed this Pact."

Initially, in 1945, there were only six members. Today, the Arab League has 22 members, including three African countries among the largest by area (Sudan, Algeria and Libya) and the largest country in the Middle East (Saudi Arabia).

Five countries have observer status that entitles them to express their opinion and give advice but denies them voting rights.

There was a continual increase in membership during the second half of the 20th century. As of 2016, there are 22 member states:

- Algeria
- Bahrain
- Comoros
- Djibouti
- Egypt
- Iraq
- Jordan
- Kuwait
- Lebanon
- Libya
- Mauritania
- Morocco
- Oman
- Palestine
- Qatar
- Saudi Arabia
- Somalia
- Sudan
- Syria
- Tunisia
- United Arab Emirates
- Yemen

and 5 observer states:

- Brazil
- Eritrea
- India
- Venezuela
- Armenia

Libya was suspended on 22 February 2011, following the start of the Libyan Civil War and the use of military force against civilians. The National Transitional Council, the partially recognised interim government of Libya, sent a representative to be seated at the Arab League meeting on 17 August to participate in a discussion as to whether to readmit Libya to the organisation.

Syria was suspended on 16 November 2011. On 6 March 2013, the Arab League gave the Syrian National Coalition Syria's seat in the Arab League. On 9 March 2014, secretary general Nabil al-Arabi said that Syria's seat would remain vacant until the opposition completes the formation of its institutions.

POLITICS AND ADMINISTRATION

The Arab League is a political organization which tries to help integrate its members economically, and solve conflicts involving member states without asking for foreign assistance. It possesses elements of a state representative parliament while foreign affairs are often dealt with under UN supervision.

The Charter of the Arab League endorsed the principle of an Arab homeland while respecting the sovereignty of the individual member states. The internal regulations of the Council of the League and the committees were agreed in October 1951. Those of the Secretariat-General were agreed in May 1953.

Since then, governance of the Arab League has been based on the duality of supra-national institutions and the sovereignty of the member states. Preservation of individual statehood derived its strengths from the natural preference of ruling elites to maintain their power and independence in decision making. Moreover, the fear of the richer that the poorer may share their wealth in the name of Arab nationalism, the feuds among Arab rulers, and the influence of external powers that might oppose Arab unity can be seen as obstacles towards a deeper integration of the league.

Mindful of their previous announcements in support of the Arabs of Palestine the framers of the Pact were determined to include them within the League from its inauguration. This was done by means of an annex that declared: "Even though

Palestine was not able to control her own destiny, it was on the basis of the recognition of her independence that the Covenant of the League of Nations determined a system of government for her. Her existence and her independence among the nations can, therefore, no more be questioned *de jure* than the independence of any of the other Arab States. [...] Therefore, the States signatory to the Pact of the Arab League consider that in view of Palestine's special circumstances, the Council of the League should designate an Arab delegate from Palestine to participate in its work until this country enjoys actual independence"

At the Cairo Summit of 1964, the Arab League initiated the creation of an organisation representing the Palestinian people. The first Palestinian National Council convened in East Jerusalem on 29 May 1964. The Palestinian Liberation Organization was founded during this meeting on 2 June 1964. Palestine was shortly admitted in to the Arab League, represented by the PLO. Today, State of Palestine is a full member of the Arab League.

At the Beirut Summit on 28 March 2002, the league adopted the Arab Peace Initiative, a Saudi-inspired peace plan for the Arab–Israeli conflict. The initiative offered full normalisation of the relations with Israel. In exchange, Israel was required to withdraw from all occupied territories, including the Golan Heights, to recognise Palestinian independence in the West Bank and Gaza Strip, with East Jerusalem as its capital, as well as a "just solution" for the Palestinian refugees. The Peace Initiative was again endorsed at 2007 in the Riyadh Summit. In July 2007, the Arab League sent a mission, consisting of the Jordanian and Egyptian foreign ministers, to Israel to promote the initiative. Following Venezuela's move to expel Israeli diplomats amid the 2008–2009 Israel–Gaza conflict, Kuwaiti member of parliament Waleed Al-Tabtabaie proposed moving Arab League headquarters to Caracas, Venezuela. On 13 June 2010, Amr Mohammed Moussa, Secretary-General of the Arab League, visited the Gaza Strip, the first visit by an official of the Arab League since Hamas' armed takeover in 2007.

In 2015, the Arab League voiced support for Saudi Arabian-led military intervention in Yemen against the Shia Houthis and forces loyal to former President Ali Abdullah Saleh, who was deposed in the 2011 uprising.

On 15 April 2018, in response to the Turkish invasion of northern Syria aimed at ousting U.S.-backed Syrian Kurds from the enclave of Afrin, the Arab League passed a resolution calling on Turkish forces to withdraw from Afrin.

SUMMITS

No.	Date	Host Country	Host City
1	13–17 January 1964	Egypt	Cairo
2	5–11 September 1964	Egypt	Alexandria
3	13–17 September 1965	Morocco	Casablanca
4	29 August 1967	Sudan	Khartoum
5	21–23 December 1969	Morocco	Rabat
6	26–28 November.1973	Algeria	Algiers
7	29 October 1974	Morocco	Rabat
8	25–26 October 1976	Egypt	Cairo
9	2–5 November.1978	Iraq	Baghdad
10	20–22 November 1979	Tunisia	Tunis
11	21–22 November 1980	Jordan	Amman
12	6–9 September 1982	Morocco	Fes
13	1985	Morocco	Casablanca
14	1987	Jordan	Amman
15	June 1988	Algeria	Algiers
16	1989	Morocco	Casablanca
17	1990	Iraq	Baghdad
18	1996	Egypt	Cairo
19	27–28 March 2001	Jordan	Amman
20	27–28 March 2002	Lebanon	Beirut
21	1 March 2003	Egypt	Sharm el-Sheikh
22	22–23 May 2004	Tunisia	Tunis
23	22–23 March 2005	Algeria	Algiers

24	28–30 March 2006	Sudan	Khartoum
25	27–28 March 2007	Saudi Arabia	Riyadh
26	29–30 March 2008	Syria	Damascus
27	28–30 March 2009	Qatar	Doha
28	27–28 March 2010	Libya	Sirte
29	27–29 March 2012	Iraq	Baghdad
30	21–27 March 2013	Qatar	Doha
31	25–26 March 2014	Kuwait	Kuwait City
32	28–29 March 2015	Egypt	Sharm El Sheikh
33	20 July 2016	Mauritania	Nouakchott
34	23–29 March 2017	Jordan	Amman
35	15 April 2018	Saudi Arabia	Dhahran
36	April 2019	Tunisia	Tunis

MILITARY

The Joint Defence Council of the Arab League is one of the Institutions of the Arab League. It was established under the terms of the Joint Defence and Economic Co-operation Treaty of 1950 to coordinate the joint defence of the Arab League member states.

The Arab League as an Organization has no military Force, like the UN or EU, but at the 2007 summit, the Leaders decided to reactivate their joint defense and establish a peacekeeping force to deploy in South Lebanon, Darfur, Iraq, and other hot spots.

At a 2015 summit in Egypt, member nations agreed in principle to form a joint military force.

Emergency summits

No.	Date	Host Country	Host City
1	21–27 September 1970	Egypt	Cairo
2	17–28 October 1976	Saudi Arabia	Riyadh
3	7–9 September 1985	Morocco	Casablanca
4	8–12 November 1987	Jordan	Amman

5	7–9 June 1988	Algeria	Algiers
6	23–26 June 1989	Morocco	Casablanca
7	28–30 March 1990	Iraq	Baghdad
8	9–10 August 1990	Egypt	Cairo
9	22–23 June 1996	Egypt	Cairo
10	21–22 October 2000	Egypt	Cairo
11	7 January 2016	Saudi Arabia	Riyadh

Two summits are not added to the system of Arab League summits:

- Anshas, Egypt: 28–29 May 1946.
- Beirut, Lebanon: 13 – 15 November 1958.
- Summit 14 in Fes, Morocco, occurred in two stages:
- On 25 November 1981: the 5-hour meeting ended without an agreement on document.
- On 6–9 September 1982.

ECONOMIC RESOURCES

The Arab League is rich in resources, such as enormous oil and natural gas resources in certain member states. Another industry that is growing steadily in the Arab League is telecommunications. Within less than a decade, local companies such as Orascom and Etisalat have managed to compete internationally.

Economic achievements initiated by the League amongst member states have been less impressive than those achieved by smaller Arab organisations such as the Gulf Cooperation Council (GCC). Among them is the Arab Gas Pipeline, that will transport Egyptian and Iraqi gas to Jordan, Syria, Lebanon, and Turkey. As of 2013, a significant difference in economic conditions exist between the developed oil states of Algeria, Qatar, Kuwait and the UAE, and developing countries like Comoros, Djibouti, Mauritania, Somalia, Sudan and Yemen.

The Arab League also includes great fertile lands in the southern part of Sudan. It is referred to as the food basket of the Arab World, the region's instability including the independence of South Sudan has not affected its tourism industry, that is considered the fastest growing industry in the region, with Egypt, UAE, Lebanon, Tunisia, and Jordan leading the way. Another industry that is growing steadily in the Arab League is telecommunications.

Economical achievements within members have been low in the league's history, other smaller Arab Organizations have achieved more than the league has, such as the GCC, but lately several major economic projects that are promising are to be completed, the Arab Gas Pipelineis to end by the year 2010, Connecting Egyptian and Iraqi Gas to Jordan, Syria and Lebanon, and then to Turkey thus Europe, a free trade Agreement (GAFTA) is to be completed by 1 January 2008, making 95% of all Arab Products tax free of customs.

Transport

The Arab League is divided into five parts when it comes to transport, with the Arabian Peninsula and the Near East being entirely connected by air, sea, roads and railways. Another part of the League is the Nile Valley, made up of Egypt and Sudan. These two member states have started to improve the River Nile's navigation system to improve accessibility and thus foster trading. A new railway system is also set to connect the southern Egyptian city of Abu Simbel with the northern Sudanese city of Wadi Halfa and then to Khartoum and Port Sudan. The third division of the League is the Maghreb, where a 3,000 km stretch of railway runs from the southern cities of Morocco to Tripoli in Western Libya. The fourth division of the League is the Horn of Africa, whose member states include Djibouti and Somalia. These two Arab League states are separated by only ten nautical miles from the Arabian Peninsula by the Bab el Mandeb and this is quickly changing as Tarik bin Laden, the brother of Osama bin Laden, has initiated the construction of the ambitious Bridge of the Horns project, which ultimately aims to connect the Horn of Africa with the Arabian Peninsula via a massive bridge. The project is intended to facilitate and accelerate the already centuries-old trade and commerce between the two regions. The last division of the

League is the isolated island of Comoros, which is not physically connected to any other Arab state, but still trades with other League members.

LITERACY IN ARAB LEAGUE COUNTRIES

In collecting literacy data, many countries estimate the number of literate people based on self-reported data. Some use educational attainment data as a proxy, but measures of school attendance or grade completion may differ. Because definitions and data collection methods vary across countries, literacy estimates should be used with caution. United Nations Development Programme, Human Development Report 2010. It is also important to note that the Persian Gulf region has had an oil boom, enabling more schools and universities to be set up.

Rank	Country	Literacy rate
1	Qatar	97.3
2	Palestine	96.5
3	Kuwait	96.3
4	Bahrain	95.7
5	Jordan	95.4
6	Saudi Arabia	94.4
7	Lebanon	93.9
8	United Arab Emirates	93.8
9	Oman	91.1
10	Libya	91
11	Syria	86.4
12	Iraq	85.7
13	Tunisia	81.8
14	Comoros	81.8
15	Algeria	80.2
16	Sudan	75.9
17	Egypt	73.8
18	Yemen	70.1
19	Djibouti	70.0

20	Morocco	68.5
21	Mauritania	52.1
22	Somalia	44–72

DEMOGRAPHICS

The Arab League is a culturally and ethnically one association of 22 member states, with the overwhelming majority of the League's population identified as Arab (on a cultural ethnoracial basis). As of July 1, 2013, about 359 million people live in the states of the Arab League. Its population grows faster than in most other global regions. The most populous member state is Egypt, with a population of about 91 million. The least populated is the Comoros, with over 0.6 million inhabitants.

Rank	Country	Population	Density (/km^2)	Density (sq mi)
1	Egypt	97,075,300	100	259
2	Algeria	40,400,000	16	41
3	Iraq	37,202,572	80	207
4	Morocco	35,740,000	71	184
5	Sudan	39,578,828	16	41
6	Saudi Arabia	33,000,000	12	31
7	Yemen	27,584,213	45	117
8	Syria*	21,906,000	118	306
9	Tunisia	11,304,482	65	168
10	Somalia	14,317,996	18	47
11	UAE	9,269,612	99	256
12	Libya	6,293,253	3.8	9.8
13	Jordan	10,159,967	71	184
14	Palestine	4,550,368	756	1,958
15	Lebanon	6,006,668	404	1,046
16	Kuwait	4,052,584	200	518
17	Mauritania	4,301,018	3.2	8.3
18	Oman	4,424,762	9.2	24
19	Qatar	2,641,669	154	399

20	Bahrain	1,425,171	1,646	4,263
21	Djibouti	942,333	37	96
22	Comoros	795,601	309	800
Total	Arab League	412,972,397	30.4	78.7

•Syrian demographics are before the Syrian civil war.

Religion

Almost all of the Arab League's citizens adhere to Islam, with Christianity being the second largest religion. At least 15 million Christians combined live in Egypt, Iraq, Jordan, Lebanon, Palestine, Sudan and Syria. In addition, there are smaller but significant numbers of Druze, Yazidis, Shabaks and Mandaeans. Numbers for nonreligious Arabs are generally not available, but research by the Pew Forum suggests around 1% of people in the MENA region are "unaffiliated".

Linguistics

The official language of the Arab League is Literary Arabic, based on Classical Arabic. However, several Arab League member states have other co-official or national languages, such as Somali, Berber, Kurdish, Assyrian, and Nubian. Additionally, various different Arabic dialects are spoken, such as Egyptian Arabic, Levantine Arabic and Moroccan Arabic.

CULTURE

Sports

The Pan Arab Games are considered the biggest Arab sporting event, which brings together athletes from all the Arab countries to participate in a variety of different sports.

The Union of Arab Football Associations organises the Arab Nations Cup (for national teams) and the Arab Club Champions Cup (for clubs). Arab sport federations also exist for several games, include basketball, volleyball, handball, table tennis, tennis, squash and swimming.

11

League of Nations

The League of Nations was an intergovernmental organisation founded on 10 January 1920 as a result of the Paris Peace Conference that ended the First World War. It was the first international organisation whose principal mission was to maintain world peace. Its primary goals, as stated in its Covenant, included preventing wars through collective security and disarmament and settling international disputes through negotiation and arbitration. Other issues in this and related treaties included labour conditions, just treatment of native inhabitants, human and drug trafficking, the arms trade, global health, prisoners of war, and protection of minorities in Europe. At its greatest extent from 28 September 1934 to 23 February 1935, it had 58 members.

The diplomatic philosophy behind the League represented a fundamental shift from the preceding hundred years. The League lacked its own armed force and depended on the victorious Great Powers of World War I (France, the UK, Italy and Japan were the permanent members of the executive Council) to enforce its resolutions, keep to its economic sanctions, or provide an army when needed. The Great Powers were often reluctant to do so. Sanctions could hurt League members, so they were reluctant to comply with them. During the Second Italo-Abyssinian War, when the League accused Italian soldiers of targeting Red Cross medical tents, Benito Mussoliniresponded that "the League is very well when sparrows shout, but no good at all when eagles fall out."

After some notable successes and some early failures in the 1920s, the League ultimately proved incapable of preventing aggression by the Axis powers in the 1930s. The credibility of the organization was weakened by the fact that the United States never officially joined the League and the Soviet Union joined late and only briefly. Germany withdrew from the League, as did Japan, Italy, Spain and others. The onset of the Second World War showed that the League had failed its primary purpose, which was to prevent any future world war. The League lasted for 26 years; the United Nations (UN) replaced it after the end of the Second World War and inherited several agencies and organisations founded by the League.

ORIGINS

Background

The concept of a peaceful community of nations had been proposed as far back as 1795, when Immanuel Kant's *Perpetual Peace: A Philosophical Sketch* outlined the idea of a league of nations to control conflict and promote peace between states. Kant argued for the establishment of a peaceful world community, not in a sense of a global government, but in the hope that each state would declare itself a free state that respects its citizens and welcomes foreign visitors as fellow rational beings, thus promoting peaceful society worldwide.International co-operation to promote collective security originated in the Concert of Europe that developed after the Napoleonic Wars in the 19th century in an attempt to maintain the *status quo* between European states and so avoid war. This period also saw the development of international law, with the first Geneva Conventions establishing laws dealing with humanitarian relief during wartime, and the international Hague Conventions of 1899 and 1907 governing rules of war and the peaceful settlement of international disputes. As historians William H. Harbaugh and Ronald E. Powaski point out, Theodore Roosevelt was the first American President to call for an international league. At the acceptance for his Nobel

Prize, Roosevelt said: "it would be a masterstroke if those great powers honestly bent on peace would form a League of Peace."

The forerunner of the League of Nations, the Inter-Parliamentary Union (IPU), was formed by the peace activists William Randal Cremer and Frédéric Passy in 1889 (and is currently still in existence as an international body with a focus on the various elected legislative bodies of the world.) The IPU was founded with an international scope, with a third of the members of parliaments (in the 24 countries that had parliaments) serving as members of the IPU by 1914. Its foundational aims were to encourage governments to solve international disputes by peaceful means. Annual conferences were established to help governments refine the process of international arbitration. Its structure was designed as a council headed by a president, which would later be reflected in the structure of the League.

Initial proposals

At the start of the First World War the first schemes for international organisation to prevent future wars began to gain considerable public support, particularly in Great Britain and the United States. Goldsworthy Lowes Dickinson, a British political scientist, coined the term "League of Nations" in 1914 and drafted a scheme for its organisation. Together with Lord Bryce, he played a leading role in the founding of the group of internationalist pacifists known as the Bryce Group, later the League of Nations Union. The group became steadily more influential among the public and as a pressure group within the then governing Liberal Party. In Dickinson's 1915 pamphlet *After the War* he wrote of his "League of Peace" as being essentially an organisation for arbitration and conciliation. He felt that the secret diplomacy of the early twentieth century had brought about war and thus could write that, "the impossibility of war, I believe, would be increased in proportion as the issues of foreign policy should be known to and controlled by public opinion." The 'Proposals' of the Bryce Group were circulated widely, both in England and the US, where they had a profound influence on the nascent international movement.

Within two weeks of the start of the war, feminists began to mobilise against the war. Having been barred from participating in prior peace organizations, American women formed a Women's Peace Parade Committee to plan a silent protest to the war. Led by chairwoman Fanny Garrison Villard, women from trade unions, feminist organizations, and social reform organizations, such as Kate Waller Barrett, Mary Ritter Beard, Carrie Chapman Catt, Rose Schneiderman, Lillian Wald, and others, organized 1500 women, who marched down Manhattan's Fifth Avenue on August 29, 1914. As a result of the parade, Jane Addams became interested in proposals by two European suffragists—Hungarian Rosika Schwimmer and British Emmeline Pethick-Lawrence—to hold a peace conference. On 9–10 January 1915, a peace conference directed by Addams was held in Washington, D. C., where the delegates adopted a platform calling for creation of international bodies with administrative and legislative powers to develop a "permanent league of neutral nations" to work for peace and disarmament.

Within months a call was made for an international women's conference to be held in The Hague. Coordinated by Mia Boissevain, Aletta Jacobs and Rosa Manus, the Congress, which opened on April 28, 1915 was attended by 1,136 participants from both neutral and non-belligerent nations, and resulted in the establishment of an organization which would become the Women's International League for Peace and Freedom (WILPF). At the close of the conference, two delegations of women were dispatched to meet European heads of state over the next several months. They secured agreement from reluctant Foreign Ministers, who overall felt that such a body would be ineffective, but agreed to participate or not impede creation of a neutral mediating body, if other nations agreed and if President Woodrow Wilson would initiate a body. In the midst of the War, Wilson refused.

In 1915, a similar body to the Bryce group proposals was set up in the United States by a group of like-minded individuals, including William Howard Taft. It was called the League to Enforce Peace and was substantially based on the proposals of the Bryce Group. It advocated the use of arbitration in conflict resolution and the imposition of sanctions on aggressive countries. None of these early organisations envisioned a continuously functioning body; with the exception of the Fabian Society in England, they maintained a legalistic approach that would limit the international body to a court of justice. The Fabians were the first to argue for a "Council" of states, necessarily the Great Powers, who would adjudicate world affairs, and for the creation of a permanent secretariat to enhance international co-operation across a range of activities.

In the course of the diplomatic efforts surrounding World War I, both sides had to clarify their long-term war aims. By 1916 in Britain, the leader of the Allies, and in neutral United States, long-range thinkers had begun to design a unified international organisation to prevent future wars. Historian Peter Yearwood argues that when the new coalition government of David Lloyd George took power in December 1916, there was widespread discussion among intellectuals and diplomats of the desirability of establishing such an organisation, when Lloyd George was challenged by Wilson to state his position With an eye on the postwar situation, he endorsed such an organisation. Wilson himself Included in his Fourteen Points in January 1918 a "league of nations to insure peace and justice." British foreign secretary, Arthur Balfour, argued that, as a condition of durable peace, "behind international law, and behind all treaty arrangements for preventing or limiting hostilities, some form of international sanction should be devised which would give pause to the hardiest aggressor."

By the time Germany gave up in November 1918, the war had had a profound impact, affecting the social, political and economic systems of Europe and inflicting psychological and physical damage. Anti-war sentiment rose across the world; the First World War was described as "the war to end all wars", and its possible causes were vigorously investigated. The causes identified included arms races, alliances, militaristic nationalism, secret diplomacy, and the freedom of sovereign states to enter into war for their own benefit. One proposed remedy was the creation of an international organisation whose aim was to prevent future war through disarmament, open diplomacy, international co-operation, restrictions on the right to wage war, and penalties that made war unattractive.

In London Balfour commissioned the first official report into the matter in early 1918, under the initiative of Lord Robert Cecil. The British committee was finally appointed in February 1918. It was led by Walter Phillimore (and became known as the Phillimore Committee), but also included Eyre Crowe, William Tyrrell, and Cecil Hurst. The recommendations of the so-called Phillimore Commission included the establishment of a "Conference of Allied States" that would arbitrate disputes and impose sanctions on offending states. The proposals were approved by the British government, and much of the commission's results were later incorporated into the Covenant of the League of Nations.

The French also drafted a much more far-reaching proposal in June 1918; they advocated annual meetings of a council to settle all disputes, as well as an "international army" to enforce its decisions.

The American President Woodrow Wilson instructed Edward M. House to draft a US plan which reflected Wilson's own idealistic views (first articulated in the Fourteen Points of January 1918), as well as the work of the Phillimore Commission. The outcome of House's work, and Wilson's own first draft, proposed the termination of "unethical" state behaviour, including forms of espionage and dishonesty. Methods of compulsion against recalcitrant states would include severe measures, such as "blockading and closing the frontiers of that power to commerce or intercourse with any part of the world and to use any force that may be necessary..."

The two principal drafters and architects of the covenant of the League of Nations were the British politician Lord Robert Cecil and the South African statesman Jan Smuts. Smuts' proposals included the creation of a Council of the great powers as permanent members and a non-permanent selection of the minor states. He also proposed the creation of a Mandate system for captured colonies of the Central Powers during the war. Cecil focused on the administrative side, and proposed annual Council meetings and quadrennial meetings for the Assembly of all members. He also argued for a large and permanent secretariat to carry out the League's administrative duties.

Establishment

At the Paris Peace Conference in 1919, Wilson, Cecil and Smuts all put forward their draft proposals. After lengthy negotiations between the delegates, the Hurst-Miller draft was finally produced as a basis for the Covenant. After more negotiation and compromise, the delegates finally approved of the proposal to create the League of Nations (French: *Société des Nations*, German: *Völkerbund*) on 25 January 1919.The final Covenant of the League of Nations was drafted by a special commission, and the League was established by Part I of the Treaty of Versailles. On 28 June 1919, 44 states signed the Covenant, including 31 states which had taken part in the war on the side of the Triple Entente or joined it during the conflict.

French women's rights advocates invited international feminists to participate in a parallel conference to the Paris Conference in hopes that they could gain permission to participate in the official conference. The Inter-Allied Women's Conference asked to be allowed to submit suggestions to the peace negotiations and commissions and were granted the right to sit on commissions dealing specifically with women and children. Though they asked for enfranchisement and full legal protection under the law equal with men, those rights were ignored. Women won the right to serve in all capacities, including as staff or delegates in the League of Nations organization. They also won a declaration that member nations should prevent trafficking of women and children and should equally support humane conditions for children, women and men labourers.At the Zürich Peace Conference held between 17–19 May 1919, the women of the WILPF condemned the terms of the Treaty of Versailles for both is punitive measures, as well as its failure to provide for condemnation of violence and exclusion of women from civil and political participation. Upon reading the Rules of Procedure for the League of Nations, Catherine Marshall, a British suffragist, discovered that the guidelines were completely undemocratic and they were modified based on her suggestion.

The League would be made up of a General Assembly (representing all member states), an Executive Council (with membership limited to major powers), and a permanent secretariat.

Member states were expected to "respect and preserve as against external aggression" the territorial integrity of other members and to disarm "to the lowest point consistent with domestic safety." All states were required to submit complaints for arbitration or judicial inquiry before going to war. The Executive Council would create a Permanent Court of International Justice to make judgements on the disputes.

Despite Wilson's efforts to establish and promote the League, for which he was awarded the Nobel Peace Prize in October 1919, the United States never joined. Senate Republicans led by Henry Cabot Lodge wanted a League with the reservation that only Congress could take the U.S. into war. Lodge gained a majority of Senators. Wilson refused to allow a compromise and the needed 2/3 majority was lacking.

The League held its first council meeting in Paris on 16 January 1920, six days after the Versailles Treaty and the Covenant of the League of Nations came into force. On 1 November 1920, the headquarters of the League was moved from London to Geneva, where the first General Assembly was held on 15 November 1920. The Palais Wilson on Geneva's western lakeshore, named after US President Woodrow Wilson in recognition of his efforts towards the establishment of the League, was the League's first permanent home.

FAILURE OF DISARMAMENT

Article 8 of the Covenant gave the League the task of reducing "armaments to the lowest point consistent with national safety and the enforcement by common action of international obligations". A significant amount of the League's time and energy was devoted to this goal, even though many member governments were uncertain that such extensive disarmament could be achieved or was even desirable.

The Allied powers were also under obligation by the Treaty of Versailles to attempt to disarm, and the armament restrictions imposed on the defeated countries had been described as the first step toward worldwide disarmament. The League Covenant assigned the League the task of creating a disarmament plan for each state, but the Council devolved this responsibility to a special commission set up in 1926 to prepare for the 1932–1934 World Disarmament Conference.

Members of the League held different views towards the issue. The French were reluctant to reduce their armaments without a guarantee of military help if they were attacked; Poland and Czechoslovakia felt vulnerable to attack from the west and wanted the League's response to aggression against its members to be strengthened before they disarmed. Without this guarantee, they would not reduce armaments because they felt the risk of attack from Germany was too great. Fear of attack increased as Germany regained its strength after the First World War, especially after Adolf Hitler gained power and became German Chancellor in 1933. In particular, Germany's attempts to overturn the Treaty of Versailles and the reconstruction of the German military made France increasingly unwilling to disarm.

The World Disarmament Conference was convened by the League of Nations in Geneva in 1932, with representatives from 60 states. A one-year moratorium on the expansion of armaments, later extended by a few months, was proposed at the start of the conference. The Disarmament Commission obtained initial agreement from France, Italy, Spain, Japan, and Britain to limit the size of their navies. The Kellogg–Briand Pact, facilitated by the commission in 1928, failed in its objective of outlawing war. Ultimately, the Commission failed to halt the military build-up by Germany, Italy, Spain and Japan during the 1930s. The League was mostly silent in the face of major events leading to the Second World War, such as Hitler's remilitarisation of the Rhineland, occupation of the Sudetenland and *Anschluss* of Austria, which had been forbidden by the Treaty of Versailles. In fact, League members themselves re-armed. In 1933, Japan simply withdrew from the League rather than submit to its judgement, as did Germany the same year (using the failure of the World Disarmament Conference to agree to arms parity between France and Germany as a pretext), Italy and Spain in 1937. The final significant act of the League was to expel the Soviet Union in December 1939 after it invaded Finland.

GENERAL WEAKNESSES

The onset of the Second World War demonstrated that the League had failed in its primary purpose, the prevention of another world war. There were a variety of reasons for this failure, many connected to general weaknesses within the organisation. Additionally, the power of the League was limited by the United States' refusal to join.

Origins and structure

The origins of the League as an organisation created by the Allied powers as part of the peace settlement to end the First World War led to it being viewed as a "League of Victors". The League's neutrality tended to manifest itself as indecision. It required a unanimous vote of nine, later fifteen, Council members to enact a resolution; hence, conclusive and effective action was difficult, if not impossible. It was also slow in coming to its decisions, as certain ones required the unanimous consent of the entire Assembly. This problem mainly stemmed from the fact that the primary members of the League of Nations were not willing to accept the possibility of their fate being decided by other countries, and by enforcing unanimous voting had effectively given themselves veto power.

Global representation

Representation at the League was often a problem. Though it was intended to encompass all nations, many never joined, or their period of membership was short. The most conspicuous absentee was the United States. President Woodrow Wilson had been a driving force behind the League's formation and strongly influenced the form it took, but the US Senate voted not to join on 19 November 1919. Ruth Henig has suggested that, had the United States become a member, it would have also provided support to France and Britain, possibly making France feel more secure, and so encouraging France and Britain to co-operate more fully regarding Germany, thus making the rise to power of the Nazi Party less likely. Conversely, Henig acknowledges that if the US had been a member, its reluctance to engage in war with European states or to enact economic sanctions might have hampered the ability of the League to deal with international incidents. The structure of the US federal government might also have made its membership problematic, as its representatives at the League could not have made decisions on behalf of the executive branch without having the prior approval of the legislative branch.

In January 1920, when the League was born, Germany was not permitted to join because it was seen as having been the aggressor in the First World War. Soviet Russia was also initially excluded, as Communist regimes were not welcomed. The League was further weakened when major powers left in the 1930s. Japan began as a permanent member of the Council, but withdrew in 1933 after the League voiced opposition to its occupation of Manchuria. Italy began as a permanent member of the Council, but withdrew in 1937. Spain also began as a permanent member of the Council, but withdrew in 1939. The League had accepted Germany, also as a permanent member of the Council, in 1926, deeming it a "peace-loving country", but Adolf Hitler pulled Germany out when he came to power in 1933.

Collective security

Another important weakness grew from the contradiction between the idea of collective security that formed the basis of the League and international relations between individual states. The League's collective security system required nations to act, if necessary, against states they considered friendly, and in a way that might endanger their national interests, to support states for which they had no normal affinity. This weakness was exposed during the Abyssinia Crisis, when Britain and France had to balance maintaining the security they had attempted to create for themselves in Europe "to defend against the enemies of internal order", in which Italy's support played a pivotal role, with their obligations to Abyssinia as a member of the League.

On 23 June 1936, in the wake of the collapse of League efforts to restrain Italy's war against Abyssinia, the British Prime Minister, Stanley Baldwin, told the House of Commons that collective security had

> failed ultimately because of the reluctance of nearly all the nations in Europe to proceed to what I might call military sanctions ... The real reason, or the main reason, was that we discovered in the process of weeks that there was no country except the aggressor country which was ready for war ... [I]f collective action is to be a reality and not merely a thing to be talked about, it means not only that every country is to be ready for war; but must be ready to go to war at once. That is a terrible thing, but it is an essential part of collective security.

Ultimately, Britain and France both abandoned the concept of collective security in favour of appeasement in the face of growing German militarism under Hitler. In this context, the League of Nations was also the institution where the first international debate on terrorism took place following the 1934 assassination of King Alexander I of Yugoslavia in Marseille, showing its conspiratorial features, many of which are detectable in the discourse of terrorism among states after 9/11.

American diplomatic historian Samuel Flagg Bemis originally supported the League, but after two decades changed his mind:

The League of Nations has been a disappointing failure.... It has been a failure, not because the United States did not join it; but because the great powers have been unwilling to apply sanctions except where it suited their individual national interests to do so, and because Democracy, on which the original concepts of the League rested for support, has collapsed over half the world.

Pacifism and disarmament

The League of Nations lacked an armed force of its own and depended on the Great Powers to enforce its resolutions, which they were very unwilling to do. Its two most important members, Britain and France, were reluctant to use sanctions and even more reluctant to resort to military action on behalf of the League. Immediately after the First World War, pacifism became a strong force among both the people and governments of the two countries. The British Conservatives were especially tepid to the League and preferred, when in government, to negotiate treaties without the involvement of that organisation. Moreover, the League's advocacy of disarmament for Britain, France, and its other members, while at the same time advocating collective security, meant that the League was depriving itself of the only forceful means by which it could uphold its authority.

When the British cabinet discussed the concept of the League during the First World War, Maurice Hankey, the Cabinet Secretary, circulated a memorandum on the subject. He started by saying, "Generally it appears to me that any such scheme is dangerous to us, because it will create a sense of security which is wholly fictitious". He attacked the British pre-war faith in the sanctity of treaties as delusional and concluded by claiming:

It [a League of Nations] will only result in failure and the longer that failure is postponed the more certain it is that this country will have been lulled to sleep. It will put a very strong lever into the hands of the well-meaning idealists who are to be found in almost every Government, who deprecate expenditure on armaments, and, in the course of time, it will almost certainly result in this country being caught at a disadvantage.

The Foreign Office minister Sir Eyre Crowe also wrote a memorandum to the British cabinet claiming that "a solemn league and covenant" would just be "a treaty, like other treaties". "What is there to ensure that it will not, like other treaties, be broken?" Crowe went on to express scepticism of the planned "pledge of common action" against aggressors because he believed the actions of individual states would still be determined by national interests and the balance of power. He also criticised the proposal for League economic sanctions because it would be ineffectual and that "It is all a question of real military preponderance". Universal disarmament was a practical impossibility, Crowe warned.

DEMISE AND LEGACY

As the situation in Europe escalated into war, the Assembly transferred enough power to the Secretary General on 30 September 1938 and 14 December 1939 to allow the League to continue to exist legally and carry on reduced operations. The headquarters of the League, the Palace of Nations, remained unoccupied for nearly six years until the Second World War ended.

At the 1943 Tehran Conference, the Allied powers agreed to create a new body to replace the League: the United Nations. Many League bodies, such as the International Labour Organisation, continued to function and eventually became affiliated with the UN. The designers of the structures of the United Nations intended to make it more effective than the League.

The final meeting of the League of Nations took place on 18 April 1946 in Geneva. Delegates from 34 nations attended the assembly.This session concerned itself with liquidating the

League: it transferred assets worth approximately $22,000,000 (U.S.) in 1946 (including the Palace of Nations and the League's archives) to the UN, returned reserve funds to the nations that had supplied them, and settled the debts of the League. Robert Cecil, addressing the final session, said:

Let us boldly state that aggression wherever it occurs and however it may be defended, is an international crime, that it is the duty of every peace-loving state to resent it and employ whatever force is necessary to crush it, that the machinery of the Charter, no less than the machinery of the Covenant, is sufficient for this purpose if properly used, and that every well-disposed citizen of every state should be ready to undergo any sacrifice in order to maintain peace ... I venture to impress upon my hearers that the great work of peace is resting not only on the narrow interests of our own nations, but even more on those great principles of right and wrong which nations, like individuals, depend.

The League is dead. Long live the United Nations.

The Assembly passed a resolution that "With effect from the day following the close of the present session of the Assembly [i.e., April 19], the League of Nations shall cease to exist except for the sole purpose of the liquidation of its affairs as provided in the present resolution." A Board of Liquidation consisting of nine persons from different countries spent the next 15 months overseeing the transfer of the League's assets and functions to the United Nations or specialised bodies, finally dissolving itself on July 31, 1947.

The archive of the League of Nations was transferred to the United Nations Office at Geneva and is now an entry in the UNESCO Memory of the World Register.

In the past few decades, by research using the League Archives at Geneva, historians have reviewed the legacy of the League of Nations as the United Nations has faced similar troubles to those of the interwar period. Current consensus views that, even though the League failed to achieve its ultimate goal of world peace, it did manage to build new roads towards expanding the rule of law across the globe; strengthened the concept of collective security, giving a voice to smaller nations; helped to raise awareness to problems like epidemics, slavery, child labour, colonial tyranny, refugee crisis and general working conditions through its numerous commissions and committees; and paved the way for new forms of statehood, as the mandate system put the colonial powers under international observation.

Professor David Kennedy portrays the League as a unique moment when international affairs were "institutionalised", as opposed to the pre–First World War methods of law and politics. The principal Allies in the Second World War (the UK, the USSR, France, the U.S., and the Republic of China) became permanent members of the United Nations Security Council in 1946. (In 1971 the People's Republic of China replaced the Republic of China (then only in control of Taiwan) as permanent member of the UN Security Council, and in 1991 the Russian Federation replaced the USSR.) Decisions of the Security Council are binding on all members of the UN; unanimous decisions are not required, unlike in the League Council. Permanent members of the Security Council can wield a veto to protect their vital interests.

12

International Labour Organization (ILO)

The International Labour Organization (ILO) is a United Nations agency dealing with labour problems, particularly international labour standards, social protection, and work opportunities for all. The ILO has 187 member states: 186 of the 193 UN member states plus the Cook Islands are members of the ILO.

In 1969, the organisation received the Nobel Peace Prize for improving peace among classes, pursuing decent work and justice for workers, and providing technical assistance to other developing nations. The ILO registers complaints against entities that are violating international rules; however, it does not impose sanctions on governments.

GOVERNANCE, ORGANIZATION, AND MEMBERSHIP

Unlike other United Nations specialised agencies, the International Labour Organisation has a tripartite governing structure – representing governments, employers, and workers (usually with a ratio of 2:1:1). The rationale behind the tripartite structure is the creation of free and open debate among governments and social partners.

The ILO secretariat (staff) is referred to as the International Labour Office.

Governing body

The governing body decides the agenda of the International Labour Conference, adopts the draft programme and budget of the organization for submission to the conference, elects the director-general, requests information from member states concerning labour matters, appoints commissions of inquiry and supervises the work of the International Labour Office.

Juan Somavía was the ILO's director-general from 1999 until October 2012, when Guy Ryder was elected as his replacement.

This governing body is composed of 48 government representatives, 14 workers' representatives, and 14 employers' representatives.

Ten of the government seats are held by member states that are nations of "chief industrial importance", as first considered by an "impartial committee". The nations are Brazil, China, France, Germany, India, Italy, Japan, the Russian Federation, the United Kingdom and the United States. The terms of office are three years.

International Labour Conference

The ILO organises the International Labour Conference in Geneva every year in June, where conventions and recommendations are crafted and adopted. Also known as the "parliament of labour", the conference also makes decisions about the ILO's general policy, work programme and budget.

Each member state has four representatives at the conference: two government delegates, an employer delegate and a worker delegate. All of them have individual voting rights, and all votes are equal, regardless of the population of the delegate's member state. The employer and worker delegates are normally chosen in agreement with the "most representative" national organizations of employers and workers. Usually, the workers' delegates coordinate their voting, as do the employers' delegates. All delegates have the same rights, and are not required to vote in blocs.

Conventions

Through July 2011, the ILO had adopted 189 conventions. If these conventions are ratified by enough governments, they come in force. However, ILO conventions are considered international labour standards regardless of ratification. When a convention comes into force, it creates a legal obligation for ratifying nations to apply its provisions.

Every year the International Labour Conference's Committee on the Application of Standards examines a number of alleged breaches of international labour standards. Governments are required to submit reports detailing their compliance with the obligations of the conventions they have ratified. Conventions that have not been ratified by member states have the same legal force as recommendations.

In 1998, the 86th International Labour Conference adopted the *Declaration on Fundamental Principles and Rights at Work*. This declaration contains four fundamental policies:

- The right of workers to associate freely and bargain collectively
- The end of forced and compulsory labour
- The end of child labour
- The end of unfair discrimination among workers

The ILO asserts that its members have an obligation to work towards fully respecting these principles, embodied in relevant ILO conventions. The ILO conventions which embody the fundamental principles have now been ratified by most member states.

Recommendations

Recommendations do not have the binding force of conventions and are not subject to ratification. Recommendations may be adopted at the same time as conventions to supplement the latter with additional or more detailed provisions. In other cases recommendations may be adopted separately and may address issues separate from particular conventions.

Membership

As of April 2016, the ILO has 187 state members. 186 of the 193 member states of the United Nations plus the Cook Islands are members of the ILO. The UN member states which are not members of the ILO are Andorra, Bhutan, Liechtenstein, Micronesia, Monaco, Nauru, and North Korea.

The ILO constitution permits any member of the UN to become a member of the ILO. To gain membership, a nation must inform the director-general that it accepts all the obligations of the ILO constitution. Other states can be admitted by a two-thirds vote of all delegates, including a two-thirds vote of government delegates, at any ILO General Conference. The Cook Islands, a non-UN state, joined in June 2015.

Members of the ILO under the League of Nations automatically became members when the organisation's new constitution came into effect after World War II.

Position within the UN

The International Labour Organisation (ILO) is a specialised agency of the United Nations (UN). As with other UN specialised agencies (or programmes) working on international development, the ILO is also a member of the United Nations Development Group.

HISTORY

Origins

While the ILO was established as an agency of the League of Nations following World War I, its founders had made great strides in social thought and action before 1919. The core members all knew one another from earlier private professional and ideological networks, in which they exchanged knowledge, experiences, and ideas on social policy. Prewar "epistemic communities", such as the International Association for Labour Legislation (IALL), founded in 1900, and political networks, such as the socialist Second International, were a decisive factor in the institutionalization of international labour politics.

In the post–World War I euphoria, the idea of a "makeable society" was an important catalyst behind the social engineering of the ILO architects. As a new discipline, international labour law became a useful instrument for putting social reforms into practice. The utopian ideals of the founding members—social justice and the right to decent work—were changed by diplomatic and political compromises made at the Paris Peace Conference of 1919, showing the ILO's balance between idealism and pragmatism.

Over the course of the First World War, the international labour movement proposed a comprehensive programme of protection for the working classes, conceived as compensation for labour's support during the war. Post-war reconstruction and the protection of labour unions occupied the attention of many nations during and immediately after World War I. In Great Britain, the Whitley Commission, a subcommittee of the Reconstruction Commission, recommended in its July 1918 Final Report that "industrial councils" be established throughout the world. The British Labour Party had issued its own reconstruction programme in the document titled *Labour and the New Social Order*. In February 1918, the third Inter-Allied Labour and Socialist Conference (representing delegates from Great Britain, France, Belgium and Italy) issued its report, advocating an international labour rights body, an end to secret diplomacy, and other goals. And in December 1918, the American Federation of Labor (AFL) issued its own distinctively apolitical report, which called for the achievement of numerous incremental improvements via the collective bargaining process.

IFTU Bern Conference

As the war drew to a close, two competing visions for the post-war world emerged. The first was offered by the International Federation of Trade Unions (IFTU), which called for a meeting in Bern, Switzerland, in July 1919. The Bern meeting would consider both the future of the IFTU and the various proposals which had been made in the previous few years. The IFTU also proposed including delegates from the

Central Powers as equals. Samuel Gompers, president of the AFL, boycotted the meeting, wanting the Central Powers delegates in a subservient role as an admission of guilt for their countries' role in the bringing about war. Instead, Gompers favoured a meeting in Paris which would only consider President Woodrow Wilson's Fourteen Points as a platform. Despite the American boycott, the Bern meeting went ahead as scheduled. In its final report, the Bern Conference demanded an end to wage labour and the establishment of socialism. If these ends could not be immediately achieved, then an international body attached to the League of Nations should enact and enforce legislation to protect workers and trade unions.

Commission on International Labour Legislation

Meanwhile, the Paris Peace Conference sought to dampen public support for communism. Subsequently, the Allied Powers agreed that clauses should be inserted into the emerging peace treaty protecting labour unions and workers' rights, and that an international labour body be established to help guide international labour relations in the future. The advisory Commission on International Labour Legislation was established by the Peace Conference to draft these proposals. The Commission met for the first time on 1 February 1919, and Gompers was elected chairman.

Two competing proposals for an international body emerged during the Commission's meetings. The British proposed establishing an international parliament to enact labour laws which each member of the League would be required to implement. Each nation would have two delegates to the parliament, one each from labour and management. An international labour office would collect statistics on labour issues and enforce the new international laws. Philosophically opposed to the concept of an international parliament and convinced that international standards would lower the few protections achieved in the United States, Gompers proposed that the international labour body be authorized only to make recommendations, and that enforcement be left up to the League of Nations. Despite vigorous opposition from the British, the American proposal was adopted.

Gompers also set the agenda for the draft charter protecting workers' rights. The Americans made 10 proposals. Three were adopted without change: That labour should not be treated as a commodity; that all workers had the right to a wage sufficient to live on; and that women should receive equal pay for equal work. A proposal protecting the freedom of speech, press, assembly, and association was amended to include only freedom of association. A proposed ban on the international shipment of goods made by children under the age of 16 was amended to ban goods made by children under the age of 14. A proposal to require an eight-hour work day was amended to require the eight-hour work day *or* the 40-hour work week (an exception was made for countries where productivity was low). Four other American proposals were rejected. Meanwhile, international delegates proposed three additional clauses, which were adopted: One or more days for weekly rest; equality of laws for foreign workers; and regular and frequent inspection of factory conditions.

The Commission issued its final report on 4 March 1919, and the Peace Conference adopted it without amendment on 11 April. The report became Part XIII of the Treaty of Versailles.

Interwar period

The first annual conference, referred to as the International Labour Conference (ILC), began on 29 October 1919 at the Pan American Union Building in Washington, D.C. and adopted the first six International Labour Conventions, which dealt with hours of work in industry, unemployment, maternity protection, night work for women, minimum age, and night work for young persons in industry. The prominent French socialist Albert Thomas became its first director-general.

Despite open disappointment and sharp critique, the revived International Federation of Trade Unions(IFTU) quickly adapted itself to this mechanism. The IFTU increasingly oriented its international activities around the lobby work of the ILO.

At the time of establishment, the U.S. government was not a member of ILO, as the US Senate rejected the covenant of the League of Nations, and the United States could not join any of its agencies. Following the election of Franklin Delano Roosevelt to the U.S. presidency, the new administration made renewed efforts to join the ILO without league membership. On 19 June, 1934, the U.S. Congress passed a joint resolution authorizing the president to join ILO without joining the League of Nations as a whole. On 22 June, 1934, the ILO adopted a resolution inviting the U.S. government to join the organization. On 20 August, 1934, the U.S. government responded positively and took its seat at the ILO.

Wartime and the United Nations

During the Second World War, when Switzerland was surrounded by German troops, ILO director John G. Winant made the decision to leave Geneva. In August 1940, the government of Canada officially invited the ILO to be housed at McGill University in Montreal. Forty staff members were transferred to the temporary offices and continued to work from McGill until 1948.

The ILO became the first specialized agency of the United Nations system after the demise of the league in 1946. Its constitution, as amended, includes the Declaration of Philadelphia (1944) on the aims and purposes of the organization.

Cold War era

In July, 1970, the United States withdrew 50% of its financial support to the ILO following the appointment of an assistant director-general from the Soviet Union. This appointment (by the ILO's British director-general, C. Wilfred Jenks) drew particular criticism from AFL–CIO president George Meany and from Congressman John E. Rooney. However, the funds were eventually paid.

On 12 June, 1975, the ILO voted to grant the Palestinian Liberation Organization observer status at its meetings.

Representatives of the United States and Israel walked out of the meeting. The U.S. House of Representatives subsequently decided to withhold funds. The United States gave notice of full withdrawal on 6 November, 1975, stating that the organization had become politicized. The United States also suggested that representation from communist countries was not truly "tripartite"—including government, workers, and employers—because of the structure of these economies. The withdrawal became effective on 1 November, 1977.

The United States returned to the organization in 1980 after extracting some concessions from the organization. It was partly responsible for the ILO's shift away from a human rights approach and towards support for the Washington Consensus. Economist Guy Standing wrote "the ILO quietly ceased to be an international body attempting to redress structural inequality and became one promoting employment equity".

PROGRAMMES

Labour statistics

The ILO is a major provider of labour statistics. Labour statistics are an important tool for its member states to monitor their progress toward improving labour standards. As part of their statistical work, ILO maintains several databases. This database covers 11 major data series for over 200 countries. In addition, ILO publishes a number of compilations of labour statistics, such as the Key Indicators of Labour Markets (KILM). KILM covers 20 main indicators on labour participation rates, employment, unemployment, educational attainment, labour cost, and economic performance. Many of these indicators have been prepared by other organizations. For example, the Division of International Labour Comparisons of the U.S. Bureau of Labor Statistics prepares the hourly compensation in manufacturing indicator.

The U.S. Department of Labor also publishes a yearly report containing a *List of Goods Produced by Child Labor or Forced Labor* issued by the Bureau of International Labor

Affairs. The December 2014 updated edition of the report listed a total of 74 countries and 136 goods.

Training and teaching units

The International Training Centre of the International Labour Organization (ITCILO) is based in Turin, Italy. Together with the University of Turin Department of Law, the ITC offers training for ILO officers and secretariat members, as well as offering educational programmes. For instance, the ITCILO offers a Master of Laws programme in management of development, which aims specialize professionals in the field of cooperation and development.

Child labour

The term *child labour* is often defined as work that deprives children of their childhood, potential, dignity, and is harmful to their physical and mental development.

Child labour refers to work that is mentally, physically, socially or morally dangerous and harmful to children. Further, it can involve interfering with their schooling by depriving them of the opportunity to attend school, obliging them to leave school prematurely, or requiring them to attempt to combine school attendance with excessively long and heavy work.

In its most extreme forms, child labour involves children being enslaved, separated from their families, exposed to serious hazards and illnesses and left to fend for themselves on the streets of large cities – often at a very early age. Whether or not particular forms of "work" can be called *child labour* depends on the child's age, the type and hours of work performed, the conditions under which it is performed and the objectives pursued by individual countries. The answer varies from country to country, as well as among sectors within countries.

ILO's response to child labour

The ILO's International Programme on the Elimination of Child Labour (IPEC) was created in 1992 with the overall goal of the progressive elimination of child labour, which was to be achieved through strengthening the capacity of countries to deal with the problem and promoting a worldwide movement to combat child labour. The IPEC currently has operations in 88 countries, with an annual expenditure on technical cooperation projects that reached over US$74 million, €50 million in 2006. It is the largest programme of its kind globally and the biggest single operational programme of the ILO.

The number and range of the IPEC's partners have expanded over the years and now include employers' and workers' organizations, other international and government agencies, private businesses, community-based organizations, NGOs, the media, parliamentarians, the judiciary, universities, religious groups and children and their families.

The IPEC's work to eliminate child labour is an important facet of the ILO's Decent Work Agenda. Child labour not only prevents children from acquiring the skills and education they need for a better future, it also perpetuates poverty and affects national economies through losses in competitiveness, productivity and potential income.

Exceptions in indigenous communities

Because of different cultural views involving labour, the ILO developed a series of culturally sensitive mandates, including convention Nos. 169, 107, 138, and 182, to protect indigenous culture, traditions, and identities. Convention Nos. 138 and 182 lead in the fight against child labour, while Nos. 107 and 169 promote the rights of indigenous and tribal peoples and protect their right to define their own developmental priorities. The ILO recognizes these changes are necessary to respect the culture and traditions of other communities while also looking after the welfare of children.

In many indigenous communities, parents believe children learn important life lessons through the act of work and through the participation in daily life. Working is seen as a learning process preparing children of the future tasks they will eventually have to do as an adult. It is a belief that the family's and child well-being and survival is a shared responsibility between members of the whole family. They also see work as an intrinsic part of their child's developmental process. While these attitudes toward child work remain, many children and parents from indigenous communities still highly value education. The ILO wants to include these communities in the fight against exploitative child labour while being sensitive to their traditions and values. actually they know the how to learn it, normally they can do it.

ISSUES

Forced labour

The ILO has considered the fight against forced labour to be one of its main priorities. During the interwar years, the issue was mainly considered a colonial phenomenon, and the ILO's concern was to establish minimum standards protecting the inhabitants of colonies from the worst abuses committed by economic interests. After 1945, the goal became to set a uniform and universal standard, determined by the higher awareness gained during World War II of politically and economically motivated systems of forced labour, but debates were hampered by the Cold War and by exemptions claimed by colonial powers. Since the 1960s, declarations of labour standards as a component of human rights have been weakened by government of postcolonial countries claiming a need to exercise extraordinary powers over labour in their role as emergency regimes promoting rapid economic development.

In June 1998 the International Labour Conference adopted a Declaration on Fundamental Principles and Rights at Work and its follow-up that obligates member states to respect, promote and realize freedom of association and the right to collective bargaining, the elimination of all forms of forced or compulsory labour, the effective abolition of child labour, and the elimination of discrimination in respect of employment and occupation.

With the adoption of the declaration, the ILO created the InFocus Programme on Promoting the Declaration which is responsible for the reporting processes and technical cooperation activities associated with the declaration; and it carries out awareness raising, advocacy and knowledge functions.

In November 2001, following the publication of the InFocus Programme's first global report on forced labour, the ILO's governing body created a special action programme to combat forced labour (SAP-FL), as part of broader efforts to promote the 1998 Declaration on Fundamental Principles and Rights at Work and its follow-up.

Since its inception, the SAP-FL has focused on raising global awareness of forced labour in its different forms, and mobilizing action against its manifestation. Several thematic and country-specific studies and surveys have since been undertaken, on such diverse aspects of forced labour as bonded labour, human trafficking, forced domestic work, rural servitude, and forced prison labour.

The SAP-FL has spearheaded the ILO's work in this field since early 2002. The programme is designed to:

- Raise global awareness and understanding of modern forced labour
- Assist governments in developing and implementing new laws, policies and action plans
- Develop and disseminate guidance and training materials on key aspects of forced labour and trafficking
- Implement innovative programmes that combine policy development, capacity building of law enforcement and labour market institutions, and targeted, field-based projects of direct support for both prevention of forced labour and identification and rehabilitation of its victims

Minimum wage law

To protect the right of labours for fixing minimum wage, ILO has created Minimum Wage-Fixing Machinery Convention, 1928, Minimum Wage Fixing Machinery (Agriculture) Convention, 1951 and Minimum Wage Fixing Convention, 1970 as minimum wage law.

HIV/AIDS

The International Labour Organization (ILO) is the lead UN-agency on HIV workplace policies and programmes and private sector mobilization. The ILO recognizes that HIV has a potentially devastating impact on labour and productivity and represents an enormous burden for working people, their families and communities. ILOAIDS is the branch of the ILO dedicated to this issue.

The ILO has been involved with the HIV response since 1998. In June 2001, the ILO's governing body adopted a pioneering code of practice on HIV/AIDS and the world of work,which was launched during a special session of the UN General Assembly.

The same year, ILO became a cosponsor of the Joint United Nations Programme on HIV/AIDS (UNAIDS).

In 2010, the 99th International Labour Conference adopted the ILO's recommendation concerning HIV and AIDS and the world of work, 2010 (No. 200), the first international labour standard on HIV and AIDS.

The recommendation lays out a comprehensive set of principles to protect the rights of HIV-positive workers and their families, while scaling up prevention in the workplace. Working under the theme of *Preventing HIV, Protecting Human Rights at Work*, ILOAIDS undertakes a range of policy advisory, research and technical support functions in the area of HIV and AIDS and the world of work.

The ILO also works on promoting social protection as a means of reducing vulnerability to HIV and mitigating its impact on those living with or affected by HIV.

ILOAIDS is currently engaged in the "Getting to Zero" campaign to arrive at zero new infections, zero AIDS-related deaths and zero-discrimination by 2015. Building on this campaign, ILOAIDS is executing a programme of voluntary and confidential counselling and testing at work, known as VCT@WORK.

Migrant workers

As the word "migrant" suggests, migrant workers refer to those who moves from one country to another to do their job. For the rights of migrant workers, ILO has adopted conventions, including Migrant Workers (Supplementary Provisions) Convention, 1975 and United Nations Convention on the Protection of the Rights of All Migrant Workers and Members of Their Families in 1990.

Domestic workers

Domestic workers are those who perform a variety of tasks for and in other peoples' homes. For example, they may cook / clean the house and look after children. Yet they are often the ones with the least consideration, excluded from labour and social protection. This is mainly due to the fact that women have traditionally carried out the tasks without pay. For the rights and decent work of domestic workers including migrant domestic workers, ILO has adopted Convention on domestic workers on 16 June 2011.

ILO and globalization

Seeking a process of globalization that is inclusive, democratically governed and provides opportunities and tangible benefits for all countries and people. The World Commission on the Social Dimension of Globalization was established by the ILO's governing body in February 2002 at the initiative of the director-general in response to the fact that there did not appear to be a space within the multilateral system that would cover adequately and comprehensively the social dimension of the various aspects of globalization. The World Commission Report, A Fair Globalization: Creating Opportunities for All, is the first attempt at structured dialogue among representatives of constituencies with different interests and opinions on the social dimension of globalization, aimed at finding common ground on one of the most controversial and divisive subjects of our time.

13

International Monetary Fund (IMF)

The International Monetary Fund (IMF) is an international organization headquartered in Washington, D.C., consisting of "189 countries working to foster global monetary cooperation, secure financial stability, facilitate international trade, promote high employment and sustainable economic growth, and reduce poverty around the world." Formed in 1945 at the Bretton Woods Conference primarily by the ideas of Harry Dexter White and John Maynard Keynes, it came into formal existence in 1945 with 29 member countries and the goal of reconstructing the international payment system. It now plays a central role in the management of balance of payments difficulties and international financial crises. Countries contribute funds to a pool through a quota system from which countries experiencing balance of payments problems can borrow money. As of 2016, the fund had SDR477 billion (about $666 billion).

Through the fund, and other activities such as the gathering of statistics and analysis, surveillance of its members' economies and the demand for particular policies, the IMF works to improve the economies of its member countries. The organisation's objectives stated in the Articles of Agreement are: to promote international monetary co-operation, international trade, high employment, exchange-rate stability, sustainable economic growth, and making resources available to member countries in financial difficulty.

The current Managing Director (MD) and Chairman of the International Monetary Fund is noted French lawyer and former politician, Christine Lagarde, who has held the post since 5 July 2011.

FUNCTIONS

According to the IMF itself, it works to foster global growth and economic stability by providing policy, advice and financing the members, by working with developing nations to help them achieve macroeconomic stability and reduce poverty. The rationale for this is that private international capital markets function imperfectly and many countries have limited access to financial markets. Such market imperfections, together with balance-of-payments financing, provide the justification for official financing, without which many countries could only correct large external payment imbalances through measures with adverse economic consequences. The IMF provides alternate sources of financing.

Upon the founding of the IMF, its three primary functions were: to oversee the fixed exchange rate arrangements between countries, thus helping national governments manage their exchange rates and allowing these governments to prioritise economic growth, and to provide short-term capital to aid the balance of payments. This assistance was meant to prevent the spread of international economic crises. The IMF was also intended to help mend the pieces of the international economy after the Great Depression and World War II. As well, to provide capital investments for economic growth and projects such as infrastructure.

The IMF's role was fundamentally altered by the floating exchange rates post-1971. It shifted to examining the economic policies of countries with IMF loan agreements to determine if a shortage of capital was due to economic fluctuations or economic policy. The IMF also researched what types of government policy would ensure economic recovery. A particular concern of the IMF was to prevent financial crisis, such as those in Mexico 1982, Brazil in 1987, East Asia in 1997–98 and

Russia in 1998, from spreading and threatening the entire global financial and currency system. The challenge was to promote and implement policy that reduced the frequency of crises among the emerging market countries, especially the middle-income countries which are vulnerable to massive capital outflows. Rather than maintaining a position of oversight of only exchange rates, their function became one of surveillance of the overall macroeconomic performance of member countries. Their role became a lot more active because the IMF now manages economic policy rather than just exchange rates.

In addition, the IMF negotiates conditions on lending and loans under their policy of conditionality, which was established in the 1950s. Low-income countries can borrow on concessional terms, which means there is a period of time with no interest rates, through the Extended Credit Facility (ECF), the Standby Credit Facility (SCF) and the Rapid Credit Facility (RCF). Nonconcessional loans, which include interest rates, are provided mainly through Stand-By Arrangements (SBA), the Flexible Credit Line (FCL), the Precautionary and Liquidity Line (PLL), and the Extended Fund Facility. The IMF provides emergency assistance via the Rapid Financing Instrument (RFI) to members facing urgent balance-of-payments needs.

Surveillance of the global economy

The IMF is mandated to oversee the international monetary and financial system and monitor the economic and financial policies of its member countries. This activity is known as surveillance and facilitates international co-operation. Since the demise of the Bretton Woods system of fixed exchange rates in the early 1970s, surveillance has evolved largely by way of changes in procedures rather than through the adoption of new obligations. The responsibilities changed from those of guardian to those of overseer of members' policies.

The Fund typically analyses the appropriateness of each member country's economic and financial policies for achieving orderly economic growth, and assesses the consequences of these policies for other countries and for the global economy.

In 1995 the International Monetary Fund began work on data dissemination standards with the view of guiding IMF member countries to disseminate their economic and financial data to the public. The International Monetary and Financial Committee (IMFC) endorsed the guidelines for the dissemination standards and they were split into two tiers: The General Data Dissemination System (GDDS) and the Special Data Dissemination Standard (SDDS).

The executive board approved the SDDS and GDDS in 1996 and 1997 respectively, and subsequent amendments were published in a revised *Guide to the General Data Dissemination System*. The system is aimed primarily at statisticians and aims to improve many aspects of statistical systems in a country. It is also part of the World Bank Millennium Development Goals and Poverty Reduction Strategic Papers.

The primary objective of the GDDS is to encourage member countries to build a framework to improve data quality and statistical capacity building to evaluate statistical needs, set priorities in improving the timeliness, transparency, reliability and accessibility of financial and economic data. Some countries initially used the GDDS, but later upgraded to SDDS.

Some entities that are not themselves IMF members also contribute statistical data to the systems:

1. Palestinian Authority – GDDS
2. Hong Kong – SDDS
3. Macau – GDDS
4. EU institutions:
    - the European Central Bank for the Eurozone – SDDS
    - Eurostat for the whole EU – SDDS, thus providing data from Cyprus (not using any DDSystem on its own) and Malta (using only GDDS on its own)

Conditionality of loans

IMF conditionality is a set of policies or conditions that the IMF requires in exchange for financial resources. The IMF does require collateral from countries for loans but also requires the government seeking assistance to correct its macroeconomic imbalances in the form of policy reform. If the conditions are not met, the funds are withheld. The concept of conditionality was introduced in a 1952 Executive Board decision and later incorporated into the Articles of Agreement.

Conditionality is associated with economic theory as well as an enforcement mechanism for repayment. Stemming primarily from the work of Jacques Polak, the theoretical underpinning of conditionality was the "monetary approach to the balance of payments".

Structural adjustment

Some of the conditions for structural adjustment can include:

- Cutting expenditures, also known as austerity.
- Focusing economic output on direct export and resource extraction,
- Devaluation of currencies,
- Trade liberalisation, or lifting import and export restrictions,
- Increasing the stability of investment (by supplementing foreign direct investment with the opening of domestic stock markets),
- Balancing budgets and not overspending,
- Removing price controls and state subsidies,
- Privatization, or divestiture of all or part of state-owned enterprises,
- Enhancing the rights of foreign investors vis-a-vis national laws,
- Improving governance and fighting corruption.

These conditions are known as the Washington Consensus.

Benefits

These loan conditions ensure that the borrowing country will be able to repay the IMF and that the country will not attempt to solve their balance-of-payment problems in a way that would negatively impact the international economy. The incentive problem of moral hazard—when economic agents maximise their own utility to the detriment of others because they do not bear the full consequences of their actions—is mitigated through conditions rather than providing collateral; countries in need of IMF loans do not generally possess internationally valuable collateral anyway.

Conditionality also reassures the IMF that the funds lent to them will be used for the purposes defined by the Articles of Agreement and provides safeguards that country will be able to rectify its macroeconomic and structural imbalances. In the judgment of the IMF, the adoption by the member of certain corrective measures or policies will allow it to repay the IMF, thereby ensuring that the resources will be available to support other members.

As of 2004, borrowing countries have had a very good track record for repaying credit extended under the IMF's regular lending facilities with full interest over the duration of the loan. This indicates that IMF lending does not impose a burden on creditor countries, as lending countries receive market-rate interest on most of their quota subscription, plus any of their own-currency subscriptions that are loaned out by the IMF, plus all of the reserve assets that they provide the IMF.

HISTORY

The IMF was originally laid out as a part of the Bretton Woods system exchange agreement in 1944. During the Great Depression, countries sharply raised barriers to trade in an attempt to improve their failing economies. This led to the devaluation of national currencies and a decline in world trade.

This breakdown in international monetary co-operation created a need for oversight. The representatives of 45 governments met at the Bretton Woods Conference in the Mount Washington Hotel in Bretton Woods, New Hampshire, in the United States, to discuss a framework for postwar international economic co-operation and how to rebuild Europe.

There were two views on the role the IMF should assume as a global economic institution. American delegate Harry Dexter White foresaw an IMF that functioned more like a bank, making sure that borrowing states could repay their debts on time.

Most of White's plan was incorporated into the final acts adopted at Bretton Woods. British economist John Maynard Keynes imagined that the IMF would be a cooperative fund upon which member states could draw to maintain economic activity and employment through periodic crises. This view suggested an IMF that helped governments and to act as the United States government had during the New Deal in response to World War II.

The IMF formally came into existence on 27 December 1945, when the first 29 countries ratified its Articles of Agreement. By the end of 1946 the IMF had grown to 39 members. On 1 March 1947, the IMF began its financial operations, and on 8 May France became the first country to borrow from it.

The IMF was one of the key organisations of the international economic system; its design allowed the system to balance the rebuilding of international capitalism with the maximisation of national economic sovereignty and human welfare, also known as embedded liberalism.The IMF's influence in the global economy steadily increased as it accumulated more members. The increase reflected in particular the attainment of political independence by many African countries and more recently the 1991 dissolution of the Soviet Union because most countries in the Soviet sphere of influence did not join the IMF.

The Bretton Woods system prevailed until 1971, when the United States government suspended the convertibility of the US$ (and dollar reserves held by other governments) into gold. This is known as the Nixon Shock. The changes to the IMF articles of agreement reflecting these changes were ratified by the 1976 Jamaica Accords.

Since 2000

The IMF provided two major lending packages in the early 2000s to Argentina (during the 1998–2002 Argentine great depression) and Uruguay (after the 2002 Uruguay banking crisis). However, by the mid-2000s, IMF lending was at its lowest share of world GDP since the 1970s.

In May 2010, the IMF participated, in 3:11 proportion, in the first Greek bailout that totalled €110 billion, to address the great accumulation of public debt, caused by continuing large public sector deficits. As part of the bailout, the Greek government agreed to adopt austerity measures that would reduce the deficit from 11% in 2009 to "well below 3%" in 2014. The bailout did not include debt restructuring measures such as a haircut, to the chagrin of the Swiss, Brazilian, Indian, Russian, and Argentinian Directors of the IMF, with the Greek authorities themselves (at the time, PM George Papandreou and Finance Minister Giorgos Papakonstantinou) ruling out a haircut.

A second bailout package of more than €100 billion was agreed over the course of a few months from October 2011, during which time Papandreou was forced from office. The so-called Troika, of which the IMF is part, are joint managers of this programme, which was approved by the Executive Directors of the IMF on 15 March 2012 for SDR23.8 billion, and which saw private bondholders take a haircutof upwards of 50%. In the interval between May 2010 and February 2012 the private banks of Holland, France and Germany reduced exposure to Greek debt from €122 billion to €66 billion.

As of January 2012, the largest borrowers from the IMF in order were Greece, Portugal, Ireland, Romania, and Ukraine.

On 25 March 2013, a €10 billion international bailout of Cyprus was agreed by the Troika, at the cost to the Cypriots of its agreement: to close the country's second-largest bank; to impose a one-time bank deposit levy on Bank of Cyprus uninsured deposits. No insured deposit of €100k or less were to be affected under the terms of a novel bail-in scheme.

The topic of sovereign debt restructuring was taken up by the IMF in April 2013 for the first time since 2005, in a report entitled "Sovereign Debt Restructuring: Recent Developments and Implications for the Fund's Legal and Policy Framework". The paper, which was discussed by the board on 20 May, summarised the recent experiences in Greece, St Kitts and Nevis, Belize, and Jamaica. An explanatory interview with Deputy Director Hugh Bredenkamp was published a few days later, as was a deconstruction by Matina Stevis of the *Wall Street Journal*.

In the October 2013 Fiscal Monitor publication, the IMF suggested that a capital levy capable of reducing Euro-area government debt ratios to "end-2007 levels" would require a very high tax rate of about 10%.

The Fiscal Affairs department of the IMF, headed at the time by Acting Director Sanjeev Gupta, produced a January 2014 report entitled "Fiscal Policy and Income Inequality" that stated that "Some taxes levied on wealth, especially on immovable property, are also an option for economies seeking more progressive taxation ... Property taxes are equitable and efficient, but underutilized in many economies ... There is considerable scope to exploit this tax more fully, both as a revenue source and as a redistributive instrument."

At the end of March 2014, the IMF secured an $18 billion bailout fund for the provisional government of Ukraine in the aftermath of the 2014 Ukrainian revolution.

MEMBER COUNTRIES

Not all member countries of the IMF are sovereign states, and therefore not all "member countries" of the IMF are members of the United Nations. Amidst "member countries" of the IMF that are not member states of the UN are non-sovereign areas with special jurisdictions that are officially under the sovereignty of full UN member states, such as Aruba, Curaçao, Hong Kong, and Macau, as well as Kosovo. The corporate members appoint *ex-officio* voting members, who are listed below. All members of the IMF are also International Bank for Reconstruction and Development (IBRD) members and vice versa.

Former members are Cuba (which left in 1964), and the Republic of China (Taiwan), which was ejected from the UN in 1980 after losing the support of then United States President Jimmy Carter and was replaced by the People's Republic of China. However, "Taiwan Province of China" is still listed in the official IMF indices. Apart from Cuba, the other UN states that do not belong to the IMF are Andorra, Liechtenstein, Monaco and North Korea.

The former Czechoslovakia was expelled in 1954 for "failing to provide required data" and was readmitted in 1990, after the Velvet Revolution. Poland withdrew in 1950—allegedly pressured by the Soviet Union—but returned in 1986.

Qualifications

Any country may apply to be a part of the IMF. Post-IMF formation, in the early postwar period, rules for IMF membership were left relatively loose. Members needed to make periodic membership payments towards their quota, to refrain from currency restrictions unless granted IMF permission, to abide by the Code of Conduct in the IMF Articles of Agreement, and to provide national economic information. However, stricter rules were imposed on governments that applied to the IMF for funding.

The countries that joined the IMF between 1945 and 1971 agreed to keep their exchange rates secured at rates that could be adjusted only to correct a "fundamental disequilibrium" in the balance of payments, and only with the IMF's agreement.

Some members have a very difficult relationship with the IMF and even when they are still members they do not allow themselves to be monitored.

Benefits

Member countries of the IMF have access to information on the economic policies of all member countries, the opportunity to influence other members' economic policies, technical assistance in banking, fiscal affairs, and exchange matters, financial support in times of payment difficulties, and increased opportunities for trade and investment.

LEADERSHIP

Board of Governors

The Board of Governors consists of one governor and one alternate governor for each member country. Each member country appoints its two governors. The Board normally meets once a year and is responsible for electing or appointing executive directors to the Executive Board. While the Board of Governors is officially responsible for approving quota increases, Special Drawing Right allocations, the admittance of new members, compulsory withdrawal of members, and amendments to the Articles of Agreement and By-Laws, in practice it has delegated most of its powers to the IMF's Executive Board.

The Board of Governors is advised by the International Monetary and Financial Committee and the Development Committee. The International Monetary and Financial Committee has 24 members and monitors developments in global liquidity and the transfer of resources to developing countries. The Development Committee has 25 members and advises on critical development issues and on financial resources required to promote economic development in developing countries. They also advise on trade and environmental issues.

Executive Board

24 Executive Directors make up the Executive Board. The Executive Directors represent all 189 member countries in a geographically based roster. Countries with large economies have their own Executive Director, but most countries are grouped in constituencies representing four or more countries.

Following the *2008 Amendment on Voice and Participation* which came into effect in March 2011, eight countries each appoint an Executive Director: the United States, Japan, China,

Germany, France, the United Kingdom, Russia, and Saudi Arabia. The remaining 16 Directors represent constituencies consisting of 4 to 22 countries. The Executive Director representing the largest constituency of 22 countries accounts for 1.55% of the vote. This Board usually meets several times each week. The Board membership and constituency is scheduled for periodic review every eight years.

Managing Director

The IMF is led by a managing director, who is head of the staff and serves as Chairman of the Executive Board. The managing director is assisted by a First Deputy managing director and three other Deputy Managing Directors.

Historically the IMF's managing director has been European and the president of the World Bank has been from the United States. However, this standard is increasingly being questioned and competition for these two posts may soon open up to include other qualified candidates from any part of the world.

In 2011 the world's largest developing countries, the BRIC nations, issued a statement declaring that the tradition of appointing a European as managing director undermined the legitimacy of the IMF and called for the appointment to be merit-based.

Previous managing director Dominique Strauss-Kahn was arrested in connection with charges of sexually assaulting a New York hotel room attendant and resigned on 18 May. The charges were later dropped. On 28 June 2011 Christine Lagarde was confirmed as managing director of the IMF for a five-year term starting on 5 July 2011.

Voting power

Voting power in the IMF is based on a quota system. Each member has a number of basic votes (each member's number of basic votes equals 5.502% of the total votes), plus one additional vote for each Special Drawing Right (SDR) of 100,000 of a member country's quota. The Special Drawing Right is the unit of account of the IMF and represents a claim to currency. It is based on a basket of key international currencies. The basic votes generate a slight bias in favour of small countries, but the additional votes determined by SDR outweigh this bias. Changes in the voting shares require approval by a supermajority of 85% of voting power.

In December 2015, the United States Congress adopted a legislation authorising the 2010 Quota and Governance Reforms. As a result,

- all 188 members' quotas will increase from a total of about SDR 238.5 billion to about SDR 477 billion, while the quota shares and voting power of the IMF's poorest member countries will be protected.
- more than 6 percent of quota shares will shift to dynamic emerging market and developing countries and also from over-represented to under-represented members.
- four emerging market countries (Brazil, China, India, and Russia) will be among the ten largest members of the IMF. Other top 10 members are the United States, Japan, Germany, France, the United Kingdom and Italy.

SCANDALS

Both Lagarde and her two predecessors Strauss-Kahn and Rato have been investigated by the authorities and have either faced trial or are scheduled to go on trial for a variety of offences.

Lagarde had been accused of giving preferential treatment to businessman-turned-politician Bernard Tapie as he pursued a legal challenge against the French government. At the time, Lagarde was the French economic minister. Within hours of her conviction, in which she escaped any punishment, the fund's 24-member executive board put to rest any speculation that she might have to resign, praising her "outstanding leadership" and the "wide respect" she commands around the world.

ALTERNATIVES

In March 2011 the Ministers of Economy and Finance of the African Union proposed to establish an African Monetary Fund.

At the 6th BRICS summit in July 2014 the BRICS nations (Brazil, Russia, India, China, and South Africa) announced the BRICS Contingent Reserve Arrangement (CRA) with an initial size of US$100 billion, a framework to provide liquidity through currency swaps in response to actual or potential short-term balance-of-payments pressures.

In 2014, the China-led Asian Infrastructure Investment Bank was established.

IN THE MEDIA

Life and Debt, a documentary film, deals with the IMF's policies' influence on Jamaica and its economy from a critical point of view. *Debtocracy*, a 2011 independent Greek documentary film, also criticises the IMF. Portuguese musician José Mário Branco's 1982 album FMI is inspired by the IMF's intervention in Portugal through monitored stabilisation programs in 1977–78. In the 2015 film, *Our Brand Is Crisis*, the IMF is mentioned as a point of political contention.

14

World Trade Organization (WTO)

The World Trade Organization (WTO) is an intergovernmental organization that regulates international trade. The WTO officially commenced on 1 January 1995 under the Marrakesh Agreement, signed by 124 nations on 15 April 1994, replacing the General Agreement on Tariffs and Trade (GATT), which commenced in 1948. It is the largest international economic organization in the world.

The WTO deals with regulation of trade in goods, services and intellectual property between participating countries by providing a framework for negotiating trade agreements and a dispute resolution process aimed at enforcing participants' adherence to WTO agreements, which are signed by representatives of member governments and ratified by their parliaments. The WTO prohibits discrimination between trading partners, but provides exceptions for environmental protection, national security, and other important goals. Trade-related disputes are resolved by independent judges at the WTO through a dispute resolution process.

The WTO's current Director-General is Roberto Azevêdo, who leads a staff of over 600 people in Geneva, Switzerland. A trade facilitation agreement, part of the Bali Package of decisions, was agreed by all members on 7 December 2013, the first comprehensive agreement in the organization's history.

On 23 January 2017, the amendment to the WTO Trade Related Aspects of Intellectual Property Rights (TRIPS) Agreement marks the first time since the organization opened in 1995 that WTO accords have been amended, and this change should secure for developing countries a legal pathway to access affordable remedies under WTO rules.

Studies show that the WTO boosted trade, and that barriers to trade would be higher in the absence of the WTO. The WTO has highly influenced the text of trade agreements, as "nearly all recent [preferential trade agreements (PTAs)] reference the WTO explicitly, often dozens of times across multiple chapters... in many of these same PTAs we find that substantial portions of treaty language—sometime the majority of a chapter—is copied verbatim from a WTO agreement."

HISTORY

The economists Harry White (left) and John Maynard Keynes at the Bretton Woods Conference.

The WTO's predecessor, the General Agreement on Tariffs and Trade (GATT), was established after World War II in the wake of other new multilateral institutions dedicated to international economic cooperation – such as the World Bank and the International Monetary Fund. A comparable international institution for trade, named the International Trade Organization never started as the treaty was not approved by the U.S. and other signatories, and so GATT slowly became a de facto international organization.

GATT Negotiations before Uruguay

Seven rounds of negotiations occurred under GATT. The first real GATT trade rounds concentrated on further reducing tariffs. Then, the Kennedy Round in the mid-sixties brought about a GATT anti-dumping Agreement and a section on development. The Tokyo Round during the seventies was the first major attempt to tackle trade barriers that do not take the form of tariffs, and to improve the system, adopting a series of agreements on non-tariff barriers, which in some cases interpreted existing GATT rules, and in others broke entirely new ground. Because these plurilateral agreements were not accepted by the full GATT membership, they were often informally called "codes". Several of these codes were amended in the Uruguay Round, and turned into multilateral commitments accepted by all WTO members. Only four remained plurilateral (those on government procurement, bovine meat, civil aircraft and dairy products), but in 1997 WTO members agreed to terminate the bovine meat and dairy agreements, leaving only two. Despite attempts in the mid-1950s and 1960s to create some form of institutional mechanism for international trade, the GATT continued to operate for almost half a century as a semi-institutionalized multilateral treaty regime on a provisional basis.

Uruguay Round

Well before GATT's 40th anniversary, its members concluded that the GATT system was straining to adapt to a new globalizing world economy. In response to the problems identified in the 1982 Ministerial Declaration (structural deficiencies, spill-over impacts of certain countries' policies on world trade GATT could not manage etc.), the eighth GATT round – known as the Uruguay Round – was launched in September 1986, in Punta del Este, Uruguay.

During the Doha Round, the US government blamed Brazil and India for being inflexible and the EU for impeding agricultural imports.

It was the biggest negotiating mandate on trade ever agreed: the talks were going to extend the trading system into several new areas, notably trade in services and intellectual property, and to reform trade in the sensitive sectors of agriculture and textiles; all the original GATT articles were up for review. The Final Act concluding the Uruguay Round and officially establishing the WTO regime was signed 15 April 1994, during the ministerial meeting at Marrakesh, Morocco, and hence is known as the Marrakesh Agreement.

The GATT still exists as the WTO's umbrella treaty for trade in goods, updated as a result of the Uruguay Round negotiations (a distinction is made between *GATT 1994*, the updated parts of GATT, and *GATT 1947*, the original agreement which is still the heart of GATT 1994).GATT 1994 is not however the only legally binding agreement included via the Final Act at Marrakesh; a long list of about 60 agreements, annexes, decisions and understandings was adopted. The agreements fall into six main parts, the Agreement Establishing the WTO, the Multilateral Agreements on Trade in Goods, the General Agreement on Trade in Services, the Agreement on Trade-Related Aspects of Intellectual Property Rights, Dispute settlement and reviews of governments' trade policies

In terms of the WTO's principle relating to tariff "ceiling-binding" (No. 3), the Uruguay Round has been successful in increasing binding commitments by both developed and developing countries, as may be seen in the percentages of tariffs bound before and after the 1986–1994 talks.

Ministerial conferences

The World Trade Organization Ministerial Conference of 1998, in the Palace of Nations (Geneva, Switzerland).

The highest decision-making body of the WTO is the Ministerial Conference, which usually meets every two years. It brings together all members of the WTO, all of which are countries or customs unions. The Ministerial Conference can take decisions on all matters under any of the multilateral trade agreements. Some of these such as the inaugural ministerial conference in Singapore and the Cancun conference in 2003 involved arguments between developed and developing economies referred to as the "Singapore issues" such as agricultural subsidies while others such as the Seattle conference in 1999 created large demonstrations. The fourth ministerial conference in Doha in 2001 approved China's entry to the WTO and launched the Doha Development Round which was supplemented by the sixth WTO ministerial conference (in Hong Kong) when agricultural export subsidies were agreed to be phased out and adoption of the European Union's Everything but Arms initiative to phase out tariffs for goods from the Least Developed Countries.

Doha Round (Doha Agenda)

The WTO launched the current round of negotiations, the Doha Development Round, at the fourth ministerial conference in Doha, Qatar in November 2001. This was to be an ambitious effort to make globalization more inclusive and help the world's poor, particularly by slashing barriers and subsidies in farming. The initial agenda comprised both further trade liberalization and new rule-making, underpinned by commitments to strengthen substantial assistance to developing countries.

Progress stalled after over differences between developed nations and the major developing countries on issues such as industrial tariffs and non tariff barriers to trade particularly against and between the EU and the US over their maintenance of agricultural subsidies—seen to operate effectively as trade barriers. Repeated attempts to revive the talks were unsuccessful though the adoption of the Bali Ministerial Declaration in 2013 addressed bureaucratic barriers to commerce

As of June 2012, the future of the Doha Round remained uncertain: the work programme lists 21 subjects in which the original deadline of 1 January 2005 was missed, and the round is still incomplete. The conflict between free trade on industrial goods and services but retention of protectionism on farm subsidies to domestic agricultural sector (requested by developed countries) and the substantiation of fair trade on agricultural products (requested by developing countries) remain the major obstacles. This impasse has made it impossible to launch new WTO negotiations beyond the Doha Development Round. As a result, there have been an increasing number of bilateral free trade agreements between governments. As of July 2012, there were various negotiation groups in the WTO system for the current agricultural trade negotiation which is in the condition of stalemate.

FUNCTIONS

Among the various functions of the WTO, these are regarded by analysts as the most important:

- It oversees the implementation, administration and operation of the covered agreements.
- It provides a forum for negotiations and for settling disputes.

Additionally, it is WTO's duty to review and propagate the national trade policies, and to ensure the coherence and transparency of trade policies through surveillance in global economic policy-making. Another priority of the WTO is the assistance of developing, least-developed and low-income countries in transition to adjust to WTO rules and disciplines through technical cooperation and training.

1. The WTO shall facilitate the implementation, administration and operation and further the objectives of this Agreement and of the Multilateral Trade Agreements, and shall also provide the framework for the implementation, administration and operation of the multilateral Trade Agreements.
2. The WTO shall provide the forum for negotiations among its members concerning their multilateral trade relations in matters dealt with under the Agreement in the Annexes to this Agreement.
3. The WTO shall administer the Understanding on Rules and Procedures Governing the Settlement of Disputes.
4. The WTO shall administer Trade Policy Review Mechanism.
5. With a view to achieving greater coherence in global economic policy making, the WTO shall cooperate, as appropriate, with the international Monetary Fund (IMF) and with the International Bank for Reconstruction and Development (IBRD) and its affiliated agencies.

The above five listings are the additional functions of the World Trade Organization. As globalization proceeds in today's society, the necessity of an International Organization to manage the trading systems has been of vital importance. As the trade volume increases, issues such as protectionism, trade barriers, subsidies, violation of intellectual property arise due to the differences in the trading rules of every nation. The World Trade Organization serves as the mediator between the nations when such problems arise. WTO could be referred to as the product of globalization and also as one of the most important organizations in today's globalized society.

The WTO is also a centre of economic research and analysis: regular assessments of the global trade picture in its annual publications and research reports on specific topics are produced by the organization. Finally, the WTO cooperates closely with the two other components of the Bretton Woods system, the IMF and the World Bank.

PRINCIPLES OF THE TRADING SYSTEM

The WTO establishes a framework for trade policies; it does not define or specify outcomes. That is, it is concerned with setting the rules of the trade policy games. Five principles are of particular importance in understanding both the pre-1994 GATT and the WTO:

1. Non-discrimination. It has two major components: the most favoured nation (MFN) rule, and the national treatment policy. Both are embedded in the main WTO rules on goods, services, and intellectual property, but their precise scope and nature differ across these areas. The MFN rule requires that a WTO member must apply the same conditions on all trade with other WTO members, i.e. a WTO member has to grant the most favourable conditions under which it allows trade in a certain product type to all other WTO members. "Grant someone a special favour and you have to do the same for all other WTO members." National treatment means that imported goods should be treated no less favourably than domestically produced goods (at least after the foreign goods have entered the market) and was introduced to tackle non-tariff barriers to trade (e.g. technical standards, security standards et al. discriminating against imported goods).

2. Reciprocity. It reflects both a desire to limit the scope of free-riding that may arise because of the MFN rule, and a desire to obtain better access to foreign markets. A related point is that for a nation to negotiate, it is necessary that the gain from doing so be greater than the gain available from unilateral liberalization; reciprocal concessions intend to ensure that such gains will materialise.
3. Binding and enforceable commitments. The tariff commitments made by WTO members in a multilateral trade negotiation and on accession are enumerated in a schedule (list) of concessions. These schedules establish "ceiling bindings": a country can change its bindings, but only after negotiating with its trading partners, which could mean compensating them for loss of trade. If satisfaction is not obtained, the complaining country may invoke the WTO dispute settlement procedures.
4. Transparency. The WTO members are required to publish their trade regulations, to maintain institutions allowing for the review of administrative decisions affecting trade, to respond to requests for information by other members, and to notify changes in trade policies to the WTO. These internal transparency requirements are supplemented and facilitated by periodic country-specific reports (trade policy reviews) through the Trade Policy Review Mechanism (TPRM). The WTO system tries also to improve predictability and stability, discouraging the use of quotas and other measures used to set limits on quantities of imports.
5. Safety values. In specific circumstances, governments are able to restrict trade. The WTO's agreements permit members to take measures to protect not only the environment but also public health, animal health and plant health.

There are three types of provision in this direction:

1. articles allowing for the use of trade measures to attain non-economic objectives;

2. articles aimed at ensuring "fair competition"; members must not use environmental protection measures as a means of disguising protectionist policies.
3. provisions permitting intervention in trade for economic reasons.

Exceptions to the MFN principle also allow for preferential treatment of developing countries, regional free trade areas and customs unions.

ORGANIZATIONAL STRUCTURE

The General Council has the following subsidiary bodies which oversee committees in different areas:

Council for Trade in Goods

There are 11 committees under the jurisdiction of the Goods Council each with a specific task. All members of the WTO participate in the committees. The Textiles Monitoring Body is separate from the other committees but still under the jurisdiction of Goods Council. The body has its own chairman and only 10 members. The body also has several groups relating to textiles.

Council for Trade-Related Aspects of Intellectual Property Rights

Information on intellectual property in the WTO, news and official records of the activities of the TRIPS Council, and details of the WTO's work with other international organizations in the field.

Trade Negotiations Committee

The Trade Negotiations Committee (TNC) is the committee that deals with the current trade talks round. The chair is WTO's director-general. As of June 2012 the committee was tasked with the Doha Development Round.

The Service Council has three subsidiary bodies: financial services, domestic regulations, GATS rules and specific commitments. The council has several different committees, working groups, and working parties. There are committees on the following: Trade and Environment; Trade and Development (Subcommittee on Least-Developed Countries); Regional Trade Agreements; Balance of Payments Restrictions; and Budget, Finance and Administration. There are working parties on the following: Accession. There are working groups on the following: Trade, debt and finance; and Trade and technology transfer.

Council for Trade in Services

The Council for Trade in Services operates under the guidance of the General Council and is responsible for overseeing the functioning of the General Agreement on Trade in Services (GATS). It is open to all WTO members, and can create subsidiary bodies as required.

DECISION-MAKING

The WTO describes itself as "a rules-based, member-driven organization—all decisions are made by the member governments, and the rules are the outcome of negotiations among members". The WTO Agreement foresees votes where consensus cannot be reached, but the practice of consensus dominates the process of decision-making.

Richard Harold Steinberg (2002) argues that although the WTO's consensus governance model provides law-based initial bargaining, trading rounds close through power-based bargaining favouring Europe and the U.S., and may not lead to Pareto improvement.

DISPUTE SETTLEMENT

The WTO's dispute-settlement system "is the result of the evolution of rules, procedures and practices developed over almost half a century under the GATT 1947". In 1994, the WTO members agreed on the Understanding on Rules and Procedures Governing the Settlement of Disputes (DSU) annexed to the "Final Act" signed in Marrakesh in 1994.Dispute settlement is regarded by the WTO as the central pillar of the multilateral trading system, and as a "unique contribution to the stability of the global economy". WTO members have agreed that, if they believe fellow-members are violating trade rules, they will use the multilateral system of settling disputes instead of taking action unilaterally.

The operation of the WTO dispute settlement process involves case-specific panels appointed by the Dispute Settlement Body (DSB), the Appellate Body, The Director-General and the WTO Secretariat, arbitrators, and advisory experts.

The priority is to settle disputes, preferably through a mutually agreed solution, and provision has been made for the process to be conducted in an efficient and timely manner so that "If a case is adjudicated, it should normally take no more than one year for a panel ruling and no more than 16 months if the case is appealed... If the complainant deems the case urgent, consideration of the case should take even less time. WTO member nations are obliged to accept the process as exclusive and compulsory.

According to a 2018 study in the *Journal of Politics*, states are less likely and slower to enforce WTO violations when the violations affect states in a diffuse manner. This is because states face collective action problems with pursuing litigation: they all expect other states to carry the costs of litigation. A 2016 study in *International Studies Quarterly*challenges that the WTO dispute settlement system leads to greater increases in trade.

AGREEMENTS

The WTO oversees about 60 different agreements which have the status of international legal texts. Member countries must sign and ratify all WTO agreements on accession. A discussion of some of the most important agreements follows.

The Agreement on Agriculture came into effect with the establishment of the WTO at the beginning of 1995. The AoA has three central concepts, or "pillars": domestic support, market access and export subsidies.

The General Agreement on Trade in Services was created to extend the multilateral trading system to service sector, in the same way as the General Agreement on Tariffs and Trade (GATT) provided such a system for merchandise trade. The agreement entered into force in January 1995.

The Agreement on Trade-Related Aspects of Intellectual Property Rights sets down minimum standards for many forms of intellectual property (IP) regulation. It was negotiated at the end of the Uruguay Round of the General Agreement on Tariffs and Trade (GATT) in 1994.The Agreement on the Application of Sanitary and Phytosanitary Measures—also known as the SPS Agreement—was negotiated during the Uruguay Round of GATT, and entered into force with the establishment of the WTO at the beginning of 1995.

Under the SPS agreement, the WTO sets constraints on members' policies relating to food safety (bacterial contaminants, pesticides, inspection and labelling) as well as animal and plant health (imported pests and diseases). The Agreement on Technical Barriers to Trade is an international treaty of the World Trade Organization. It was negotiated during the Uruguay Round of the General Agreement on Tariffs and Trade, and entered into force with the establishment of the WTO at the end of 1994. The object ensures that technical negotiations and standards, as well as testing and certification procedures, do not create unnecessary obstacles to trade".

The Agreement on Customs Valuation, formally known as the Agreement on Implementation of Article VII of GATT, prescribes methods of customs valuation that Members are to follow. Chiefly, it adopts the "transaction value" approach.

In December 2013, the biggest agreement within the WTO was signed and known as the Bali Package.

OFFICE OF DIRECTOR-GENERAL

The procedures for the appointment of the WTO director-general were published in January 2003. Additionally, there are four deputy directors-general. As of 13 June 2018, under director-general Roberto Azevêdo, the four deputy directors-general are

- Yi Xiaozhun of China (since 1 October 2017),
- Karl Brauner of Germany (since 1 October 2013),
- Yonov Frederick Agah of Nigeria (since 1 October 2013) and
- Alan W. Wolff of the United States (since 1 October 2017).

List of directors-general

Source: Official website

- Roberto Azevêdo, 2013–present
- Pascal Lamy, 2005–2013
- Supachai Panitchpakdi, 2002–2005
- Mike Moore, 1999–2002
- Renato Ruggiero, 1995–1999
- Peter Sutherland, 1995

(Heads of the precursor organization, GATT):

- Peter Sutherland, 1993–1995
- Arthur Dunkel, 1980–1993
- Olivier Long, 1968–1980
- Eric Wyndham White, 1948–1968

IMPACT

Studies show that the WTO boosted trade. Research shows that in the absence of the WTO, the average country would face an increase in tariffs on their exports by 32 percentage points.

According to a 2017 study in the *Journal of International Economic Law*, "nearly all recent [preferential trade agreements (PTAs)] reference the WTO explicitly, often dozens of times across multiple chapters. Likewise, in many of these same PTAs we find that substantial portions of treaty language—sometime the majority of a chapter—is copied verbatim from a WTO agreement... the presence of the WTO in PTAs has increased over time."

15

United Nations High Commissioner for Refugees (UNHCR)

UNHCR, the UN Refugee Agency, is a United Nations programme with the mandate to protect refugees, forcibly displaced communities and stateless people, and assist in their voluntary repatriation, local integration or resettlement to a third country. UNHCR stands for the Office of the United Nations High Commissioner for Refugees and was created in 1950, during the aftermath of World War II. Its headquarters are in Geneva, Switzerland and it is a member of the United Nations Development Group. The UNHCR has won two Nobel Peace Prizes, once in 1954 and again in 1981.

HISTORY

Following the demise of the League of Nations and the formation of the United Nations the international community was acutely aware of the refugee crisis following the end of World War II. In 1947, the International Refugee Organization (IRO) was founded by the United Nations.The IRO was the first international agency to deal comprehensively with all aspects of refugees' lives. Preceding this was the United Nations Relief and Rehabilitation Administration, which was established in 1944 to address the millions of people displaced across Europe as a result of World War II.

In the late 1940s, the IRO fell out of favor, but the UN agreed that a body was required to oversee global refugee issues. Despite many heated debates in the General Assembly, the United Nations High Commissioner for Refugees was founded as a subsidiary organ of the General Assembly by Resolution 319 (IV) of the United Nations General Assembly of December 1949. However, the organization was only intended to operate for 3 years, from January 1951, due to the disagreement of many UN member states over the implications of a permanent body.

UNHCR's mandate was originally set out in its statute, annexed to resolution 428 (V) of the United Nations General Assembly of 1950. This mandate has been subsequently broadened by numerous resolutions of the General Assembly and its Economic and Social Council (ECOSOC). According to UNHCR, [its] mandate is to provide, on a non-political and humanitarian basis, international protection to refugees and to seek permanent solutions for them.

Soon after the signing of the 1951 Convention relating to the Status of Refugees, it became clear that refugees were not solely restricted to Europe. In 1956, UNHCR was involved in coordinating the response to the uprising in Hungary. Just a year later, UNHCR was tasked with dealing with Chinese refugees in Hong Kong, while also responding Algerian refugees who had fled to Morocco and Tunisia in the wake of Algeria's war for independence. The responses marked the beginning of a wider, global mandate in refugee protection and humanitarian assistance.

Decolonization in the 1960s triggered large refugee movements in Africa, creating a massive challenge that would transform UNHCR; unlike the refugee crises in Europe, there were no durable solutions in Africa and many refugees who fled one country only found instability in their new country of asylum. By the end of the decade, two-thirds of UNHCR's budget was focused on operations in Africa and in just one decade, the organization's focus had shifted from an almost exclusive focus on Europe.

In 1967, the Protocol Relating to the Status of Refugees was ratified to remove the geographical and temporal restrictions of UNHCR under the 1951 Convention relating to the Status of Refugees. As the Convention was confined to the refugee crisis in the aftermath of World War II in Europe, the Protocol was made to address the "new refugee situations that have arisen since the Convention was adopted and the refugees concerned that may therefore not fall within the scope of the Convention". In the 1970s, UNHCR refugee operations continued to spread around the globe, with the mass exodus of East Pakistanis to India shortly before the birth of Bangladesh. Adding to the woes in Asia was the Vietnam war, with millions fleeing the war-torn country.

The 1980s saw new challenges for UNHCR, with many member states unwilling to resettle refugees due to the sharp rise in refugee numbers over the 1970s. Often, these refugees were not fleeing wars between states, but inter-ethnic conflict in newly independent states. The targeting of civilians as military strategy added to the displacement in many nations, so even 'minor' conflicts could result in a large number of displaced persons. Whether in Asia, Central America or Africa, these conflicts, fueled by superpower rivalry and aggravated by socio-economic problems within the concerned countries, durable solutions continued to prove a massive challenge for the UNHCR. As a result, the UNHCR became more heavily involved with assistance programs within refugee camps, often located in hostile environments.

The end of the Cold War marked continued inter-ethnic conflict and contributed heavily to refugee flight. In addition, humanitarian intervention by multinational forces became more frequent and the media began to play a big role, particularly in the lead up to the 1999 NATO mission in Yugoslavia, while by contrast, the 1994 Rwandan Genocide had little attention. The genocide in Rwanda caused a massive refugee crisis, again highlighting the difficulties for UNHCR to uphold its mandate, and the UNHCR continued to battle against restrictive asylum policies in so called 'rich' nations.

FUNCTION

UNHCR packages containing tents, tarps, and mosquito netting sit in a field in Dadaab, Kenya, on 11 December 2006, following disastrous flooding

UNHCR was established on 14 December 1950 and succeeded the earlier United Nations Relief and Rehabilitation Administration. The agency is mandated to lead and co-ordinate international action to protect refugees and resolve refugee problems worldwide. Its primary purpose is to safeguard the rights and well-being of refugees. It strives to ensure that everyone can exercise the right to seek asylum and find safe refuge in another state, with the option to return home voluntarily, integrate locally or to resettle in a third country.

UNHCR's mandate has gradually been expanded to include protecting and providing humanitarian assistance to whom it describes as other persons "of concern," including internally displaced persons (IDPs) who would fit the legal definition of a refugee under the 1951 United Nations Convention Relating to the Status of Refugees and 1967 Protocol, the 1969 Organization for African Unity Convention, or some other treaty if they left their country, but who presently remain in their country of origin. UNHCR presently has major missions in Lebanon, South Sudan, Chad/Darfur, Democratic Republic of Congo, Iraq, Afghanistan as well as Kenya to assist and provide services to IDPs and refugees in camps and in urban settings.

UNHCR maintains a database of refugee information, ProGres, which was created during the Kosovo War in the 1990s. The database today contains data on over 11 million refugees, or about 11% of all displaced persons globally. The database contains biometric data, including fingerprints and iris scans and is used to determine aid distribution for recipients.The results of using biometric verification has been successful. When introduced in Kenyan refugee camps of Kakuma and Dadaab in the year 2013, the UN World Food Programme was able to eliminate $1.4m in waste and fraud.

To achieve its mandate, the UNHCR engaged in activities both in the countries of interest and in countries with donors. For example, the UNHCR hosts expert roundtables to discuss issues of concern to the international refugee community.

Palestine refugee mandate

Most Palestinian refugees – those in the West Bank, Gaza Strip, Lebanon, Syria, and Jordan – do not come within the responsibility of the UNHCR, but instead come under an older body, the United Nations Relief and Works Agency for Palestine Refugees in the Near East (UNRWA). The UNRWA has a much broader definition of "refugee" than the UNHCR, including not only refugees themselves but their descendants in perpetuity; however, it only covers refugees stemming from the 1948 and 1967 Arab-Israeli wars. Other Palestinian refugees outside of UNRWA's area of operations do fall under UNHCR's mandate, if they meet the UNHCR's more limited definition of refugee.

Public awareness

Several new programs have recently been introduced to support and to heighten awareness of the issues faced by refugees around the world. These two new programs are a product of the benchmarks set out by the United Nations Millennium Development Goals.

The UNHCR works in different regions of the world to raise awareness about the refugee crisis and the needs of these refugees.

Since 2009, the UNHCR acknowledged a large presence of migration and refugees in the Caribbean, where the refugee crisis remained largely unreported. Many refugees in search for asylum in the United States are unable to reach their destination and end up in the Caribbean. However, migrant laws in most of these nations lacked any protections for asylum-seekers, even the ability to be recognized as a refugee or asylum seeker itself. The UNHCR organized talks with these nations in Costa Rica in 2009, in an effort to bring forward the lack of protections for refugees, who are often labeled as "illegal" and prosecuted as unauthorized migrants.

In 2007, UNHCR offices in Canada launched an aggressive media campaign to shed light on the plight of refugees. This campaign was meant to humanize the refugee crisis by showing refugees living in the midst of disturbing conditions. Using emotional appeals to raise public awareness, the campaign hoped to increase the interest of particularly "30 to 45-year-old professionals who are generally well educated, well read, but have not had direct experience or knowledge of refugee issues," according to fund-raising officer Jonathan Wade.

In Ireland, the UNHCR works to inform the public through different channels. The UNHCR in Ireland actively pursues media relations and "[they] supply the media with accurate and reliable information coupled with our unique insight based on our refugee protection mandate and role as one of the world's leading humanitarian agencies". It also engages its community by holding public events in aims of informing people of current refugee crises. One of these is the annual UNHCR/SARI Fair play Football Cup.

Cooperation within the United Nations

As UNHCR is a program governed by the UN General Assembly, and the UN Economic and Social Council, it cooperates with many other programs and agencies under the United Nations in order to effectively protect the rights of refugees.

On 19 September 2016, UN General Assembly hosted the UN Summit for Refugees and Migrants, a high-level summit to address large movements of refugees and migrants, with the aim of bringing countries together behind a more humane and coordinated approach. Leaders of the UN High Commissioner for Human Rights, UN Entity for Gender Equality and the Empowerment of Women, UN Office on Drugs and Crime, and The World Bank were present. The summit addressed the root causes and drive for migration and the necessity of global cooperation. As a result of this summit, the United Nations unveiled a draft set of principles that urge the international community to build on the momentum set by the adoption of the New York Declaration for Refugees and Migrants. Specifically, the 20 draft principles focus on human rights; non-discrimination; rescue and assistance; access to justice; border governance; returns; violence; detention; family unity; child migrants; women migrants; right to health; adequate standard of living; decent work; right to education; right to information; monitoring and accountability; migrants' human rights defenders; data; and international cooperation.

On 28 September 2016, the UNHCR partnered with the UN Food and Agricultural Organization in Tehran for the Solutions Strategy for Afghan Refugees. FAO highlighted the contributions to be made by FAO towards SSAR objectives on livelihood related activities including livestock and fishery initiatives as well as nutritional projects in Iranian schools.

FAO and UNHCR are committed towards increasing refugees' access to livelihood opportunities and reducing dependency on humanitarian aid. Of late, a joint livelihood strategy for South Sudan was launched looking to address this issue with a clearly defined action plan. The strategy targets both refugees (70 percent) and local communities (30 percent) in refugee-hosting areas across the country.

Awards

Since 1954, the UNHCR Nansen Refugee Award has been annually awarded to a person or an organization in recognition of outstanding service to the cause of refugees, displaced or stateless people.

The UNHCR itself was awarded the Nobel Peace Prize in 1954 and 1981.The UNHCR has been chosen for the prestigious Indira Gandhi Prize for Peace, Disarmament and Development 2015.

Persons of concern to UNHCR

The UNHCR's Mid-Year Trends report of June 2015 (based on information for mid-2015 or latest available information up to that date) reported an "unprecedented" 57,959,702 individuals falling under its mandate (for reference, on January the 1st, 2007, 21,018,589 people - or less than half of the number in 2015 - fell under the mandate of the UNHCR). The sharp increase was mainly attributed to the Syrian Civil War, "with the outbreak of armed crises or the deterioration of ongoing ones in countries like Afghanistan, Burundi, Democratic Republic of the Congo, Mali, Somalia, South Sudan and the Ukraine contributing to prevailing trends."

Persons of concern include refugees and asylum-seekers, people in refugee-like conditions, internally-displaced people (IDPs), stateless persons and "others of concern to the UNHCR".

Sorted by the UNHCR bureau in which asylum is sought, the number for June 2015 included:

1. 16,796,426 in the Middle East and North Africa, of which
   - 2,941,121 are refugees
   - 64,166 are in refugee-like situations

- 109,847 have pending asylum cases
- 374,309 are stateless ("persons not considered as nationals by any State")
- 13,297,101 are IDPs or people in IDP-like situations assisted by the UNHCR

2. 9,694,535 in the Asia and Pacific bureau, of which
   - 3,506,644 are refugees
   - 278,350 are in refugee-like situations
   - 133,894 have pending asylum cases
   - 1,801,802 are stateless ("persons not considered as nationals by any State")
   - 2,965,211 are IDPs or people in IDP-like situations assisted by the UNHCR
3. 8,451,275 in East and Horn of Africa, of which
   - 2,713,748 are refugees
   - 33,553 are in refugee-like situations
   - 108,016 have pending asylum cases
   - 233,726 are stateless ("persons not considered as nationals by any State"
   - 5,119,463 are IDPs or people in IDP-like situations assisted by the UNHCR
4. 7,726,594 in the Americas, of which
   - 501,049 are refugees
   - 251,888 are in refugee-like situations
   - 276,394 have pending asylum cases
   - 136,413 are stateless ("persons not considered as nationals by any State")
   - 6,520,270 are IDPs or people in IDP-like situations assisted by the UNHCR
5. 7,585,581 in Europe, of which
   - 3,506,644 are refugees
   - 14,261 are in refugee-like situations
   - 827,374 are asylum-seekers

- 610,532 are stateless ("persons not considered as nationals by any State"
- 2,574,886 are IDPs or people in IDP-like situations assisted by the UNHCR

6. 3,580,181 in Central Africa-Great Lakes, of which
   - 865,112 are refugees
   - 13,741 are in refugee-like situations
   - 18,623 have pending asylum cases
   - 1,302 are stateless ("persons not considered as nationals by any State"
   - 2,021,269 are IDPs or people in IDP-like situations assisted by the UNHCR
7. 2,754,893 in Western Africa of which
   - 258,893 are refugees
   - (Information not applicable/unavailable) on number in refugee-like situations
   - 9,298 have pending asylum cases
   - 700,116 are stateless ("persons not considered as nationals by any State")
   - 1,549,516 are IDPs or people in IDP-like situations assisted by the UNHCR
8. 1,370,217 in Southern Africa, of which
   - 179,837 are refugees
   - (Information not applicable/unavailable) on number in refugee-like situations
   - 860,500 have pending asylum cases
   - 300,000 are stateless ("persons not considered as nationals by any State")
   - (Information not applicable/unavailable) on number of IDPs or people in IDP-like situations assisted by the UNHCR

STAFFING

As of April 2008, the UNHCR employed a staff of 6,351 people in 117 countries.

High Commissioners

The UN General Assembly elects High Commissioners every five years. High Commissioners are supported by the 'Executive Committee to the High Commissioner's Programme' and he or she has to make annual reports to the UN General Assembly and needs to follow their directives. The current High Commissioner is Filippo Grandi, who has held the post since 1 January 2016. Prior to the establishment of the UNHCR, Fridtjof Nansen was the League of Nations High Commissioner of the Nansen International Office for Refugees, from 1922. The post of High Commissioner has been held by:

Fridtjof Nansen as the League of Nations' high commissioner for prisoners of war and refugees, during a stay in Sofia, where he discussed problems regarding the exchange of prisoners of war and refugees.

16

International Cricket Council (ICC)

The International Cricket Council (ICC) is the global governing body of Cricket. It was founded as the Imperial Cricket Conferencein 1909 by representatives from Australia, England and South Africa. It was renamed as the International Cricket Conference in 1965, and took up its current name in 1989.

The ICC has 103 members: 12 Full Members that play Test matches and 91 Associate Members. The ICC is responsible for the organisation and governance of cricket's major international tournaments, most notably the Cricket World Cup. It also appoints the umpires and referees that officiate at all sanctioned Test matches, One Day International and Twenty20 Internationals. It promulgates the ICC Code of Conduct, which sets professional standards of discipline for international cricket, and also co-ordinates action against corruption and match-fixing through its Anti-Corruption and Security Unit (ACSU).

The ICC does not control bilateral fixtures between member countries (which include all Test matches), it does not govern domestic cricket in member countries, and it does not make the laws of the game, which remain under the control of the Marylebone Cricket Club.

The Chairman heads the board of directors and on 26 June 2014, N.Srinivasan, the former president of BCCI, was announced as the first chairman of the council. The role of ICC president has become a largely honorary position since the establishment of the chairman role and other changes were made to the ICC constitution in 2014. It has been claimed that the 2014 changes have handed control to the so-called 'Big Three' nations of England, India and Australia. The last ICC president was Zaheer Abbas, who was appointed in June 2015 following the resignation of Mustafa Kamal in April 2015. The post of ICC president was abolished in April 2016 and Shashank Manohar who replaced Mr. Srinivasan in October 2015 became the first independent chairman of the ICC since then. The current CEO is David Richardson, who succeeded Haroon Lorgat.

HISTORY

1909 - 1963 - Imperial Cricket Conference

On 30th November 1907, Abe Bailey, the President of South African Cricket Association, wrote a letter to the Marylebone Cricket Club's (MCC, England) secretary, F.E Lacey. Bailey suggested the formation of an 'Imperial Cricket Board'. In the letter, he suggested that the board would be responsible for formulation of rules and regulations which will govern the international matches between the three members; Australia, England and South Africa. Bailey, wanted to host a Triangular Test series between the participant countries in South Africa. Australia rejected the offer. However, Bailey did not lose hope. He saw an opportunity of getting the three members together during the Australia's tour of England in 1909. After continued lobbying and efforts, Bailey was successful.

On 15th June 1909, representatives from England, Australia and South Africa met at Lord's and founded the *Imperial Cricket Conference.* A month later, a second meeting between the three members was held. The rules were agreed amongst the nations, and the first ever Tri -Test series was decided to be held in England in 1912.

In 1926, West Indies, New Zealand and India were elected as Full Members, doubling the number of Test-playing nations to six. After the formation of Pakistan in 1947, it was given Test status in 1952, becoming the seventh Test-playing nation. In May 1961 South Africa left the Commonwealth and therefore lost membership.

1964 - 1988 - International Cricket Conference

In 1964, the ICC agreed upon including the non - Test playing countries. The following year, the ICC changed it's name to the International Cricket Conference. Under the new type of membership, the Associate. USA, Ceylon and Fiji were admitted.

In 1966, Denmark, Bermuda, Netherlands, and East Africa were admitted as Associate. South Africa had still not applied to rejoin the ICC.

In 1969, the basic rules of ICC were amended.

In 1971 meeting, the idea of organizing a World Cup was introduced. In 1973 meeting, it was decided that a World Cup will be played in 1975 in England. The six Test playing nations and East Africa and Sri Lanka were invited to take part.

New members were added regularly during this period:

In 1974, Argentina, Israel and Singapore were admitted as Associate.

In 1976, West Africa was admitted as Associate.

In 1977, Bangladesh was admitted as Associate.

In 1978, Papua-New Guinea was admitted as Associate. South Africa applied to rejoin, however their application was rejected.

In 1981, Sri-Lanka was promoted to being a Full Member. They played their first Test in 1982.

In 1984, the third type of membership; Affiliate category of membership was added to the ICC. Italy was the first member, followed by Switzerland in 1985. In 1987, Bahamas and France were admitted, followed by Nepal in 1988.

1989 - present

In the July meeting of 1989, the ICC renamed itself to the International Cricket Council and the trend of the MCC President automatically becoming the Chairman of ICC was terminated.

In 1990, UAE joined as an associate.

In 1991, for the first time in ICC history the meeting was held away from England - in Melbourne. South Africa was re-elected as a Full Member of the ICC in July, after the end of apartheid.

In 1992, Zimbabwe was admitted as the ninth Test-playing nation (Full Member). Namibia joined as Associate member. Austria, Belgium, Brunei and Spain joined as Affiliates.

In 1993, the *Chief Executive of ICC* was created with Sir David Richards of the Australian Cricket Board the first person appointed to the position.

In July, Sir Clyde Walcott, from Barbados, was elected as the first non-British Chairman. The emergence of new technology saw the introduction of a third umpire who was equipped with video playback facilities.

By 1995, TV replays were made available for run outs and stumpings in Test matches with the third umpire required to signal out or not out with red and green lights respectively. The following year, the cameras were used to determine if the ball had crossed the boundary, and in 1997 decisions on the cleanness of catches could be referred to the third umpire. This year also saw the introduction of the Duckworth-Lewis method of adjusting targets in rain-affected ODI matches.

In 2000, Bangladesh received Test status (Full Member).

In 2005, ICC moved its new headquarters in Dubai.

In 2017, Afghanistan Cricket Board and Cricket Ireland were confirmed as Full Members of the International Cricket Council after a unanimous vote at the ICC Full Council meeting at The Oval.

MEMBERS

Full Members - The twelve governing bodies of teams that play official Test matches;

The 12 full members are:

- Afghanistan
- Australia
- Bangladesh
- England
- India
- Ireland
- New Zealand
- Pakistan
- South Africa
- Sri Lanka
- West Indies
- Zimbabwe

Associate Members - The 92 governing bodies in countries where cricket is firmly established and organized, but have not been granted Full membership yet. There were previously three classes of membership, but the ICC removed the Affiliate Membership in 2017, with all previous Affiliates becoming Associate Members.

LOCATION

From its formation, the ICC had Lord's Cricket Ground as its home, and from 1993 had its offices in the "Clock Tower" building at the nursery end of the ground. The independent ICC was funded initially by commercial exploitation of the rights to the World Cup of One Day International cricket. As not all Member countries had double-tax agreements with the United Kingdom, it was necessary to protect cricket's revenues by creating a company, ICC Development (International) Pty Ltd – known as IDI, outside the UK. This was established in January 1994 and was based in Monaco.

For the remainder of the nineties, the administration of IDI was a modest affair. But with the negotiation of a bundle of rights to all ICC events from 2001–2008, revenues available to International cricket and the ICC member countries rose substantially. This led to a growth in the number of commercial staff employed by IDI in Monaco. It also had the disadvantage that the Council's cricket administrators, who remained at Lord's, were separated from their commercial colleagues in Monaco. The Council decided to seek ways of bringing all of their staff together in one office while protecting their commercial income from tax.

The option of staying at Lord's was investigated and a request was made, through Sport England, to the British Government to allow the ICC to have all its personnel (including those working on commercial matters) in London – but be given special exemption from paying UK corporation tax on its commercial income. The British Government was unwilling to create a precedent and would not agree to this request. As a consequence, the ICC examined other locations and eventually settled on the emirate of Dubai in the United Arab Emirates. ICC is registered in British Virgin Islands. In August 2005, the ICC moved its offices to Dubai, and subsequently closed its offices at Lord's and Monaco. The move to Dubai was made after an 11–1 vote by the ICC's Executive Board in favour.

While the principal driver of the ICC's move to Dubai was the wish to bring its main employees together in one tax efficient location, a secondary reason was the wish to move offices closer to the increasingly important new centres of cricketing power in South Asia. Lord's had been a logical venue when the ICC had been administered by the Marylebone Cricket Club (MCC) (a situation that lasted until 1993). But the growing power of India and Pakistan in world cricket had made the continued control of international cricket by a British private members club (the MCC) anachronistic and unsustainable. A direct consequence of the changes and reforms instituted in 1993 was eventually to be the move away from Lord's to a more neutral venue.

INCOME GENERATION

The ICC generates income from the tournaments it organises, primarily the Cricket World Cup, and it distributes the majority of that income to its members. Sponsorship and television rights of the World Cup brought in over US$1.6 billion between 2007 and 2015, by far the ICC's main source of income.

In the nine-month accounting period to 31 December 2007 the ICC had operating income of USD 12.66 million, mainly from member subscriptions and sponsorship. In contrast, event income was USD 285.87 million, including USD 239 million from the 2007 World Cup. There was also investment income of USD 6.695 million in the period.

The ICC has no income streams from the bilateral international cricket matches (Test matches, One Day International and Twenty20 Internationals), that account for the great majority of the international playing schedule, as they are owned and run by its members.

It has sought to create other new events to augment its World Cup revenues. These include the ICC Champions Trophy and the ICC Super Series played in Australia in 2005. However these events have not been as successful as the ICC hoped.

The Super Series was widely seen as a failure and is not expected to be repeated, and India called for the Champions Trophy to be scrapped in 2006. The Champions Trophy 2004 event was referred to in *Wisden 2005* by the editor as a "turkey of a tournament" and a "fiasco"; although the 2006 edition was seen as a greater success due to a new format.

The ICC World Twenty20, first played in 2007, was a success. The ICC's current plan is to have an international tournament every year, with a Twenty20 World Cup played in even number years, the World Cup continuing to be held the year before the Olympic Games, and the ICC Champions Trophy in the remaining year of the cycle. This cycle will begin in 2010, one year after the 2009 edition.

RULES AND REGULATION

The International Cricket Council oversees playing conditions, bowling reviews, and other ICC regulations. The ICC does not have copyright to the Laws of Cricket: only the MCC may change the Laws, though this is usually done in consultation with the game's global governing body. The ICC maintains a set of playing conditions for international cricket which make slight amendments to the Laws. They also have a "Code of Conduct" to which teams and players in international matches are required to adhere. Where breaches of this code occur the ICC can apply sanctions, usually fines. In 2008, the ICC imposed 19 penalties on players.

UMPIRES AND REFEREES

The ICC appoints international umpires and Match referees who officiate at all sanctioned Test matches, One-Day Internationals and Twenty20 Internationals. The ICC operates 3 panels of umpires: namely the Elite Panel, the International Panel, and the Associates and Affiliates Panel.

As of April 2012, the Elite Panel includes twelve umpires. In theory, two umpires from the Elite Panel officiate at every Test match, while one Elite Panel umpire stands in ODI matches together with an umpire from the International Panel. In practice, members of the International Panel stand in occasional Test matches, as this is viewed as a good opportunity to see whether they can cope at the Test level, and whether they should be elevated to the Elite Panel. The Elite Panel are full-time employees of the ICC, although do still, very occasionally umpire first-class cricket in their country of residence. The average, annual, officiating schedule for Elite Umpires is 8–10 Test matches and 10–15 ODIs, a potential on-field workload of 75 days plus travel and preparation time per year.

The International Panel is made up of officials nominated from each of the ten Test-playing cricket boards. The Panel Members officiate in ODI matches in their home country, and assist the Elite Panel at peak times in the cricket calendar when they can be appointed to overseas ODI and Test matches. International Panel members also undertake overseas umpiring assignments such as the ICC Under 19 Cricket World Cup to improve their knowledge and understanding of overseas conditions, and help them prepare for possible promotion onto the Elite Panel. Some of these umpires also officiate in the Cricket World Cup. Each of the Test cricket boards nominates a "third umpire" who can be called upon to review certain on-field decisions through instant television replays. All third umpires are first-class umpires in their own county, and the role is seen as a step onto the International Panel, and then the Elite Panel.

The inaugural ICC Associate and Affiliate International Umpires Panel was formed in June 2006. It superseded the ICC Associate and Affiliate International Umpires Panel, created in 2005, and serves as the pinnacle for umpires from non-Test playing Members, with selection achieved through each of the five ICC Development Program Regional Umpires Panels. Members of the Associate and Affiliate International Umpires Panel are eligible for appointments to ODIs involving ICC Associate Members, ICC Intercontinental Cup matches and other Associate and Affiliate tournaments. High-performing umpires may also be considered for other ICC events, including the ICC U/19 Cricket World Cup, and could also be invited to be involved in the ICC Champions Trophy and ICC Cricket World Cup.

There is also an Elite Panel of ICC Referees who act as the independent representative of the ICC at all Test and ODI matches. As of January 2009, it has 6 members, all highly experienced former international cricketers. The Referees do not have the power to report players or officials (which has to be done by the umpires), but they are responsible for conducting hearings under the ICC Code of Conduct and imposing penalties as required at matches, ranging from an official reprimand to a lifetime ban from cricket. Decisions can be appealed, but the original decision is upheld in most cases.

The Council failed to achieve consensus among the cricket playing nations – as of June 2012 – on the universal application of Umpire's Decision Review System, due to opposition by BCCI. It will continue to be applied subject to mutual agreement of the playing countries. In July 2012, ICC decided to send a delegation to show the ball tracking research done by Dr Ed Rosten, an expert on computer vision and technology, to BCCI to remove the scepticism about the use of DRS technology.

REGIONAL BODIES

These regional bodies aim to organise, promote and develop the game of cricket:

- African Cricket Association
- Asian Cricket Council
- ICC Americas
- ICC East Asia-Pacific
- European Cricket Council

Two further regional bodies were disestablished following the creation of the African Cricket Association:

- East and Central Africa Cricket Council
- West Africa Cricket Council

COMPETITIONS AND AWARDS

The ICC organises various international *First-Class*, *One-Day* and *Twenty20* cricket competitions:

Format	Tournament	Notes
First-Class	ICC Test Championship	Notional league (for Test rankings)
	ICC Intercontinental Cup	Test league for associate members
	ICC World Test Championship	Premier Test league
One Day	ICC ODI Championship	Notional league (for ODI rankings)
	ICC Cricket World Cup	Premier ODI league

	ICC Women's Cricket World Cup	Premier ODI league for women
	ICC Champions Trophy	ODI league for Test-playing nations
	ICC Under-19 Cricket World Cup	Premier ODI league for youth
	ICC World Cricket League	ODI league for associate members
	ICC World Cup Qualifier	Qualifier league for teams ranked below 8
Twenty20	ICC T20I Championship	Notional league (for T20I rankings)
	ICC World Twenty20	Premier T20 league
	ICC Women's World Twenty20	Premier T20 league for women
	ICC World Twenty20 Qualifier	Qualifier league for teams ranked below 8

The ICC has instituted the ICC Awards to recognise and honour the best international cricket players of the previous 12 months. The inaugural ICC Awards ceremony was held on 7 September 2004, in London.

The ICC Player Rankings are a widely followed system of rankings for international cricketers based on their recent performances. The current sponsor is MRF Tyres who signed a 4-year deal with the ICC that will last until 2020.

Prize breakdown for ICC Cricket World Cup.

Winner	US$ 3,750,000
Runner-Up	US$ 1,750,000
Losing Semi-Finalists (Two)	US$ 600,000
Losing Quarter-Finalists (Four)	US$ 600,000
Winner of each Group Match	US$ 45,000 X 42
Team eliminated after Group Stage	US$ 35,000 X 6 Teams
TOTAL	US$ 10,000,000

In the 2015 ICC Cricket World Cup; Australia, the title winner, won the prize money of 3,975,000 US dollars. While New Zealand as Runners-up won 1,750,000 US dollars as prize money.

ANTI-CORRUPTION AND SECURITY

The ICC has also had to deal with drugs and bribery scandals involving top cricketers.

Following the corruption scandals by cricketers connected with the legal and illegal bookmaking markets, the ICC set up an Anti-Corruption and Security Unit (ACSU) in 2000 under the retired Commissioner of the London Metropolitan Police, Lord Condon. Among the corruption on which they have reported was that of former South African captain Hansie Cronje who had accepted substantial sums of money from an Indian bookmaker for under-performing or ensuring that certain matches had a pre-determined result.

Similarly, the former Indian captain Mohammad Azharuddin and Ajay Jadeja were investigated, found guilty of match-fixing, and banned from playing cricket (for life and for five years, respectively). The ACSU continues to monitor and investigate any reports of corruption in cricket and protocols have been introduced, which for example prohibit the use of mobile telephones in dressing rooms.

Prior to the 2007 Cricket World Cup ICC chief executive Malcolm Speed warned against any corruption and said that the ICC would be vigilant and intolerant against it.

Following a scandal that occurred during the 2010 Pakistan tour of England, 3 Pakistani players, Mohammad Amir, Mohammad Asif and Salman Butt were found to be guilty of spot-fixing, and were banned for 5 years, 7 years and 10 years respectively. On 3 November 2011, jail terms were handed down of 30 months for Butt, one year for Asif, six months for Amir and two years eight months for Majeed, the sports agent that facilitated the bribes.

GLOBAL CRICKET ACADEMY

The ICC Global Cricket Academy (GCA) is located at Dubai Sports City in the United Arab Emirates. The GCA's facilities include two ovals, each with 10 turf pitches, outdoor turf and synthetic practice facilities, indoor practice facilities including hawk eye technology and a cricket specific gymnasium. Rod Marsh has been appointed as the Academy's Director of Coaching. The opening, originally planned for 2008, took place in 2010.

ICC CRICKET WORLD PROGRAM

The International Cricket Council telecasts a weekly program on television called ICC Cricket World. It is produced by Sportsbrand.

It is a weekly 30-minute program providing the latest cricket news, recent cricket action including all Test and One-Day International matches, as well as off-field features and interviews

CRITICISM

Journalist Peter Della Penna, of ESPN Cricinfo, has criticised the ICC for what he has perceived as attempts to minimise reports of security issues relating to unruly fans at matches.

In 2015, Sam Collins and Jarrod Kimber made the documentary *Death of a Gentleman* on the internal organization of the ICC.

17

BRICS

BRICS is the acronym coined by British Economist Jim O'Neill meant for an association of five major emerging national economies: Brazil, Russia, India, China and South Africa. Originally the first four were grouped as "BRIC" (or "the BRICs"), before the induction of South Africa in 2010. The BRICS members are known for their significant influence on regional affairs; all are members of G20. Since 2009, the BRICS nations have met annually at formal summits. China hosted the 9th BRICS summit in Xiamen on September 2017, while South Africa hosted the most recent 10th BRICS summit in July 2018. The term does not include countries such as South Korea, Mexico and Turkey for which other acronyms and group associations were later created.

In 2015, the five BRICS countries represent over 3.1 billion people, or about 41% of the world population; four out of five members (excluding South Africa at #24) are in the top 10 of the world by population. As of 2018, these five nations have a combined nominal GDP of US$18.6 trillion, about 23.2% of the gross world product, combined GDP (PPP) of around US$40.55 trillion (32% of World's GDP PPP) and an estimated US$4.46 trillion in combined foreign reserves. Overall the BRICS are forecasted to expand 4.6% in 2016, from an estimated growth of 3.9% in 2015. The World Bank expected BRICS growth to increase to 5.3% in 2017. The BRICS have received both praise and criticism from numerous commentators. Bilateral relations among BRICS nations have mainly been conducted on the basis of non-interference, equality, and mutual benefit.

HISTORY

The term "BRIC" was coined in 2001 by then-chairman of Goldman Sachs Asset Management, Jim O'Neill, in his publication *Building Better Global Economic BRICs.* The foreign ministers of the initial four BRIC states (Brazil, Russia, India, and China) met in New York City in September 2006 at the margins of the General Debate of the UN General Assembly, beginning a series of high-level meetings. A full-scale diplomatic meeting was held in Yekaterinburg, Russia, on 16 June 2009.

First BRIC summit

The BRIC grouping's first formal summit, also held in Yekaterinburg, commenced on 16 June 2009, with Luiz Inácio Lula da Silva, Dmitry Medvedev, Manmohan Singh, and Hu Jintao, the respective leaders of Brazil, Russia, India and China, all attending. The summit's focus was on means of improving the global economic situation and reforming financial institutions, and discussed how the four countries could better co-operate in the future. There was further discussion of ways that developing countries, such as 3/4 of the BRIC members, could become more involved in global affairs.

In the aftermath of the Yekaterinburg summit, the BRIC nations announced the need for a new global reserve currency, which would have to be "diverse, stable and predictable".Although the statement that was released did not directly criticise the perceived "dominance" of the US dollar – something that Russia had criticised in the past – it did spark a fall in the value of the dollar against other major currencies.

Entry of South Africa

In 2010, South Africa began efforts to join the BRIC grouping, and the process for its formal admission began in August of that year. South Africa officially became a member nation on 24 December 2010, after being formally invited by the BRIC countries to join the group. The group was renamed BRICS – with the "S" standing for South Africa – to reflect the group's expanded membership. In April 2011, the President of South Africa, Jacob Zuma, attended the 2011 BRICS summit in Sanya, China, as a full member.

Developments

The BRICS leaders in 2016. Left to right: Temer, Modi, Xi, Putin and Zuma.

The BRICS Forum, an independent international organisation encouraging commercial, political and cultural cooperation between the BRICS nations, was formed in 2011. In June 2012, the BRICS nations pledged $75 billion to boost the lending power of the International Monetary Fund (IMF). However, this loan was conditional on IMF voting reforms. In late March 2013, during the fifth BRICS summit in Durban, South Africa, the member countries agreed to create a global financial institution which they intended to rival the western-dominated IMF and World Bank. After the summit, the BRICS stated that they planned to finalise the arrangements for this New Development Bank by 2014. However, disputes relating to burden sharing and location slowed down the agreements.

At the BRICS leaders meeting in St Petersburg in September 2013, China committed $41 billion towards the pool; Brazil, India and Russia $18 billion each; and South Africa $5 billion. China, holder of the world's largest foreign exchange reserves and who is to contribute the bulk of the currency pool, wants a greater managing role, said one BRICS official. China also wants to be the location of the reserve. "Brazil and India want the initial capital to be shared equally. We know that China wants more," said a Brazilian official. "However, we are still negotiating, there are no tensions arising yet." On 11 October 2013, Russia's Finance Minister Anton Siluanov said that a decision on creating a $100 billion fund designated to steady currency markets would be taken in early 2014. The Brazilian finance minister, Guido Mantega stated that the fund would be created by March 2014.However, by April 2014, the currency reserve pool and development bank had yet to be set up, and the date was rescheduled to 2015. One driver for the BRICS development bank is that the existing institutions primarily benefit extra-BRICS corporations, and the political significance is notable because it allows BRICS member states "to promote their interests abroad... and can highlight the strengthening positions of countries whose opinion is frequently ignored by their developed American and European colleagues."

In March 2014, at a meeting on the margins of the Nuclear Security Summit in The Hague, the BRICS Foreign Ministers issued a communique that "noted with concern, the recent media statement on the forthcoming G20 Summit to be held in Brisbane in November 2014. The custodianship of the G20 belongs to all Member States equally and no one Member State can unilaterally determine its nature and character." In light of the tensions surrounding the 2014 Crimean crisis, the Ministers remarked that "The escalation of hostile language, sanctions and counter-sanctions, and force does not contribute to a sustainable and peaceful solution, according to international law, including the principles and purposes of the United Nations Charter." This was in response to the statement of Australian Foreign Minister Julie Bishop, who had said earlier that Russian President Vladimir Putin might be barred from attending the G20 Summit in Brisbane.

In July 2014, the Governor of the Russian Central Bank, Elvira Nabiullina, claimed that the "BRICS partners the establishment of a system of multilateral swaps that will allow to transfer resources to one or another country, if needed" in an article which concluded that "If the current trend continues, soon the dollar will be abandoned by most of the significant global economies and it will be kicked out of the global trade finance."

Over the weekend of 13 July 2014, when the final game of the FIFA World Cup was held, and in advance of the BRICS Fortaleza summit, Putin met fellow leader Dilma Rouseff to discuss the BRICS development bank, and sign some other bilateral accords on air defence, gas and education. Rouseff said that the BRICS countries "are among the largest in the world and cannot content themselves in the middle of the 21st century with any kind of dependency." The Fortaleza summit was followed by a BRICS meeting with the Union of South American Nations president's in Brasilia, where the development bank and the monetary fund were introduced. The development bank will have capital of US$50 billion with each country contributing US$10 billion, while the monetary fund will have US$100 billion at its disposal.

The BRICS leaders in 2017. Left to right: Temer, Putin, Xi, Zuma and Modi.

On 15 July, the first day of the BRICS 6th summit in Fortaleza, Brazil, the group of emerging economies signed the long-anticipated document to create the US$100 billion New Development Bank (formerly known as the "BRICS Development Bank") and a reserve currency pool worth over another US$100 billion. Documents on cooperation between

BRICS export credit agencies and an agreement of cooperation on innovation were also inked.

At the end of October 2014, Brazil trimmed down its US government holdings to US$261.7 billion; India, US$77.5 billion; China, US$1.25 trillion; South Africa, US$10.3 billion.

In March 2015, Morgan Stanley stated that India and Indonesia had escaped from the 'fragile five' (the five major emerging markets with the most fragile currencies) by instituting economic reforms. Previously, in August 2013, Morgan Stanley rated India and Indonesia, together with Brazil, Turkey and South Africa, as the 'fragile five' due to their vulnerable currencies.

But since then, India and Indonesia have reformed their economies, completing 85% and 65% of the necessary adjustments respectively, while Brazil had only achieved 15%, Turkey only 10%, and South Africa even less.

After the 2015 summit, the respective communications ministers, under a Russian proposal, had a first summit for their ministries in Moscow in October where the host minister, Nikolai Nikiforov, proposed an initiative to further tighten their information technology sectors and challenge the monopoly of the United States in the sector.

Since 2012, the BRICS group of countries have been planning an optical fibre submarine communications cable system to carry telecommunications between the BRICS countries, known as the BRICS Cable. Part of the motivation for the project was the spying of the National Security Agency on all telecommunications that flowed across the US.

GEOGRAPHY

The BRICS is an association formed by countries in four continents: Brazil in the Americas, Russia in Europe, India and China in Asiaand South Africa in Africa. Its member states cover an area of over 39,000,000 square kilometers, which is approximately 27% of the world's land surface.

SUMMITS

The grouping has held annual summits since 2009, with member countries taking turns to host. Prior to South Africa's admission, two BRIC summits were held, in 2009 and 2010. The first five-member BRICS summit was held in 2011. The most recent BRICS summit took place in Xiamen, China, from 3 to 5 September 2017.

FINANCIAL STRUCTURE

Currently, there are two components that make up the financial architecture of BRICS, namely, the New Development Bank (NDB) or sometimes referred to as the BRICS Development Bank and the Contingent Reserve Arrangement (CRA). Both of these components were signed into treaty in 2014 and became active in 2015.

New Development Bank

The New Development Bank (NDB), formerly referred to as the BRICS Development Bank, is a multilateral development bank operated by the BRICS states. The bank's primary focus of lending will be infrastructure projects with authorized lending of up to $34 billion annually. South Africa will be the African Headquarters of the Bank named the "New Development Bank Africa Regional Centre". The bank will have starting capital of $50 billion, with capital increased to $100 billion over time. Brazil, Russia, India, China and South Africa will initially contribute $10 billion each to bring the total to $50 billion.

BRICS CRA

The BRICS Contingent Reserve Arrangement (CRA) is a framework for providing protection against global liquidity pressures. This includes currency issues where members' national currencies are being adversely affected by global financial pressures. It is found that emerging economies that experienced rapid economic liberalization went through increased economic volatility, bringing uncertain macroeconomic environment. The CRA is generally seen as a competitor to the International Monetary Fund (IMF) and along with the New Development Bank is viewed as an example of increasing South-South cooperation. It was established in 2015 by the BRICS countries. The legal basis is formed by the *Treaty for the Establishment of a BRICS Contingent Reserve Arrangement*, signed at Fortaleza, Brazil on 15 July 2014. With its inaugural meetings of the BRICS CRA Governing Council and Standing Committee, held on September 4, 2015, in Ankara, Turkey it entered into force upon ratification by all BRICS states, announced at the 7th BRICS summit in July 2015.

BRICS payment system

At the 2015 BRICS summit in Russia, ministers from BRICS nations, initiated consultations for a payment system that would be an alternative to the SWIFT system. Russian Deputy Foreign Minister Sergey Ryabkov stated in an interview, "The finance ministers and executives of the BRICS central banks are negotiating ... setting up payment systems and moving on to settlements in national currencies. SWIFT or not, in any case we're talking about ... a transnational multilateral payment system that would provide greater independence, would create a definite guarantee for BRICS."

The Central Bank of Russia (CBR) also started consultations with BRICS nations for a payment system that would be an alternative to the SWIFT system. The main benefits highlighted were backup and redundancy in case there were disruptions to the SWIFT system. The Deputy Governor of the Central Bank of the Russia, Olga Skorobogatova stated in an interview, "The only topic that may be of interest to all of us within BRICS is to consider and talk over the possibility of setting up a system that would apply to the BRICS countries, used as a backup."

China has also initiated development of their own payment system called CIPS that would be an alternative to the SWIFT system. The Cross-Border Inter-Bank Payments System(CIPS) is a planned alternative payments system to SWIFT which would provide a network that enables financial institutions worldwide to send and receive information about financial transactions in a secure, standardized and reliable environment.

RECEPTION

In 2012, Hu Jintao, the then President of China and Paramount leader, described the BRICS countries as defenders and promoters of developing countries and a force for world peace. Western analysts have highlighted potential divisions and weaknesses in the grouping, including significant economic instabilities, disagreements between the members over UN Security Council reform, and India and China's disputes over territorial issues.

In June 2015, Jim Rogers said that he does not see any current alternative to the US dollar and that "The world needs something to compete with the US-dominated institutions, some of them - the World Bank and the IMF. So, if BRICS offer any new structures that can compete with these long-standing...institutions, it will be very good."

On 9 April 2013, Isobel Coleman from the Council on Foreign Relations, director of CFR's Civil Society, Markets and Democracy Program said that members of BRICS share a lack of consensus. They uphold drastically different political systems, from active democracy in Brazil to entrenched Oligarchy in Russia, and their economies are little integrated and are different in size by orders of magnitude. Also she states that the great difference in GDP, influences the reserves, for China taking up of over 41% of the contribution, which in turn leads to bigger political say within the association.

BRICS Pro Tempore Presidency

The group at each summit elects one of the heads of state of the component countries to serve as President Pro Tempore of the BRICS, currently in 2018, the pro tempore presidency is held by the president of South Africa.

18

The National Aeronautics and Space Administration (NASA)

The National Aeronautics and Space Administration (NASA) is an independent agency of the executive branch of the Federal government of the United States responsible for the civilian space program, as well as aeronautics and aerospaceresearch.

President Dwight D. Eisenhower established NASA in 1958 with a distinctly civilian (rather than military) orientation encouraging peaceful applications in space science. The National Aeronautics and Space Act was passed on July 29, 1958, disestablishing NASA's predecessor, the National Advisory Committee for Aeronautics (NACA). The new agency became operational on October 1, 1958.Since that time, most U.S. space exploration efforts have been led by NASA, including the Apollo Moon landing missions, the Skylabspace station, and later the Space Shuttle. Currently, NASA is supporting the International Space Station and is overseeing the development of the Orion Multi-Purpose Crew Vehicle, the Space Launch System and Commercial Crew vehicles. The agency is also responsible for the Launch Services Program (LSP) which provides oversight of launch operations and countdown management for unmanned NASA launches.

NASA science is focused on better understanding Earth through the Earth Observing System, advancing heliophysics through the efforts of the Science Mission Directorate's

Heliophysics Research Program, exploring bodies throughout the Solar System with advanced robotic spacecraft missions such as *New Horizons*, and researching astrophysics topics, such as the Big Bang, through the Great Observatories and associated programs. NASA shares data with various national and international organizations such as from the Greenhouse Gases Observing Satellite.

CREATION

From 1946, the National Advisory Committee for Aeronautics (NACA) had been experimenting with rocket planes such as the supersonic Bell X-1. In the early 1950s, there was challenge to launch an artificial satellite for the International Geophysical Year (1957–58). An effort for this was the American Project Vanguard. After the Soviet launch of the world's first artificial satellite (*Sputnik 1*) on October 4, 1957, the attention of the United States turned toward its own fledgling space efforts. The US Congress, alarmed by the perceived threat to national security and technological leadership (known as the "Sputnik crisis"), urged immediate and swift action; President Dwight D. Eisenhowerand his advisers counseled more deliberate measures. On January 12, 1958, NACA organized a "Special Committee on Space Technology", headed by Guyford Stever. On January 14, 1958, NACA Director Hugh Dryden published "A National Research Program for Space Technology" stating:

It is of great urgency and importance to our country both from consideration of our prestige as a nation as well as military necessity that this challenge [*Sputnik*] be met by an energetic program of research and development for the conquest of space... It is accordingly proposed that the scientific research be the responsibility of a national civilian agency... NACA is capable, by rapid extension and expansion of its effort, of providing leadership in space technology.

While this new federal agency would conduct all non-military space activity, the Advanced Research Projects Agency (ARPA) was created in February 1958 to develop space technology for military application.

On July 29, 1958, Eisenhower signed the National Aeronautics and Space Act, establishing NASA. When it began operations on October 1, 1958, NASA absorbed the 43-year-old NACA intact; its 8,000 employees, an annual budget of US$100 million, three major research laboratories (Langley Aeronautical Laboratory, Ames Aeronautical Laboratory, and Lewis Flight Propulsion Laboratory) and two small test facilities. A NASA seal was approved by President Eisenhower in 1959. Elements of the Army Ballistic Missile Agencyand the United States Naval Research Laboratory were incorporated into NASA. A significant contributor to NASA's entry into the Space Race with the Soviet Union was the technology from the German rocket program led by Wernher von Braun, who was now working for the Army Ballistic Missile Agency (ABMA), which in turn incorporated the technology of American scientist Robert Goddard's earlier works. Earlier research efforts within the US Air Force and many of ARPA's early space programs were also transferred to NASA. In December 1958, NASA gained control of the Jet Propulsion Laboratory, a contractor facility operated by the California Institute of Technology.

STAFF AND LEADERSHIP

The agency's leader, NASA's administrator, is nominated by the President of the United States subject to approval of the US Senate, and reports to him or her and serves as senior space science advisor. Though space exploration is ostensibly non-partisan, the appointee usually is associated with the President's political party (Democratic or Republican), and a new administrator is usually chosen when the Presidency changes parties. The only exceptions to this have been: James C. Fletcher, appointed by Republican Richard Nixon but stayed through May 1977 into the term of Democrat Jimmy Carter; Daniel Goldin, appointed by Republican George H. W. Bush and stayed through the administration of Democrat Bill Clinton; and Robert

M. Lightfoot, Jr., associate administrator under Democrat Barack Obama kept on as acting administrator by Republican Donald Trump.Though the agency is independent, the survival or discontinuation of projects can depend directly on the will of the President.

The first administrator was Dr. T. Keith Glennan appointed by Republican President Dwight D. Eisenhower. During his term he brought together the disparate projects in American space development research.

The second administrator, James E. Webb (1961–1968), appointed by President John F. Kennedy, was a Democrat who first publicly served under President Harry S. Truman. In order to implement the Apollo program to achieve Kennedy's Moon landing goal by the end of the 1960s, Webb directed major management restructuring and facility expansion, establishing the Houston Manned Spacecraft (Johnson) Center and the Florida Launch Operations (Kennedy) Center. Capitalizing on Kennedy's legacy, President Lyndon Johnson kept continuity with the Apollo program by keeping Webb on when he succeeded Kennedy in November 1963. But Webb resigned in October 1968 before Apollo achieved its goal, and Republican President Richard M. Nixonreplaced Webb with Republican Thomas O. Paine.

James Fletcher was responsible for early planning of the Space Shuttle program during his first term as administrator under President Nixon. He was appointed for a second term as administrator from May 1986 through April 1989 by President Ronald Reagan to help the agency recover from the Space Shuttle *Challenger* disaster.

Former astronaut Charles Bolden served as NASA's twelfth administrator from July 2009 to January 20, 2017. Administrator Bolden is one of three former astronauts who became NASA administrators, along with Richard H. Truly (served 1989–1992) and Frederick D. Gregory (acting, 2005).

The agency's administration is located at NASA Headquarters in Washington, DC and provides overall guidance and direction. Except under exceptional circumstances, NASA civil service employees are required to be citizens of the United States.

SPACE FLIGHT PROGRAMS

NASA has conducted many manned and unmanned spaceflight programs throughout its history. Unmanned programs launched the first American artificial satellites into Earth orbit for scientific and communications purposes, and sent scientific probes to explore the planets of the solar system, starting with Venus and Mars, and including "grand tours" of the outer planets. Manned programs sent the first Americans into low Earth orbit (LEO), won the Space Race with the Soviet Union by landing twelve men on the Moon from 1969 to 1972 in the Apollo program, developed a semi-reusable LEO Space Shuttle, and developed LEO space station capability by itself and with the cooperation of several other nations including post-Soviet Russia. Some missions include both manned and unmanned aspects, such as the Galileo probe, which was deployed by astronauts in Earth orbit before being sent unmanned to Jupiter.

Manned programs

The experimental rocket-powered aircraft programs started by NACA were extended by NASA as support for manned spaceflight. This was followed by a one-man space capsule program, and in turn by a two-man capsule program. Reacting to loss of national prestige and security fears caused by early leads in space exploration by the Soviet Union, in 1961 President John F. Kennedy proposed the ambitious goal "of landing a man on the Moon by the end of [the 1960s], and returning him safely to the Earth." This goal was met in 1969 by the Apollo program, and NASA planned even more ambitious activities leading to a manned mission to Mars. However, reduction of the perceived threat and changing political priorities almost immediately caused the termination of most of these plans. NASA turned its attention to an Apollo-derived temporary space laboratory, and a semi-reusable Earth orbital shuttle. In the 1990s, funding was approved for NASA to develop a permanent Earth orbital space station in cooperation with the international community, which now included the former rival, post-Soviet Russia. To date, NASA has launched a total of 166 manned space missions on rockets, and thirteen X-15 rocket flights above the USAF definition of spaceflight altitude, 260,000 feet (80 km).

X-15 rocket plane (1959–1968)

The X-15 was an NACA experimental rocket-powered hypersonic research aircraft, developed in conjunction with the US Air Force and Navy. The design featured a slender fuselage with fairings along the side containing fuel and early computerized control systems. Requests for proposal were issued on December 30, 1954, for the airframe, and February 4, 1955, for the rocket engine. The airframe contract was awarded to North American Aviation in November 1955, and the XLR30 engine contract was awarded to Reaction Motors in 1956, and three planes were built. The X-15 was drop-launched from the wing of one of two NASA Boeing B-52 Stratofortresses, *NB52A* tail number 52-003, and *NB52B*, tail number 52-008 (known as the *Balls 8*). Release took place at an altitude of about 45,000 feet (14 km) and a speed of about 500 miles per hour (805 km/h).

Twelve pilots were selected for the program from the Air Force, Navy, and NACA (later NASA). A total of 199 flights were made between 1959 and 1968, resulting in the official world record for the highest speed ever reached by a manned powered aircraft (current as of 2014), and a maximum speed of Mach 6.72, 4,519 miles per hour (7,273 km/h). The altitude record for X-15 was 354,200 feet (107.96 km). Eight of the pilots were awarded Air Force astronaut wings for flying above 260,000 feet (80 km), and two flights by Joseph A. Walker exceeded 100 kilometers (330,000 ft), qualifying as spaceflight according to the International Aeronautical Federation. The X-15 program employed mechanical techniques used in the later manned spaceflight programs, including reaction control system jets for controlling the orientation of a spacecraft, space suits, and horizon definition for navigation. The reentry and landing data collected were valuable to NASA for designing the Space Shuttle.

Project Mercury (1958–1963)

Shortly after the Space Race began, an early objective was to get a person into Earth orbit as soon as possible, therefore the simplest spacecraft that could be launched by existing rockets was favored. The US Air Force's Man in Space Soonest program considered many manned spacecraft designs, ranging from rocket planes like the X-15, to small ballistic space capsules. By 1958, the space plane concepts were eliminated in favor of the ballistic capsule.

When NASA was created that same year, the Air Force program was transferred to it and renamed *Project Mercury*. The first seven astronauts were selected among candidates from the Navy, Air Force and Marine test pilot programs. On May 5, 1961, astronaut Alan Shepard became the first American in space aboard *Freedom 7*, launched by a Redstone booster on a 15-minute ballistic (suborbital) flight. John Glenn became the first American to be launched into orbit, by an Atlas launch vehicle on February 20, 1962, aboard *Friendship 7*. Glenn completed three orbits, after which three more orbital flights were made, culminating in L. Gordon Cooper's 22-orbit flight *Faith 7*, May 15–16, 1963. The Soviet Union (USSR) competed with its own single-pilot spacecraft, Vostok. They sent the first man in space, by launching cosmonaut Yuri Gagarin into a single Earth orbit aboard Vostok 1 in April 1961, one month before Shepard's flight. In August 1962, they achieved an almost four-day record flight with Andriyan Nikolayev aboard Vostok 3, and also conducted a concurrent Vostok 4 mission carrying Pavel Popovich.

Project Gemini (1961–1966)

Based on studies to grow the Mercury spacecraft capabilities to long-duration flights, developing space rendezvous techniques, and precision Earth landing, Project Gemini was started as a two-man program in 1962 to overcome the Soviets' lead and to support the Apollo manned lunar landing program, adding extravehicular activity (EVA) and rendezvous and docking to its objectives.

The first manned Gemini flight, Gemini 3, was flown by Gus Grissom and John Young on March 23, 1965. Nine missions followed in 1965 and 1966, demonstrating an endurance mission of nearly fourteen days, rendezvous, docking, and practical EVA, and gathering medical data on the effects of weightlessness on humans.

Ed White on Gemini 4: first US spacewalk, 1965

Under the direction of Soviet Premier Nikita Khrushchev, the USSR competed with Gemini by converting their Vostok spacecraft into a two- or three-man Voskhod. They succeeded in launching two manned flights before Gemini's first flight, achieving a three-cosmonaut flight in 1963 and the first EVA in 1964. After this, the program was canceled, and Gemini caught up while spacecraft designer Sergei Korolevdeveloped the Soyuz spacecraft, their answer to Apollo.

Apollo program (1961–1972)

The U.S public's perception of the Soviet lead in the space race (by putting the first man into space) motivated President John F. Kennedy to ask the Congress on May 25, 1961, to commit the federal government to a program to land a man on the Moon by the end of the 1960s, which effectively launched the Apollo program.

Apollo 11: Buzz Aldrin on the Moon, 1969.

Apollo was one of the most expensive American scientific programs ever. It cost more than $20 billion in 1960s dollars or an estimated $213 billion in present-day US dollars. (In comparison, the Manhattan Project cost roughly $27.2 billion, accounting for inflation.) It used the Saturn rockets as launch vehicles, which were far bigger than the rockets built for previous projects. The spacecraft was also bigger; it had two main parts, the combined command and service module (CSM) and the lunar landing module (LM). The LM was to be left on the Moon and only the command module (CM) containing the three astronauts would eventually return to Earth.

The second manned mission, Apollo 8, brought astronauts for the first time in a flight around the Moon in December 1968. Shortly before, the Soviets had sent an unmanned spacecraft around the Moon. On the next two missions docking maneuvers that were needed for the Moon landing were practiced and then finally the Moon landing was made on the Apollo 11 mission in July 1969.

The first person to stand on the Moon was Neil Armstrong, who was followed by Buzz Aldrin, while Michael Collins orbited above. Five subsequent Apollo missions also landed astronauts on the Moon, the last in December 1972. Throughout these six Apollo spaceflights, twelve men walked on the Moon. These missions returned a wealth of scientific data and 381.7 kilograms (842 lb) of lunar samples. Topics covered by experiments performed included soil mechanics, meteoroids, seismology, heat flow, lunar ranging, magnetic fields, and solar wind. The Moon landing marked the end of the space race; and as a gesture, Armstrong mentioned mankind when he stepped down on the Moon.

Apollo 17: LRV-003, 1972.

Apollo set major milestones in human spaceflight. It stands alone in sending manned missions beyond low Earth orbit, and landing humans on another celestial body. Apollo 8 was the first manned spacecraft to orbit another celestial body, while Apollo 17 marked the last moonwalk and the last manned mission beyond low Earth orbit to date. The program spurred advances in many areas of technology peripheral to rocketry and manned spaceflight, including avionics, telecommunications, and computers. Apollo sparked interest in many fields of engineering and left many physical facilities and machines developed for the program as landmarks. Many objects and artifacts from the program are on display at various locations throughout the world, notably at the Smithsonian's Air and Space Museums.

Skylab (1965–1979)

Skylab was the United States' first and only independently built space station. Conceived in 1965 as a workshop to be constructed in space from a spent Saturn IB upper stage, the

169,950 lb (77,088 kg) station was constructed on Earth and launched on May 14, 1973, atop the first two stages of a Saturn V, into a 235-nautical-mile (435 km) orbit inclined at 50° to the equator. Damaged during launch by the loss of its thermal protection and one electricity-generating solar panel, it was repaired to functionality by its first crew. It was occupied for a total of 171 days by 3 successive crews in 1973 and 1974. It included a laboratory for studying the effects of microgravity, and a solar observatory. NASA planned to have a Space Shuttle dock with it, and elevate Skylab to a higher safe altitude, but the Shuttle was not ready for flight before Skylab's re-entry on July 11, 1979.

Skylab space station, 1974

To save cost, NASA used one of the Saturn V rockets originally earmarked for a canceled Apollo mission to launch the Skylab. Apollo spacecraft were used for transporting astronauts to and from the station. Three three-man crews stayed aboard the station for periods of 28, 59, and 84 days. Skylab's habitable volume was 11,290 cubic feet (320 m^3), which was 30.7 times bigger than that of the Apollo Command Module.

Apollo–Soyuz Test Project (1972–1975)

On May 24, 1972, US President Richard M. Nixon and Soviet Premier Alexei Kosygin signed an agreement calling for a joint manned space mission, and declaring intent for all future international manned spacecraft to be capable of docking with each other. This authorized the Apollo-Soyuz Test Project (ASTP), involving the rendezvous and docking in Earth orbit of a surplus Apollo Command/Service Module with a Soyuz spacecraft. The mission took place in July 1975. This was the last US manned space flight until the first orbital flight of the Space Shuttle in April 1981.

The mission included both joint and separate scientific experiments, and provided useful engineering experience for future joint US–Russian space flights, such as the Shuttle–Mir Program and the International Space Station.

Space Shuttle program (1972–2011)

Launch of a Space Shuttle.

Mae Jemison working in Spacelab in 1992. Spacelab was a major NASA collaboration with Europe's space agencies

The Space Shuttle became the major focus of NASA in the late 1970s and the 1980s. Planned as a frequently launchable and mostly reusable vehicle, four space shuttle orbiters were built by 1985. The first to launch, *Columbia*, did so on April 12, 1981, the 20th anniversary of the first known human space flight.

Its major components were a spaceplane orbiter with an external fuel tank and two solid-fuel launch rockets at its side. The external tank, which was bigger than the spacecraft itself, was the only major component that was not reused. The shuttle could orbit in altitudes of 185–643 km (115–400 miles) and carry a maximum payload (to low orbit) of 24,400 kg (54,000 lb). Missions could last from 5 to 17 days and crews could be from 2 to 8 astronauts.

On 20 missions (1983–98) the Space Shuttle carried Spacelab, designed in cooperation with the European Space Agency (ESA). Spacelab was not designed for independent orbital flight, but remained in the Shuttle's cargo bay as the astronauts entered and left it through an airlock. Another famous series of missions were the launch and later successful repair of the Hubble Space Telescope in 1990 and 1993, respectively.

In 1995, Russian-American interaction resumed with the Shuttle–Mir missions (1995–1998). Once more an American vehicle docked with a Russian craft, this time a full-fledged space station. This cooperation has continued with Russia and the United States as two of the biggest partners in the largest space station built: the International Space Station (ISS). The strength of their cooperation on this project was even more evident when NASA began relying on Russian launch vehicles to service the ISS during the two-year grounding of the shuttle fleet following the 2003 Space Shuttle *Columbia* disaster.

The Shuttle fleet lost two orbiters and 14 astronauts in two disasters: *Challenger* in 1986, and *Columbia* in 2003. While the 1986 loss was mitigated by building the Space Shuttle *Endeavour* from replacement parts, NASA did not build another orbiter to replace the second loss. NASA's Space Shuttle program had

135 missions when the program ended with the successful landing of the Space Shuttle *Atlantis* at the Kennedy Space Center on July 21, 2011. The program spanned 30 years with over 300 astronauts sent into space.

DIRECTIVES

Some major NASA directives were to land people on the moon, and another one was build the space shuttle, and to build a large space station. Typically major directives mark some combination of science advisory, political, funding, and public interest that synergize into various waves of effort often heavily swayed by technical, funding, and world wide events. For example, there was a major push to build Space Station Freedom in the 1980s, but when the Cold War ended Russian and the USA and international partners came together to build the International Space Station.

In the 2010s the major shift was the retirement of the Space Shuttle and development of a new manned heavy lift rocket, the Space Launch System. Missions for the new system have varied but are overall similar, and involved a human push outward from Earth using the system. After Apollo, there is typically some combination of using space stations, the Moon, and other targets as part of an overall exploration of the solar system. An example of this was the Space Exploration Initiative of the 1980s.

Roadmaps have similarities in that there is usually a goal of Mars in the coming decades, but there are some differences over what are the best steps to take and what specific technologies to focus on. One of the options that were considered was an Asteroid Redirect Mission. ARM had largely been defunded in 2017, but key technologies developed for ARM would be utilized for future exploration, especially work on a solar electric propulsion system. The long lead times for projects usually means its up to later officials to execute on a directive, sometimes decades later. This means there is often an ebb and flow of directions and shifts. For example, a Shuttle replacement has numerous projects each making some headway before being called off for various reasons including the National Aerospace Plane, VentureStar, Orbital Space Plane, Ares I, etc.. The asteroid mission was not a major directive in the 2010s, rather there was generic support for a large heavy launch vehicle and a long term goal of getting humans to Mars. The space shuttle was retired and much of the existing roadmap was shelved including the then planned Lunar return and Ares I human launch vehicle.

Previously, in the early 2000s there was a plan called the Constellation Program but this was defunded in the early 2010s. In the 1990s there was a plan called "Faster, Better, Cheaper" In the 1980s there was a directive to build a manned space station. One of the famous directives was in 1962, delivered in the speech We choose to go to the Moon.

NASA Authorization Act of 2017

Langley's Mars Ice Dome design from 2016 for a Mars base

Orion at ISS artwork

The NASA Authorization Act of 2017 which included $19.5 billion in funding for that fiscal year, also directed NASA to get humans near or on the surface of Mars by the early 2030s.

Space Policy Directive 1

In December 2017, on the 45th anniversary of the last manned mission to the Lunar surface, the executive branch approved a directive that includes a lunar mission on the pathway to Mars and beyond.

We'll learn. The directive I'm signing today will refocus America's space program on human exploration and discovery. It marks an important step in returning American astronauts to the moon for the first time since 1972 for long-term exploration and use. This time, we will not only plant our flag and leave our footprint, we will establish a foundation for an eventual mission to Mars. And perhaps, someday, to many worlds beyond. *—President of the United States of America, 2017*

19

Group of Eight

The G8, reformatted as G7 from 2014 due to the suspension of Russia's participation, was an inter-governmental political forum from 1997 until 2014.

The forum originated with a 1975 summit hosted by France that brought together representatives of six governments: France, Germany, Italy, Japan, the United Kingdom, and the United States, thus leading to the name Group of Six or G6. The summit came to be known as the Group of Seven, or G7, in 1976 with the addition of Canada. Russia was added to the political forum from 1997, which the following year became known as the G8. In March 2014 Russia was suspended indefinitely following the annexation of Crimea, whereupon the political forum name reverted to G7. In 2017 Russia announced its permanent withdrawal from the G8. However, some representatives of G7 countries stated that they would be interested in Russia's return to the group. The European Union was represented at the G8 since the 1980s as a "nonenumerated" participant, but originally could not host or chair summits. The 40th summit was the first time the European Union was able to host and chair a summit. Collectively, in 2012 the G8 nations comprised 50.1 percent of 2012 global nominal GDP and 40.9 percent of global GDP (PPP).

"G7" can refer to the member states in aggregate or to the annual summit meeting of the G7 heads of government. G7 ministers also meet throughout the year, such as the G7 finance ministers (who meet four times a year), G7 foreign ministers, or G7 environment ministers.

Each calendar year, the responsibility of hosting the G8 was rotated through the member states in the following order: France, United States, United Kingdom, Russia (suspended), Germany, Japan, Italy, and Canada. The holder of the presidency sets the agenda, hosts the summit for that year, and determines which ministerial meetings will take place.

In 2005, the UK government initiated the practice of inviting five leading emerging markets — Brazil, China, India, Mexico, and South Africa — to participate in the G8 meetings that came to be known as G8+5, but this practice was short-lived. With the G20 major economies growing in stature since the 2008 Washington summit, world leaders from the group announced at their Pittsburgh summit in September 2009 that the group would replace the G8 as the main economic council of wealthy nations. Nevertheless, the G7 retains its relevance as a "steering group for the West", with special significance appointed to Japan.

HISTORY

Following 1994's G7 summit in Naples, Russian officials held separate meetings with leaders of the G7 after the group's summits. This informal arrangement was dubbed the Political 8 (P8)—or, colloquially, the G7+1. At the invitation of UK Prime Minister Tony Blair and U.S. President Bill Clinton, President Boris Yeltsin was invited first as a guest observer, later as a full participant. It was seen as a way to encourage Yeltsin with his capitalist reforms. Russia formally joined the group in 1998, resulting in the Group of Eight, or G8.

Food

A major focus of the G8 since 2009 has been the global supply of food. At the 2009 L'Aquila summit, the G8's members promised to contribute $22 billion to the issue. By 2015, 93% of funds had been disbursed.

Ȧt the 2012 summit, President Barack Obama asked G8 leaders to adopt the New Alliance for Food Security and Nutrition initiative to "help the rural poor produce more food and sell it in thriving local and regional markets as well as on the global market".

Russia2s participation suspension (2014)

On 24 March 2014, the G7 members cancelled the planned G8 summit that was to be held in June that year in the Russian city of Sochi, and suspended Russia2s membership of the group, due to Russia's annexation of Crimea; nevertheless, they stopped short of outright permanent expulsion. Russian foreign minister Sergei Lavrov downplayed the importance of the decision by the U.S. and its allies, and pointed up that major international decisions were taken by the G20 countries.

Later on, the Italian Foreign Affairs minister Federica Mogherini and other Italian authorities, along with the EastWest Institute board member Wolfgang Ischinger, suggested that Russia may restore its membership in the group. In April 2015, the German foreign minister Frank-Walter Steinmeier said that Russia would be welcomed to return to G8 provided the Minsk Protocol was implemented. In 2016, he added that "none of the major international conflicts can be solved without Russia", and the G7 countries will consider Russia's return to the group in 2017. The same year, Japanese Prime Minister Shinzô Abe called for Russia's return to G8, stating that Russia's involvement is "crucial to tackling multiple crises in the Middle East". In January 2017, the Italian foreign minister Angelino Alfano said that Italy hopes for "resuming the G8 format with Russia and ending the atmosphere of the Cold War". On 13 January 2017, Russia announced that it would permanently leave the G8 grouping. Nonetheless, Christian Lindner, the leader of Free Democratic Party of Germany and member of the Bundestag, said that Putin should be "asked to join the table of the G7" so that one could "talk with him and not about him", and "we cannot make all things dependent on the situation in Crimea". In April 2018, the German politicians and members of the Bundestag Sahra Wagenknecht and Alexander Graf Lambsdorff said that Russia should be invited back to the group and attend the 2018 summit in Canada: "Russia should again be at the table during the [June] summit at the latest" because "peace in Europe and also in the Middle East is only possible with Russia". The President of US Donald Trump also stated that Russia should be returned to G8; his appeal was supported by the Italian Prime Minister Giuseppe Conte.Later the 4 EU members of G7, Canada and Japan anyway didn't agree about it. After several G7 members quickly rejected US President Trump suggestion to accept again Russian Federation in the G8, Russian Foreign Minister Lavrov said Russian Federation isn't interested to rejoin the political forum G8. He also said that G20 is sufficient for Russian Federation. In the final statement of 2018 Canada meeting, the G7 members announced to recall sanctions and also to be ready to take further restrictive measures against the Russian Federation for the failure of Minsk Agreement complete implementation.

STRUCTURE AND ACTIVITIES

By design, the G8 deliberately lacked an administrative structure like those for international organizations, such as the United Nations or the World Bank. The group does not have a permanent secretariat, or offices for its members.

The presidency of the group rotates annually among member countries, with each new term beginning on 1 January of the year. The rotation order is: France, the United States, the United Kingdom, Russia (suspended), Germany, Japan, Italy, and Canada. The country holding the presidency is responsible for planning and hosting a series of ministerial-level meetings, leading up to a mid-year summit attended by the heads of government. The president of the European Commission participates as an equal in all summit events.

The ministerial meetings bring together ministers responsible for various portfolios to discuss issues of mutual or global concern. The range of topics include health, law enforcement, labor, economic and social development, energy, environment, foreign affairs, justice and interior, terrorism, and trade. There are also a separate set of meetings known as the G8+5, created during the 2005 Gleneagles, Scotland summit, that is attended by finance and energy ministers from all eight member countries in addition to the five "outreach countries" which are also known as the Group of Five—Brazil, People's Republic of China, India, Mexico, and South Africa.

In June 2005, justice ministers and interior ministers from the G8 countries agreed to launch an international database on pedophiles. The G8 officials also agreed to pool data on terrorism, subject to restrictions by privacy and security laws in individual countries.

Global energy

At the Heiligendamm Summit in 2007, the G8 acknowledged a proposal from the EU for a worldwide initiative on efficient energy use. They agreed to explore, along with the International Energy Agency, the most effective means to promote energy efficiency internationally. A year later, on 8 June 2008, the G8 along with China, India, South Korea and the European Community established the International Partnership for Energy Efficiency Cooperation, at the Energy Ministerial meeting hosted by Japan holding 2008 G8 Presidency, in Aomori.

G8 Finance Ministers, whilst in preparation for the 34th Summit of the G8 Heads of State and Government in Toyako, Hokkaido, met on the 13 and 14 June 2008, in Osaka, Japan. They agreed to the "G8 Action Plan for Climate Change to Enhance the Engagement of Private and Public Financial Institutions." In closing, Ministers supported the launch of new Climate Investment Funds (CIFs) by the World Bank, which will help existing efforts until a new framework under the UNFCCC is implemented after 2012. The UNFCCC is not on track to meeting any of its stated goals.

Annual summit

The first G8 summit was held in 1997 after Russia formally joined the G7 group, and the last one was held in 2013. The

2014 summit was scheduled to be held in Russia. However, due to the Crimean crisis, the other seven countries decided to hold a separate meeting without Russia as a G7 summit in Brussels, Belgium.

CRITICISM

Some criticism centres on the assertion that members of G8 do not do enough to help global problems, due to strict patent policy and other issues related to globalization. In *Unraveling Global Apartheid*, political analyst Titus Alexander described the G7, as it was in 1996, as the 'cabinet' of global minority rule, with a coordinating role in world affairs.

The Heritage Foundation has criticized the G8 for advocating food security without making room for economic freedom.

RELEVANCE

The G8's relevance has been subject to debate from 2008 onward. It represented the major industrialized countries but critics argued that the G8 no longer represented the world's most powerful economies, as China has surpassed every economy but the United States.

Vladimir Putin did not attend the 2012 G8 summit at Camp David, causing *Foreign Policy* (*FP*) magazine to remark that the summit has generally outlived its usefulness as a viable international gathering of foreign leaders. Two years later, Russia was suspended from the G8, then chose to leave permanently in January 2017.

The G20 major economies leaders' summit has had an increased level of international prestige and influence. However, British Prime Minister David Cameron said of the G8 in 2012:

Some people ask, does the G8 still matter, when we have a Group of 20? My answer is, yes. The G8 is a group of like-minded countries that share a belief in free enterprise as the best route to growth. As eight countries making up about half the world's gross domestic product, the standards we set, the commitments we make, and the steps we take can help solve vital global issues, fire up economies and drive prosperity all over the world.

YOUTH 8 SUMMIT

The Y8 Summit or simply Y8, formerly known as the G8 Youth Summit is the youth counterpart to the G8 summit. The first summit to use the name Y8 took place in May 2012 in Puebla, Mexico, alongside the Youth G8 that took place in Washington, D.C. the same year.

The Y8 Summit brings together young leaders from G8 nations and the European Union to facilitate discussions of international affairs, promote cross-cultural understanding, and build global friendships. The conference closely follows the formal negotiation procedures of the G8 Summit. The Y8 Summit represents the innovative voice of young adults between the age of 18 and 35. The delegates jointly come up with a consensus-based written statement in the end, the Final Communiqué. This document is subsequently presented to G8 leaders in order to inspire positive change.

The Y8 Summit is organised annually by a global network of youth-led organisations called The IDEA (The International Diplomatic Engagement Association). The organisations undertake the selection processes for their respective national delegations, while the hosting country is responsible for organising the summit. Now, several youth associations are supporting and getting involved in the project. For instance, every year, the Young European Leadership association is recruiting and sending EU Delegates.

20

United Nations Human Rights Council

The United Nations Human Rights Council (UNHRC) is a United Nations body whose mission is to promote and protect human rightsaround the world. The UNHRC has 47 members elected for staggered three-year terms on a regional group basis. The 38th session of the UNHRC began June 18, 2018. It ended on July 7, 2018. The headquarters of UNHRC is in Geneva, Switzerland.

The UNHRC investigates allegations of breaches of human rights in UN member states, and addresses important thematic human rights issues such as freedom of association and assembly, freedom of expression, freedom of belief and religion, women's rights, LGBT rights, Criminals, drug lords in Philippines and the rights of racial and ethnic minorities.

The UNHRC was established by the UN General Assembly on March 15, 2006 (by resolution A/RES/60/251) to replace the UN Commission on Human Rights (UNCHR, herein CHR) that had been strongly criticised for allowing countries with poor human rights records to be members. UN Secretaries General Kofi Annan and Ban Ki-moon, former president of the council Doru Costea, the European Union, Canada, and the United States have accused the UNHRC of focusing disproportionately on the Israeli–Palestinian conflict, and many allege an anti-Israel bias- the Council has resolved more resolutions condemning Israel than the rest of the world combined. The UNHRC works closely with the Office of the High Commissioner for Human Rights (OHCHR) and engages the UN's *special procedures.*

STRUCTURE

The members of the General Assembly elect the members who occupy the UNHRC's 47 seats. The term of each seat is three years, and no member may occupy a seat for more than two consecutive terms. The seats are distributed among the UN's regional groups as follows: 13 for Africa, 13 for Asia, six for Eastern Europe, eight for Latin America and the Caribbean (GRULAC), and seven for the Western European and Others Group (WEOG). The previous CHR had a membership of 53 elected by the Economic and Social Council (ECOSOC) through a majority of those present and voting.

The General Assembly can suspend the rights and privileges of any Council member that it decides has persistently committed gross and systematic violations of human rights during its term of membership. The suspension process requires a two-thirds majority vote by the General Assembly. The resolution establishing the UNHRC states that "when electing members of the Council, Member States shall take into account the contribution of candidates to the promotion and protection of human rights and their voluntary pledges and commitments made thereto", and that "members elected to the Council shall uphold the highest standards in the promotion and protection of human rights".

Sessions

The UNHRC holds regular sessions three times a year, in March, June, and September.

The UNHRC can decide at any time to hold a special session to address human rights violations and emergencies, at the request of one-third of the member states. To date there have been 28 special sessions.

Members

The UNHRC has 47 members, selected each year by the UN General Assembly for staggered three-year terms on a regional group basis. No member may occupy a seat for more than two consecutive three-year terms. The seats are distributed among the UN's regional groups as follows: 13 for Africa, 13 for Asia, six for Eastern Europe, eight for Latin America and the Caribbean (GRULAC), and seven for the Western European and Others Group (WEOG).

The first election of members was held on May 9, 2006. Their terms of office began on June 19, 2006. On May 19, it was announced that Mexico would serve as the Council's chair during its first year of existence.

2010 Group The replacement for the *2007 Group* was duly elected by the General Assembly on May 17, 2007, known as the *2010 Group*, the year when their terms expire.In this election, Angola and Egypt were elected to the council, whereas Belarus was rejected.

2011 Group: The replacement for the *2008 Group* was duly elected by the General Assembly on May 21, 2008, known as the *2011 Group*, the year when their terms expire.

2012 Group: The replacement for the *2009 Group* was duly elected by the General Assembly on May 12, 2009, known as the *2012 Group*, the year when their terms expire.

2013 Group: The replacement for the *2010 Group* was duly elected by the General Assembly on May 13, 2010, known as the *2013 Group*, the year when their terms expire.

2014 Group: The replacement for the *2011 Group* was duly elected by the General Assembly on May 20, 2011, known as the *2014 Group*, the year when their terms expire.

2015 Group: The replacement for the *2012 Group* was duly elected by the General Assembly on November 12, 2012, known as the *2015 Group*, the year when their terms expire.

2016 Group: The replacement for the *2013 Group* was duly elected by the General Assembly on November 12, 2013, known as the *2016 Group*, the year when their terms expire.

SUBSIDIARY BODIES THAT DIRECTLY REPORT TO THE UNHRC

Universal Periodic Review Working Group

An important component of the Council consists in a periodic review of all 193 UN member states, called the Universal Periodic Review (UPR).

The new mechanism is based on reports coming from different sources, one of them being contributions from NGOs. Each country's situation will be examined during a three-and-a-half-hour debate.

The first cycle of the UPR took place between 2008 and 2012, and the second cycle of reviews started in 2012 and is expected to be completed in 2016.

The General Assembly resolution establishing the Council, provided that "the Council shall review its work and functioning five years after its establishment". The main work of the review was undertaken in an Intergovernmental Working Group established by the Council in its Resolution 12/1 of October 1, 2009 The review was finalized in March 2011, by the adoption of an "Outcome" at the Council's sixteenth session, annexed to Resolution 16/21.

First cycle: The following terms and procedures were set out in General Assembly Resolution 60/251:

- Reviews are to occur over a four-year period (48 countries per year). Accordingly, the 192 countries that are members of the United Nations shall normally all have such a Review between 2008 and 2011;
- The order of review should follow the principles of universality and equal treatment;
- All Member States of the Council will be reviewed while they sit at the Council and the initial members of the Council will be first;
- The selection of the countries to be reviewed must respect the principle of equitable geographical allocation;

- The first Member States and the first observatory States to be examined will be selected randomly in each regional group in order to guarantee full compliance with the equitable geographical allocation. Reviews shall then be conducted alphabetically.

Second cycle: HRC Resolution 16/21 brought the following changes:

- Reviews are to occur over a four-and-a-half-year period (42 countries per year). Accordingly, the 193 countries that are members of the United Nations shall normally all have such a Review between 2012 and 2016;
- The order of review will be similar to the 1st cycle;
- The length of each Review will be extended from three to three-and-a-half hours;
- The second and subsequent cycles of the review should focus on, inter alia, the implementation of the recommendations.

Similar mechanisms exist in other organizations: International Atomic Energy Agency, Council of Europe, International Monetary Fund, Organization of American States, International Labour Bureau and the World Trade Organization.

Except for the tri-annual reports on development of human rights policies, that Member States have to submit to the Secretary General since 1956, the Human Rights Council UPR procedure constitutes a first in the area. It marks the end of the discrimination that had plagued the work of the Human Rights Commission and had caused it to be harshly criticised. Finally, this mechanism demonstrates and confirms the universal nature of human rights.

SPECIFIC ISSUES

Israel

As of 2018, Israel has been condemned in 78 resolutions by the Council since its creation in 2006—the Council has resolved more resolutions condemning Israel than the rest of the world combined. By April 2007, the Council had passed eleven resolutions condemning Israel, the only country which it had specifically condemned. Toward Sudan, a country with human rights abuses as documented by the Council's working groups, it has expressed "deep concern".

The council voted on June 30, 2006 to make a review of alleged human rights abuses by Israel a permanent feature of every council session. The Council's special rapporteur on the Israeli–Palestinian conflict is its only expert mandate with no year of expiry. The resolution, which was sponsored by Organisation of the Islamic Conference, passed by a vote of 29 to 12 with five abstentions. Human Rights Watch urged it to look at international human rights and humanitarian law violations committed by Palestinian armed groups as well. Human Rights Watch called on the Council to avoid the selectivity that discredited its predecessor and urged it to hold special sessions on other urgent situations, such as that in Darfur.

The Special Rapporteur on the question of Palestine to the previous UNCHR, the current UNHRC and the General Assembly was, between 2001 and 2008, John Dugard. Bayefski quotes him as saying that his mandate is to "investigate human rights violations by Israel only, not by Palestinians". Dugard was replaced in 2008 with Richard Falk, who has compared Israel's treatment of Palestinians with the Nazis' treatment of Jews during the Holocaust. Like his predecessor, Falk's mandate only covers Israel's human rights record. The Palestinian Authority has informally asked Falk to resign, among other reasons due to viewing him as "a partisan of Hamas". Falk disputes this and has called the reasons given "essentially untrue". In July 2011, Richard Falk posted a cartoon some critics has described as anti-Semitic onto his blog. The cartoon depicted a bloodthirsty dog with the word "USA" on it wearing a kippah, or Jewish headcovering. In response, Falk was heavily criticized by world leaders in the United States and certain European countries. The United States called Falk's behavior "shameful and outrageous" and "an embarrassment to the

United Nations", and officially called on him to resign. Ileana Ros-Lehtinen, chairwoman of the U.S. House of Representatives Committee on Foreign Affairs, called on Falk to resign as well. The Anti-Defamation League described the cartoon as a "message of hatred".

The UN Human Rights Council was castigated by Israeli Prime Minister Binyamin Netanyahu for facilitating an event featuring a Hamas politician. The Hamas parliamentarian had spoken at an NGO event in the UN Geneva building. Israel's ambassador to the United Nations Ron Prosor denounced the speech stating that Hamas was an internationally recognized terrorist organization that targeted civilians. "Inviting a Hamas terrorist to lecture to the world about human rights is like asking Charles Manson to run the murder investigation unit at the NYPD", he said.

On July 3, 2015, UNHRC voted Resolution A/HRC/29/L.35 "ensuring accountability and justice for all violations of international law in the Occupied Palestinian Territory, including East Jerusalem.". It passed by 41 votes in favor including the eight sitting EU members (France, Germany, Britain, Ireland, the Netherlands, Portugal, Latvia and Estonia), 1 against (the US) and 5 absentions (India, Kenya, Ethiopia, Paraguay and Macedonia). India precised that its abstention was due to the reference to International Criminal Court (ICC) in the Resolution whereas "India is not a signatory to the Rome Statute establishing the ICC".

UN Secretaries General

In 2006, UN Secretary-General Kofi Annan argued that the Commission should not have a "disproportionate focus on violations by Israel. Not that Israel should be given a free pass. Absolutely not. But the Council should give the same attention to grave violations committed by other states as well".

On June 20, 2007, Secretary-General Ban Ki-moon issued a statement that read: "The Secretary-General is disappointed at the council's decision to single out only one specific regional item given the range and scope of allegations of human rights violations throughout the world."

United States and UNHRC President

The Council's charter preserves the watchdog's right to appoint special investigators for countries whose human rights records are of particular concern, something many developing states have long opposed.

A Council meeting in Geneva in 2007 caused controversy after Cuba and Belarus, both accused of abuses, were removed from a list of nine special mandates. The list, which included North Korea, Cambodia and Sudan, had been carried forward from the defunct Commission. Commenting on Cuba and Belarus, the UN statement said that Ban noted "that not having a Special Rapporteur assigned to a particular country does not absolve that country from its obligations under the Universal Declaration of Human Rights."

The United States said a day before the UN statement that the Council deal raised serious questions about whether the new body could be unbiased. Alejandro Wolff, deputy U.S. permanent representative at the United Nations, accused the council of "a pathological obsession with Israel" and also denounced its action on Cuba and Belarus. "I think the record is starting to speak for itself", he told journalists.

The UNHRC President Doru Costea responded: "I agree with him. The functioning of the Council must be constantly improved". He added that the Council must examine the behaviour of all parties involved in complex disputes and not place just one state under the magnifying glass.

Netherlands

Speaking at the IDC's Herzliya Conference in Israel in January 2008, Dutch Foreign Minister Maxime Verhagen criticized the actions of the Human Rights Council actions against Israel. "At the United Nations, censuring Israel has become something of a habit, while Hamas's terror is referred to in coded language or not at all. The Netherlands believes the record should be set straight, both in New York and at the Human Rights Council in Geneva", Verhagen said.

2006 Lebanon conflict

At its Second Special Session in August 2006, the Council announced the establishment of a High-Level Commission of Inquiry charged with probing allegations that Israel systematically targeted and killed Lebanese civilians during the 2006 Israel-Lebanon conflict. The resolution was passed by a vote of 27 in favour to 11 against, with 8 abstentions. Before and after the vote several member states and NGOs objected that by targeting the resolution solely at Israel and failing to address Hezbollah attacks on Israeli civilians, the Council risked damaging its credibility. The members of the Commission of Inquiry, as announced on September 1, 2006, were Clemente Baena Soares of Brazil, Mohamed Chande Othman of Tanzania, and Stelios Perrakis of Greece. The Commission noted that its report on the conflict would be incomplete without fully investigating both sides, but that "the Commission is not entitled, even if it had wished, to construe [its charter] as equally authorizing the investigation of the actions by Hezbollah in Israel", as the Council had explicitly prohibited it from investigating the actions of Hezbollah.

January 2008 decree

The Council released a statement calling on Israel to stop its military operations in the Gaza Strip and to open the Strip's borders to allow the entry of food, fuel and medicine. The Council adopted the resolution by a vote of 30 to 1, with 15 states abstaining.

"Unfortunately, neither this resolution nor the current session addressed the role of both parties. It was regretful that the current draft resolution did not condemn the rocket attacks on Israeli civilians," said Canada's representative Terry Cormier, the lone voter against.

The United States and Israel boycotted the session. U.S. ambassador Warren Tichenor said the Council's unbalanced approach had "squandered its credibility" by failing to address continued rocket attacks against Israel. "Today's actions do nothing to help the Palestinian people, in whose name the supporters of this session claim to act," he said in a statement. "Supporters of a Palestinian state must avoid the kind of inflammatory rhetoric and actions that this session represents, which only stoke tensions and erode the chances for peace", he added. "We believe that this council should deplore the fact that innocent civilians on both sides are suffering", Slovenian Ambassador Andrej Logar said on behalf of the seven EU states on the council.

At a press conference in Geneva on Wednesday, UN Secretary General Ban Ki-moon responded when asked about its special session on Gaza, that "I appreciate that the council is looking in depth into this particular situation. And it is rightly doing so. I would also appreciate it if the council will be looking with the same level of attention and urgency at all other matters around the world. There are still many areas where human rights are abused and not properly protected", he said.

Gaza report

On April 3, 2009, South African Judge Richard Goldstone was named as the head of the independent United Nations Fact-Finding Mission to investigate international human rights and humanitarian law violations related to the Gaza War. The Mission was established by Resolution S-9/1 of the United Nations Human Rights Council.

On September 15, 2009, the UN Fact-Finding mission released its report. The report found that there was evidence "indicating serious violations of international human rights and humanitarian law were committed by Israel during the Gaza conflict, and that Israel committed actions amounting to war crimes, and possibly crimes against humanity". The mission also found that there was evidence that "Palestinian armed groups committed war crimes, as well as possibly crimes against humanity, in their repeated launching of rockets and mortars into Southern Israel". The mission called for referring either side in the conflict to the UN Security Council for prosecution at the International Criminal Court if they refuse to launch fully independent investigations by December 2009.

Goldstone has since partially retracted the reports conclusions that Israel committed war crimes, as new evidence has shed light upon the decision making by Israeli commanders. He said, "I regret that our fact-finding mission did not have such evidence explaining the circumstances in which we said civilians in Gaza were targeted, because it probably would have influenced our findings about intentionality and war crimes."

Goldstone acknowledged that Israel has "to a significant degree" implemented the reports recommendations that "each party to investigate [the incidents] transparently and in good faith," but "Hamas has done nothing". The Palestinian Authority has also implemented the reports recommendations by investigating "assassinations, torture and illegal detentions, perpetrated by Fatah in the West Bank", but Goldstone noted that "most of those allegations were confirmed by this inquiry".

March 2011 controversy

At the UNHRC's opening session in February 2011, U.S. Secretary of State Hillary Clinton criticized the council's "structural bias" against the State of Israel: "The structural bias against Israel – including a standing agenda item for Israel, whereas all other countries are treated under a common item – is wrong. And it undermines the important work we are trying to do together."

An editorial in the *Jerusalem Post* subsequently revealed that the UNHRC was "poised to adopt six resolutions ... condemning Israel," noting that it was the highest number of resolutions ever to be adopted against Israel in a single session. Human rights activist and Hudson Institute senior fellow Anne Bayefsky accused the UNHRC of failing to remove antisemitic propaganda distributed by the IHH during one of its sessions. The material in question was an illustration depicting Israel as a sinister Nazi octopus seizing control of a ship.

Chair of the United States House Committee on Foreign Affairs Rep. Ileana Ros-Lehtinen (R) said she would propose legislation making U.S. funding for the UN contingent on extensive reform. Her bill will also call for the United States to withdraw from the UNHRC, as "Israel is the only country on the council's permanent agenda, while abuses by rogue regimes like Cuba, China, and Syria are ignored".

The hosting of a Hamas member controversy

In March 2012, the UN Human Rights Council was criticised for facilitating an event featuring a Hamas politician. The Hamas parliamentarian had spoken at an NGO event in the UN Geneva building.

Israeli Prime Minister Binyamin Netanyahu castigated the UNHRC's decision stating, "He represents an organization that indiscriminately targets children and grown-ups, and women and men.

Innocents – is their special favorite target". Israel's ambassador to the UN Ron Prosor denounced the speech stating that Hamas was an internationally recognized terrorist organization that targeted civilians. "Inviting a Hamas terrorist to lecture to the world about human rights is like asking Charles Manson to run the murder investigation unit at the NYPD", he said.

March 2012 criticism

The United States urged the United Nations Human Rights Council in Geneva to stop its anti-Israel bias. It took particular exception to the council's Agenda Item 7, under which at every session, Israel's human rights record is debated. No other country has a dedicated agenda item. The US Ambassador to the UNHRC Eileen Chamberlain Donahoe said that the United States was deeply troubled by the "Council's biased and disproportionate focus on Israel." She said that the hypocrisy was further exposed in the Golan Heights resolution that was advocated by the Syrian regime at a time when it was murdering its own citizens.

"Defamation of religion"

From 1999 to 2011, the CHR and the UNHRC adopted resolutions in opposition to the "defamation of religion".

Climate change

The Human Rights Council has adopted the Resolution 10/4 about human rights and climate change.

Eritrea report

In June 2015, a 500-page UNHRC report accused Eritrea's government of widespread human rights violations. These were alleged to include extrajudicial executions, torture, indefinitely prolonged national service and forced labour, and the report also indicated that sexual harassment, rape and sexual servitude by state officials are widespread. *The Guardian* claimed that the report 'catalogues a litany of human rights violations by the "totalitarian" regime of President Isaias Afwerki "on a scope and scale seldom witnessed elsewhere"'. The report also asserted that these serial violations may amount to crimes against humanity.

The Eritrean Foreign Ministry responded by describing the Commission's report as "wild allegations" which were "totally unfounded and devoid of all merit" and countercharged the UNHRC with "vile slanders and false accusations".

The vice chairperson of the subcommittee on human rights at the European parliament said the report detailed 'very serious human rights violations', and said that EU funding for development would not continue as at present without change in Eritrea.

CANDIDACY ISSUES

Syria

In July 2012, Syria announced that it would seek a UNHRC seat. This was while there was serious evidence (provided by numerous human rights organizations including the UN itself) that Syrian President Bashar al-Assad had authorised and funded the slaughter of thousands of civilians, with estimates of 14,000 civilians being killed as of July 2012 during the Syrian civil war. According to UN Watch, Syria's candidacy was virtually assured under the prevailing election system.Syria would be responsible for promoting human rights if elected. In response, the United States and European Union drafted a resolution to oppose the move. In the end, Syria was not on the ballot for the 12 November 2012 election to UNHRC.

Sudan and Ethiopia

In July 2012, it was reported that Sudan and Ethiopia were nominated for a UNHRC seat, despite being accused by human rights organizations of grave human rights violations. UN Watch condemned the move to nominate Sudan, pointing out that Sudan's President Omar Al-Bashir was indicted for genocide by the International Criminal Court. According to UN Watch, Sudan was virtually assured of securing a seat. A joint letter of 18 African and international civil society organizations urged foreign ministers of the African Union to reverse its endorsement of Ethiopia and Sudan for a seat, accusing them of serious human rights violations and listing examples of such violations, and stating that they should not be rewarded with a seat. Sudan was not on the ballot for the 12 November 2012 election to UNHRC, but Ethiopia was elected.

Saudi Arabia

In September 2015, Faisal bin Hassan Trad, Saudi Arabia's ambassador to the UN in Geneva, was elected Chair of the UNHRC Advisory Committee, the panel that appoints independent experts. UN Watch executive director Hillel Neuer said: "It is scandalous that the UN chose a country that has beheaded more people this year [2015] than ISIS to be head of a key human rights panel. Petro-dollars and politics have trumped human rights." Saudi Arabia also shut down criticism, during the UN meeting. In January 2016, Saudi Arabia executed the prominent Shia cleric Sheikh Nimr who had called for free elections in Saudi Arabia.

In September 2017, US President Donald Trump said that 'it is an "embarrassment" that there are countries on the UN human rights panel that have themselves committed atrocities', but not naming any particular country.

COUNTRY POSITIONS

Position of the United States

In regard to the United Nations Human Rights Council, the position of the United States is: "human rights have been a cornerstone of American values since the country's birth and the United States is committed to support the work of the UN Commission in promoting the principles embodied in the Universal Declaration of Human Rights. U.S. President George W. Bush declared that the United States would not seek a seat on the Council, saying it would be more effective from the outside. He did pledge, however, to support the Council financially. State Department spokesman Sean McCormack said, "We will work closely with partners in the international community to encourage the council to address serious cases of human rights abuse in countries such as Iran, Cuba, Zimbabwe, Burma, Sudan, and North Korea".

The U.S. State Department said on March 5, 2007 that, for the second year in a row, the United States has decided not to seek a seat on the Human Rights Council, asserting the body had lost its credibility with repeated attacks on Israel and a failure to confront other rights abusers. Spokesman Sean McCormack said the council has had a "singular focus" on Israel, while countries such as Cuba, Myanmar and North Korea have been spared scrutiny. He said that though the United States will have only an observer role, it will continue to shine a spotlight on human rights issues. The most senior Republican member of the Committee on Foreign Affairs of the U.S. House of Representatives, Ileana Ros-Lehtinen, supported the administration decision. "Rather than standing as a strong defender of fundamental human rights, the Human Rights Council has faltered as a weak voice subject to gross political manipulation," she said. Upon passage of UNHRC's June 2007 institution building package, the U.S. restated its condemnation of bias in the institution's agenda. Spokesman Sean McCormack again criticised the Commission for focusing on Israel in light of many more pressing human rights issues around the world, such as Sudan or Myanmar, and went on to criticise the termination of Special Rapporteurs to Cuba and Belarus, as well as procedural irregularities that prevented member-states from voting on the issues; a similar critique was issued by the Canadian representative. On September 2007, the US Senate voted to cut off funding to the council.

The United States joined with Australia, Canada, Israel, and three other countries in opposing the UNHRC's draft resolution on working rules citing continuing misplaced focus on Israel at the expense of action against countries with poor human-rights records. The resolution passed 154–7 in a rare vote forced by Israel including the support of France, the United Kingdom, and China, although it is usually approved through consensus. United States Ambassador to the United Nations, Zalmay Khalilzad, spoke about the "council's relentless focus during the year on a single country – Israel," contrasting that with failure "to address serious human rights violations taking place in other countries such as Zimbabwe, DPRK (North Korea), Iran, Belarus and Cuba." Khalilzad said that aside from condemnation of the crackdown of the Burmese anti-government protests, the council's past year was "very bad" and it "had failed to fulfill our hopes."

On June 6, 2008, Human Rights Tribune announced that the United States had withdrawn entirely from the UNHRC, and had withdrawn its observer status.

The United States boycotted the Council during the George W. Bush administration, but reversed its position on it during the Obama administration. Beginning in 2009 however, with the United States taking a leading role in the organization, American commentators began to argue that the UNHRC was becoming increasingly relevant.

On March 31, 2009, the administration of Barack Obama announced that it would reverse the country's previous position and would join the UNHRC; New Zealand has indicated its willingness not to seek election to the council to make room for the United States to run unopposed along with Belgium and Norway for the WEOG seats.

On June 19, 2018, U.S. Secretary of State Mike Pompeo and U.S. Ambassador to the United Nations Nikki Haley announced that the United States, under President Donald Trump, was pulling out of the United Nations Human Rights Council, accusing the council being "hypocritical and self-serving" and, in the past, Haley had accused it of "chronic anti-Israel bias." "When the Human Rights Council treats Israel worse than North Korea, Iran, and Syria, it is the Council itself that is foolish and unworthy of its name. It is time for the countries who know better to demand changes," Haley said in a statement at the time, pointing to the council's adoption of five resolutions condemning Israel. "The United States continues to evaluate our membership in the Human Rights Council. Our patience is not unlimited."

Position of Sri Lanka

Sri Lanka has come under increasing scrutiny with a draft resolution tabled by the United States on reconciliation and accountability in Sri Lanka.

The draft resolution, which is under review, notes, "with concern that the LLRC report does not adequately address serious allegations of violations of international law, 1. Calls on the Government of Sri Lanka to implement the constructive recommendations in the LLRC report and take all necessary additional steps to fulfill its relevant legal obligations and commitment to initiate credible and independent actions to ensure justice, equity, accountability and reconciliation for all Sri Lankans, 2. Requests that the Government of Sri Lanka present a comprehensive action plan as expeditiously as possible detailing the steps the Government has taken and will take to implement the LLRC recommendations and also to address alleged violations of international law, 3. Encourages the Office of the High Commissioner for Human Rights and relevant special procedures to provide, and the Government of Sri Lanka to accept, advice and technical assistance on implementing those steps and requests the Office of the High Commissioner for Human Rights to present a report to the Council on the provision of such assistance at its twenty-second session."

Sri Lankan Ambassador in Geneva Tamara Kunanayakam pointed out that 80% of the UNHRC's funding requirements are supplied by powerful nations such as the United States and its allies. Also, key positions in the UNHCR are mostly held by those who have served in the foreign services of such countries. Sri Lanka's position is that this fact is significantly detrimental to the impartiality of the UNHRC activities, especially when dealing with the developing world. As a result, Sri Lanka, along with Cuba and Pakistan, sponsored a resolution seeking transparency in funding and staffing the UNHRC, during its 19th session starting in February 2012. The resolution passed on 4 April 2012.

CRITICISM

The United States boycotted the UNHRC during the George W. Bush administration to protest the repressive states among its membership, but in March 2009 the Obama administration reversed that position and decided to "reengage" and seek a seat on the UNHRC. Beginning in 2009 however, with the United States taking a leading role in the organization, American commentators began to argue that the UNHRC was becoming increasingly relevant.

The UNHRC has been criticised for the repressive states among its membership. Countries with questionable human rights records that have served on the UNHRC include Cuba, Saudi Arabia, China and Russia.

Agenda Item 7

The UNHRC has been accused of anti-Israel bias, a particular criticism being its focus on the Israeli-Palestinian conflict at each session as Agenda Item 7. The Council voted on 30 June 2006 to make a review of alleged human rights abuses by Israel a permanent feature of every council session:

Item 7. *Human rights situation in Palestine and other occupied Arab territories*

- Human rights violations and implications of the Israeli occupation of Palestine and other occupied Arab territories
- Right to self-determination of the Palestinian people

None of the nine other items deals exclusively with a specific conflict. The Council's special rapporteur on the Israeli–Palestinian conflict is the council's only expert mandate with no year of expiry. The rapporteur between 2008 and 2014, Richard A. Falk, has been accused of being antisemitic.

UN Secretaries General Kofi Annan and Ban Ki-moon, former president of the council Doru Costea, the European Union, Canada, and the United States have accused the UNHRC of focusing disproportionately on the Israeli–Palestinian conflict.

Boris Johnson, Britain's Foreign Secretary on 18 June 2018 said: "We share the view that a dedicated agenda item focused solely on Israel and the occupied Palestinian territories is disproportionate and damaging to the cause of peace."

On 19 June 2018, the United States pulled out of the UNHRC accusing the body of bias against Israel and a failure to hold human rights abusers accountable. At UNHRC's 38th Session, on 2 July 2018, Western nations held a *de facto* boycott of Agenda Item 7 by not speaking to the item.

Bloc voting

A Reuters report in 2008 said that independent human rights groups say that UNHRC is being controlled by some Middle East and African nations, supported by China, Russia and Cuba, which protect each other from criticism. This drew criticism from the UN Secretary General Ban Ki-moon at the ineffectiveness of UNHRC, saying it had fallen short of its obligations. He urged countries to 'drop rhetoric' and rise above "partisan posturing and regional divides" and get on with defending people around the world. This follows criticism since UNHRC was set up, where Israel has been condemned on most occasions and other incidences in the world such as Darfur, Tibet, North Korea, and Zimbabwe have not been discussed at the council.

Ban Ki-Moon also appealed for the United States to fully join the council and play a more active role. The UNHRC was criticized in 2009 for adopting a resolution submitted by Sri Lanka praising its conduct in Vanni that year, ignoring pleas for an international war crimes investigation.

Addressing criticism of CHR

On 18 June 2007, one year after holding its first meeting, the UNHRC adopted its *Institution-building package*, to guide it in its future work. Among its elements was the Universal Periodic Review, which assesses the human rights situations in all 193 UN Member States. Another element is an *Advisory Committee*, which serves as the UNHRC's *think tank* and provides it with expertise and advice on thematic human rights issues. A further element is a *Complaint procedure*, which allows individuals and organizations to bring complaints about human rights violations to the attention of the Council.

In the election of members, the General Assembly takes into account each candidate state's contribution to the promotion and protection of human rights, as well as their voluntary pledges and commitments in this regard. The General Assembly, by a two-thirds majority, can suspend the rights and privileges of any Council member that it decides has persistently committed gross and systematic violations of human rights during its term of membership. The resolution establishing the UNHRC states that "members elected to the Council shall uphold the highest standards in the promotion and protection of human rights".

21

The United Nations Children's Fund (UNICEF)

The United Nations Children's Fund (UNICEF) is a United Nations (UN) program headquartered in New York City that provides humanitarian and developmental assistance to children and mothers in developing countries. It is a member of the United Nations Development Group.

The United Nations International Children's Emergency Fund was created by the United Nations General Assembly on 11 December 1946, to provide emergency food and healthcare to children in countries that had been devastated by World War II. The Polish physician Ludwik Rajchman is widely regarded as the founder of UNICEF and served as its first chairman from 1946. On Rajchman's suggestion, the American Maurice Pate was appointed its first executive director, serving from 1947 until his death in 1965. In 1950, UNICEF's mandate was extended to address the long-term needs of children and women in developing countries everywhere. In 1953 it became a permanent part of the United Nations System, and the words "international" and "emergency" were dropped from the organization's name, making it simply the United Nations Children's Fund, retaining the original acronym, "UNICEF".

UNICEF relies on contributions from governments and private donors. UNICEF's total income for 2015 was US$5,009,557,471 . Governments contribute two-thirds of the organization's resources. Private groups and individuals contribute the rest through national committees. It is estimated that 92 per cent of UNICEF revenue is distributed to program services. UNICEF's programs emphasize developing community-level services to promote the health and well-being of children. UNICEF was awarded the Nobel Peace Prize in 1965 and the Prince of Asturias Award of Concord in 2006.

Most of UNICEF's work is in the field, with a presence in 190 countries and territories. UNICEF's network of over 150 country offices, headquarters and other offices, and 34 National Committees carry out UNICEF's mission through programs developed with host governments. Seven regional offices provide technical assistance to country offices as needed.

UNICEF's Supply Division is based in Copenhagen and serves as the primary point of distribution for such essential items as vaccines, antiretroviral medicines for children and mothers with HIV, nutritional supplements, emergency shelters, family reunification, and educational supplies. A 36-member executive board establishes policies, approves programs and oversees administrative and financial plans. The executive board is made up of government representatives who are elected by the United Nations Economic and Social Council, usually for three-year terms.

GOVERNANCE

Each country office carries out UNICEF's mission through a unique program of cooperation developed with the host government. This five-year program focuses on practical ways to realize the rights of children and women. Regional offices guide this work and provide technical assistance to country offices as needed. Overall management and administration of the organization takes place at headquarters, where global policy on children is shaped. Guiding and monitoring all of UNICEF's work is a 36-member Executive Board made up of government representatives. They establish policies, approve programs and decide on administrative and financial plans and budgets. Executive Board's work is coordinated by the Bureau, comprising the President and four Vice-Presidents, each officer representing one of the five regional groups. These five officers, each one representing one of the five regional groups, are elected by the Executive Board each year from among its members, with the presidency rotating among the regional groups on an annual basis.

As a matter of custom, permanent members of the Security Council do not serve as officers of the Executive Board. Office of the Secretary of the Executive Board supports and services the Executive Board. It is responsible for maintaining an effective relationship between the Executive Board and the UNICEF secretariat, and helps to organize the field visits of the Executive Board.

UNICEF NATIONAL COMMITTEES

There are national committees in 34 [industrialized] countries, each established as an independent local non-governmental organization. The national committees raise funds from the public sector.

UNICEF is funded entirely by voluntary contributions, and the National Committees collectively raise around one-third of UNICEF's annual income. This comes through contributions from corporations, civil society organizations around six million individual donors worldwide.

PROMOTION AND FUNDRAISING

In the United States, Canada and some other countries, UNICEF is known for its "Trick-Or-Treat for UNICEF" program in which children collect money for UNICEF from the houses they trick-or-treat on Halloween night, sometimes instead of candy.

UNICEF is present in 191 countries and territories around the world, but not involved in nine others (Bahamas, Brunei, Cyprus, Latvia, Liechtenstein, Malta, Mauritius, Monaco, and Singapore).

Many people in developed countries first hear about UNICEF's work through the activities of one of the 36 National Committees for UNICEF. These non-governmental organizations(NGO) are primarily responsible for fundraising, selling UNICEF greeting cards and products, creating private and public partnerships, advocating for children's rights, and providing other support. The US Fund for UNICEF is the oldest of the national committees, founded in 1947.

On 19 April 2007, Grand Duchess Maria Teresa of Luxembourg was appointed UNICEF Eminent Advocate for Children, in which role she has visited Brazil (2007), China (2008), and Burundi (2009).

In 2009, the British retailer Tesco used "Change for Good" as advertising, which is trademarked by UNICEF for charity usage but not for commercial or retail use. This prompted the agency to say, "it is the first time in Unicef's history that a commercial entity has purposely set out to capitalise on one of our campaigns and subsequently damage an income stream which several of our programs for children are dependent on". They went on to call on the public "who have children's welfare at heart, to consider carefully who they support when making consumer choices".

SPONSORSHIP

On 7 September 2006, an agreement between UNICEF and the Spanish Catalan association football club FC Barcelona was reached whereby the club would donate 1.5 million Euros per year to the organization for five years. As part of the agreement, FC Barcelona would wear the UNICEF logo on the front of their uniforms in the colour yellow (as seen in the picture on the right of Lionel Messi). This was the first time a football club sponsored an organization rather than the other way around. It was also the first time in FC Barcelona's history that they have had another organization's name across the front of their uniform. In 2016, the team signed a new four-year sponsorship deal with UNICEF guaranteeing the organization £ 1.58million per year and free advertising.

In January 2007 UNICEF struck a partnership with Canada's national tent pegging team. The team was officially re-flagged as "UNICEF Team Canada", and its riders wear UNICEF's logo in competition, and team members promote and raise funds for UNICEF's campaign against childhood HIV-AIDS. When the team became the 2008 tent pegging world champions, UNICEF's flag was raised alongside the Canadian flag at the games, the first time in the history of international Grand Prix equestrian competition that a non-state flag has flown over the medal podium.

The Swedish club Hammarby IF followed the Spanish and Canadian lead on 14 April 2007, also raising funds for UNICEF and displaying the UNICEF name on their sportswear. The Danish football club Brøndby IF participated in a similar arrangement from 2008 to 2013.

In 2007, Race driver Jacques Villeneuve has occasionally placed the UNICEF logo on the #27 Bill Davis Racing pickup truck in the NASCARCraftsman Truck Series.

Australian A-League club Sydney FC announced they would also enter into a partnership with UNICEF raising funds for children in the Asia-Pacific region, and would also display the UNICEF logo for the remainder of the 2011-12 A-League season.

Race driver Jacques Villeneuve has occasionally placed the UNICEF logo on the #27 Bill Davis Racing pickup truck in the NASCAR Craftsman Truck Series.

In Botswana, UNICEF has funded the development of new state-of-the-art HIV/AIDS education for every schoolchild in Botswana from nonprofit organization TeachAIDS.

UNICEF announced a landmark partnership with Scottish club Rangers F.C. UNICEF partnered with the Rangers Charity Foundation and pledged to raise £300,000 by 2011.

In 2010, UNICEF created a partnership with Phi Iota Alpha, making them the first Greek Lettered Organization UNICEF has ever worked with. In 2011, Phi Iota Alpha raised over $20,000 for the Tap Project and the Trick or Treats for UNICEF Campaign.

In 2013, they agreed a contract with Greek association football champions Olympiacos F.C. who will show the organization's logo on the front of their shirts.

UNICEF Kid Power

Started in 2015, Kid Power is a division of UNICEF that was created as an effort to involve kids in helping other kids in need. UNICEF Kid Power developed the world's first Wearable for Good, called Kid Power Bands, which is a kids' fitness tracker bracelet that connects to a smartphone app. The app lets users complete missions, which counts total steps and awards points. The points then unlock funding from partners, which is then used by UNICEF to deliver lifesaving packets of therapeutic food to severely malnourished children around the world.

Trick-or-Treat UNICEF box

Since 1950, when a group of children in Philadelphia, Pennsylvania, donated $17 which they received on Halloween to help post-World War II victims, the Trick-or-Treat UNICEF box has become a tradition in North America during the fall. These small orange boxes are handed to children at schools and other locations before 31 October. As of 2012, the Trick-or-Treat for UNICEF campaign has collected approximately CAD 91 million in Canada and over US$167 million in the U.S.

Cartoons for Children's Rights

In 1994, UNICEF held a summit encouraging animation studios around the world to create individual animated spots demonstrating the international rights of children. Cartoons for Children's Rights is the collection of animated shorts based on UNICEF's Convention on the Rights of the Child.

Corporate partnership

To raise money to support its Education and Literacy Programs, UNICEF collaborates with companies worldwide – international as well as small- and medium-sized businesses.

Since 2004, the organization has been supported by Montblanc, working collaboratively to help the world's children getting better access to education.

According to *Vaccine News Daily*, Merck & Co. partnered with UNICEF in June 2013 to decrease maternal mortality, HIV and tuberculosis prevalence in South Africa. Merck's program "Merck for Mothers" will give US$500 million worldwide for programs that improve health for expectant mothers and their children.

In May 2010, Crucell N.V. announced an additional US$110 million award from UNICEF to supply its pentavalent pediatric vaccine Quinvaxem to the developing world.

Corporate Social Responsibility

UNICEF works directly with companies to improve their business practices, bringing them in line with obligations under international law, and ensuring that they respect children's rights in the realms of the marketplace, workplace, and the community. In 2012, UNICEF worked with Save the Children and The United Nations Global Compact to develop the Children's Rights and Business Principles and now these guidelines form the basis UNICEF's advice to companies. UNICEF works with companies seeking to improve their social sustainability by guiding them through a due diligence process where issues throughout their supply chain, such as child labor, can be identified and actions to ratify them are put in place.

Girl Star

The Girl Star project is a series of films which documents stories of girls from the most disadvantaged communities across five northern states in India who, through via education, have managed to break socio-economic constraints to make a success of their lives and become self-sufficient. These young women have grown to become role models in their communities, inspiring younger girls to go to school and continue their education. They have selected professions from the most conventional such as teaching and nursing, to the most unconventional like archery, bee-keeping, scrap management, often entering what has traditionally been a man's domain. Girl Star is also one of UNICEF's most known projects.

Kids United

Kids United is a French musical group of four children (six children when the group was formed) born between 2000 and 2007. It has been created to support UNICEF campaigns and is sponsored by Hélène Ségara and Corneille, two Francophone singers. The first album Un monde meilleur (A better world) was launched on Universal Children's Day in 2015, it received gold certification in France.[1] The second album Tout le bonheur du monde was even certified 2x platinum.

CELEBRITY AMBASSADORS

UNICEF Ambassadors are leaders in the entertainment industry, representing the fields of film, television, music, sports and beyond. They help raise awareness of the needs of children, and use their talent and fame to fund-raise, advocate, and educate on behalf of UNICEF.

Facilities

UNICEF World Warehouse

The old UNICEF World Warehouse is a large facility in Denmark, which hosts UNICEF deliverable goods as well as co-hosts emergency goods for United Nations High Commissioner for Refugees (UNHCR) and the International Federation of Red Cross and Red Crescent Societies (IFRC). Until 2012 the facilities was a 25,000m warehouse at Marmormolen in Copenhagen. With construction of a 45,000m UN City that is to house all UN activities in Copenhagen under one roof, the warehouse service has been relocated to outer parts of the Freeport of Copenhagen. The facility houses the UNICEF Supply Division which manages strategic transport hubs in Dubai, Panama and Shanghai. The warehouse contains a variety of items, e.g., food supplements, water purification tablets, dietary and vitamin supplements, and the "School in a box" (illustrated above).

UNICEF Innocenti Research Centre

The UNICEF Innocenti Research Centre in Florence, Italy, was established in 1988. The centre, formally known as the International Child Development Centres, has as its prime objectives to improve international understanding of issues relating to children's rights, to promote economic policies that advance the cause of children, and to help facilitate the full implementation of the United Nations Convention on the Rights of the Child in industrialized and developing countries.

The program for 2006–2008 was approved by UNICEF Executive Board in September 2005.

It reaffirms the centre's academic freedom and the focus of IRC's research on knowledge gaps, emerging questions and sensitive issues which are relevant to the realization of children's rights, in developing and industrialized countries. It capitalizes on IRC's role as an interface between UNICEF field experience, international experts, research networks and policy makers and is designed to strengthen the centre's institutional collaboration with regional academic and policy institutions, pursuing the following goals:

- Generation and communication of strategic and influential knowledge on issues affecting children and the realization of their rights;
- Knowledge exchange and brokering;
- Support to UNICEF's advocacy, policy's and program development in support of the Millennium Agenda
- Securing and strengthening the centre's institutional and financial basis.

Three interrelated strategies guide the achievement of these goals:

- Evidence-based analysis drawing on quantitative and qualitative information, the application of appropriate methodologies, and the development of recommendations to assess and inform advocacy and policy action.

- Enhanced partnerships with research and policy institutions and development actors, globally and at regional level, in developing and industrialized countries.
- Communication and leveraging of research findings and recommendations to support policy development and advocacy initiatives through strategic dissemination of studies and contribution to relevant events and fora.

CONTROVERSIES

Adoption program

UNICEF has a policy preferring orphanages only be used as temporary accommodation for children when there is no alternative. UNICEF has historically opposed the creation of large-scale, permanent orphanages for children, preferring instead to find children places in their (extended) families and communities, wherever possible. This has led UNICEF to be skeptical of international adoption efforts as a solution to child care problems in developing countries; UNICEF has preferred to see children cared for in their birth countries rather than be adopted by foreign parents.

Major news outlets such as US News have asserted UNICEF's intervention that on giving large cash payments to developing countries can lead to a cessation of international adoptions until all of its recommendations are in place, and have even labeled UNICEF a "villain" for the extent of its negative impact on orphans. Elizabeth Bartholet and Paulo Barrozo have written in this context, encouraging adoption protocols to take on a more child-centric viewpoint.

Infant mortality

One concern is that the child mortality rate has not decreased in some areas as rapidly as had been planned, especially in Sub-Saharan Africa, where in 2013 "the region still has the highest child mortality rate: 92 deaths per 1000 live births". and that "Globally, nearly half of under-five deaths are attributable to undernutrition."

In 2005, Richard Horton editor-in-chief of *The Lancet*, editorialized that "over 60% of these deaths were and remain preventable" and that the coverage levels for these interventions are "appallingly low in the 42 countries that account for 90% of child deaths".

NSA surveillance

Documents released by Edward Snowden in December 2013 showed that UNICEF was among the surveillance targets of British and American intelligence agencies.

22

United Nations Educational, Scientific and Cultural Organization (UNESCO)

The United Nations Educational, Scientific and Cultural Organization (UNESCO; French: *Organisation des Nations unies pour l'éducation, la science et la culture*) is a specialized agency of the United Nations (UN) based in Paris. Its declared purpose is to contribute to peace and security by promoting international collaboration through educational, scientific, and cultural reforms in order to increase universal respect for justice, the rule of law, and human rights along with fundamental freedom proclaimed in the United Nations Charter. It is the successor of the League of Nations' International Committee on Intellectual Cooperation.

UNESCO has 195 member states and ten associate members. Most of its field offices are "cluster" offices covering three or more countries; national and regional offices also exist.

UNESCO pursues its objectives through five major programs: education, natural sciences, social/human sciences, culture and communication/information. Projects sponsored by UNESCO include literacy, technical, and teacher-training programs, international science programs, the promotion of independent media and freedom of the press, regional and cultural history projects, the promotion of cultural diversity, translations of world literature, international cooperation agreements to secure the world's cultural and natural heritage (World Heritage sites) and to preserve human rights, and attempts to bridge the worldwide digital divide. It is also a member of the United Nations Development Group.

UNESCO's aim is "to contribute to the building of peace, the eradication of poverty, sustainable development and intercultural dialogue through education, the sciences, culture, communication and information". Other priorities of the organization include attaining quality Education For All and lifelong learning, addressing emerging social and ethical challenges, fostering cultural diversity, a culture of peace and building inclusive knowledge societies through information and communication.

The broad goals and objectives of the international community—as set out in the internationally agreed development goals, including the Millennium Development Goals (MDGs)—underpin all UNESCO strategies and activities.

HISTORY

UNESCO and its mandate for international cooperation can be traced back to a League of Nations resolution on 21 September 1921, to elect a Commission to study feasibility. On 18 December 1925, the International Bureau of Education (IBE) began work as a non-governmental organization in the service of international educational development. However, the onset of World War II largely interrupted the work of these predecessor organizations.

After the signing of the Atlantic Charter and the Declaration of the United Nations, the Conference of Allied Ministers of Education (CAME) began meetings in London which continued between 16 November 1942 to 5 December 1945. On 30 October 1943, the necessity for an international organization was expressed in the Moscow Declaration, agreed upon by China, the United Kingdom, the United States and the USSR. This was followed by the Dumbarton Oaks Conference proposals of

9 October 1944. Upon the proposal of CAME and in accordance with the recommendations of the United Nations Conference on International Organization (UNCIO), held in San Francisco in April–June 1945, a United Nations Conference for the establishment of an educational and cultural organization (ECO/CONF) was convened in London 1–16 November 1945 with 44 governments represented. A prominent figure in the initiative for UNESCO was Rab Butler, the Minister of Education for the United Kingdom. At the ECO/CONF, the Constitution of UNESCO was introduced and signed by 37 countries, and a Preparatory Commission was established. The Preparatory Commission operated between 16 November 1945, and 4 November 1946—the date when UNESCO's Constitution came into force with the deposit of the twentieth ratification by a member state.

The first General Conference took place between 19 November to 10 December 1946, and elected Dr. Julian Huxley to Director-General. The Constitution was amended in November 1954 when the General Conference resolved that members of the Executive Board would be representatives of the governments of the States of which they are nationals and would not, as before, act in their personal capacity. This change in governance distinguished UNESCO from its predecessor, the CICI, in how member states would work together in the organization's fields of competence. As member states worked together over time to realize UNESCO's mandate, political and historical factors have shaped the organization's operations in particular during the Cold War, the decolonization process, and the dissolution of the USSR.

Among the major achievements of the organization is its work against racism, for example through influential statements on race starting with a declaration of anthropologists (among them was Claude Lévi-Strauss) and other scientists in 1950 and concluding with the 1978 Declaration on Race and Racial Prejudice. In 1956, the Republic of South Africa withdrew from UNESCO claiming that some of the organization's publications amounted to "interference" in the country's "racial problems."

South Africa rejoined the organization in 1994 under the leadership of Nelson Mandela.

UNESCO's early work in the field of education included the pilot project on fundamental education in the Marbial Valley, Haiti, started in 1947. This project was followed by expert missions to other countries, including, for example, a mission to Afghanistan in 1949. In 1948, UNESCO recommended that Member States should make free primary education compulsory and universal. In 1990, the World Conference on Education for All, in Jomtien, Thailand, launched a global movement to provide basic education for all children, youths and adults. Ten years later, the 2000 World Education Forum held in Dakar, Senegal, led member governments to commit to achieving basic education for all by 2015.

ACTIVITIES

UNESCO implements its activities through the five programme areas: education, natural sciences, social and human sciences, culture, and communication and information.

1. Education: UNESCO supports research in comparative education; and provide expertise and fosters partnerships to strengthen national educational leadership and the capacity of countries to offer quality education for all. This includes the

- UNESCO Chairs, an international network of 644 UNESCO Chairs, involving over 770 institutions in 126 countries.
- Environmental Conservation Organisation
- Convention against Discrimination in Education adopted in 1960
- Organization of the International Conference on Adult Education (CONFINTEA) in an interval of 12 years
- Publication of the Education for All Global Monitoring Report
- Publication of the Four Pillars of Learning seminal document

- UNESCO ASPNet, an international network of 8,000 schools in 170 countries.

UNESCO does not accredit institutions of higher learning.

2. UNESCO also issues public statements to educate the public:

- Seville Statement on Violence: A statement adopted by UNESCO in 1989 to refute the notion that humans are biologically predisposed to organised violence.

3. Designating projects and places of cultural and scientific significance, such as:

- Global Geoparks Network
- Biosphere reserves, through the Programme on Man and the Biosphere (MAB), since 1971
- City of Literature; in 2007, the first city to be given this title was Edinburgh, the site of Scotland's first circulating library. In 2008, Iowa City, Iowa became the City of Literature.
- Endangered languages and linguistic diversity projects
- Masterpieces of the Oral and Intangible Heritage of Humanity
- Memory of the World International Register, since 1997
- Water resources management, through the International Hydrological Programme (IHP), since 1965
- World Heritage sites
- World Digital Library

4. Encouraging the "free flow of ideas by images and words" by:

- Promoting freedom of expression, including freedom of the press and freedom of information legislation, through the Division of Freedom of Expression and Media Development, including the International Programme for the Development of Communication
- Promoting the safety of journalists and combatting impunity for those who attack them, through coordination of the UN Plan of Action on the Safety of Journalists and the Issue of Impunity

- Promoting universal access to and preservation of information and open solutions for sustainable development through the Knowledge Societies Division, including the Memory of the World Programme and Information for All Programme
- Promoting pluralism, gender equality and cultural diversity in the media
- Promoting Internet Universality and its principles, that the Internet should be (I) human Rights-based, (ii) Open, (iii) Accessible to all, and (iv) nurtured by Multi-stakeholderparticipation (summarized as the acronym R.O.A.M.)
- Generating knowledge through publications such as *World Trends in Freedom of Expression and Media Development*, the UNESCO Series on Internet Freedom, and the Media Development Indicators, as well as other indicator-based studies.

5. Promoting events, such as:
   - International Decade for the Promotion of a Culture of Peace and Non-Violence for the Children of the World: 2001–2010, proclaimed by the UN in 1998
   - World Press Freedom Day, 3 May each year, to promote freedom of expression and freedom of the press as a basic human right and as crucial components of any healthy, democratic and free society.
   - Criança Esperança in Brazil, in partnership with Rede Globo, to raise funds for community-based projects that foster social integration and violence prevention.
   - International Literacy Day
   - International Year for the Culture of Peace
   - Health Education for Behavior Change program in partnership with the Ministry of Education of Kenya which was financially supported by the Government of Azerbaijan to promote health education among 10-19-year-old young people who live in informal camp in Kibera, Nairobi. The project was carried out between September 2014 - December 2016.

6. Founding and funding projects, such as:
   - Migration Museums Initiative: Promoting the establishment of museums for cultural dialogue with migrant populations.
   - UNESCO-CEPES, the European Centre for Higher Education: established in 1972 in Bucharest, Romania, as a de-centralized office to promote international co-operation in higher education in Europe as well as Canada, USA and Israel. *Higher Education in Europe* is its official journal.
   - Free Software Directory: since 1998 UNESCO and the Free Software Foundation have jointly funded this project cataloguing free software.
   - FRESH Focussing Resources on Effective School Health.
   - OANA, Organization of Asia-Pacific News Agencies
   - International Council of Science
   - UNESCO Goodwill Ambassadors
   - ASOMPS, Asian Symposium on Medicinal Plants and Spices, a series of scientific conferences held in Asia
   - Botany 2000, a programme supporting taxonomy, and biological and cultural diversity of medicinal and ornamental plants, and their protection against environmental pollution
   - The UNESCO Collection of Representative Works, translating works of world literature both to and from multiple languages, from 1948 to 2005
   - GoUNESCO, an umbrella of initiatives to make heritage fun supported by UNESCO, New Delhi Office

The UNESCO transparency portal has been designed to enable public access to information regarding Organization's activities, such as its aggregate budget for a biennium, as well as links to relevant programmatic and financial documents. These two distinct sets of information are published on the IATI registry, respectively based on the IATI Activity Standard and the IATI Organization Standard.

There have been proposals to establish two new UNESCO lists. The first proposed list will focus on movable cultural heritage such as artifacts, paintings, and biofacts. The list may include cultural objects, such as the Jômon Venus of Japan, the Mona Lisa of France, the Gebel el-Arak Knife of Egypt, The Ninth Wave of Russia, the Seated Woman of Çatalhöyükof Turkey, the David (Michelangelo) of Italy, the Mathura Herakles of India, the Manunggul Jar of the Philippines, the Crown of Baekje of South Korea, The Hay Wain of the United Kingdom and the Benin Bronzes of Nigeria. The second proposed list will focus on the world's living species, such as the Komodo Dragon of Indonesia, the Panda of China, the Bald eagle of North American countries, the Aye-aye of Madagascar, the Asiatic Lion of India, the Kakapo of New Zealand, and the Mountain tapir of Colombia, Ecuador and Peru.

Media

UNESCO and its specialized institutions issue a number of magazines. *The UNESCO Courier* magazine states its mission to "promote UNESCO's ideals, maintain a platform for the dialogue between cultures and provide a forum for international debate." Since March 2006 it is available online, with limited printed issues. Its articles express the opinions of the authors which are not necessarily the opinions of UNESCO. As of 2016, the latest issue posted was October–December 2011.

In 1950, UNESCO initiated the quarterly review *Impact of Science on Society* (also known as *Impact*) to discuss the influence of science on society. The journal ceased publication in 1992. UNESCO also published museum international quarterly from the year 1948.

INTERNATIONAL DAYS OBSERVED AT UNESCO

International Days

Date	Name
27 January	International Day of Commemoration in Memory of the Victims of the Holocaust

13 February	World Radio Day
21 February	International Mother Language Day
8 March	International Women's Day
20 March	International Francophonie Day
21 March	International Day of Nowruz
21 March	World Poetry Day
21 March	International Day for the Elimination of Racial Discrimination
22 March	World Day for Water
23 April	World Book and Copyright Day
30 April	International Jazz Day
3 May	World Press Freedom Day
21 May	World Day for Cultural Diversity for Dialogue and Development
22 May	International Day for Biological Diversity
25 May	Africa Day / Africa Week
5 June	World Environment Day
8 June	World Oceans Day
17 June	World Day to Combat Desertification and Drought
9 August	International Day of the World's Indigenous People
12 August	International Youth Day
23 August	International Day for the Remembrance of the Slave Trade and its Abolition
8 September	International Literacy Day
15 September	International Day of Democracy
21 September	International Day of Peace
28 September	International Day for the Universal Access to Information
2nd October	International Day of Non-Violence
5th October	World Teachers' Day
2nd Wed in October	International Day for Disaster Reduction
17 October	International Day for the Eradication of Poverty
20 October	World Statistics Day

27 October	World Day for Audiovisual Heritage
2 November	International Day to End Impunity for Crimes Against Journalists
10 November	World Science Day for Peace and Development
3rd Thursday in November	World Philosophy Day
16 November	International Day for Tolerance
19 November	International Men's Day
25 November	International Day for the Elimination of Violence against Women
29 November	International Day of Solidarity with the Palestinian People
1 December	World AIDS Day
10 December	Human Rights Day
18 December	International Migrants Day

The World Beatles Day is celebrated on January 16. This holiday was approved by UNESCO in 2001. The list of UNESCO does not contain such date, because the members of The Beatles are alive. The event is not very known in a result. In the same time, UNESCO claims that this date is only joke to check statistics.

MEMBER STATES

UNESCO counts 195 member states and 10 associate members. Some members are not independent states and some members have additional National Organizing Committees from some of their dependent territories. UNESCO state parties are the United Nations member states (except Liechtenstein), Cook Islands, Niue, and the State of Palestine. The USA and Israel plan to leave UNESCO on 31 December 2018 over purported anti-Israel bias.

GOVERNING BODIES

Director-General

There has been no elected UNESCO Director-General from

Southeast Asia, South Asia, Central and North Asia, Middle East, North Africa, East Africa, Central Africa, South Africa, Australia-Oceania, and South America since inception.

The Director-Generals of UNESCO came from West Europe (5), Central America (1), North America (2), West Africa (1), East Asia (1), and East Europe (1). Out of the 11 Director-Generals since inception, women have held the position only twice. Qatar, the Philippines, and Iran are proposing for a Director-General bid by 2021 or 2025.

There have never been a Middle Eastern or Southeast Asian UNESCO Director-General since inception. The ASEAN bloc and some Pacific and Latin American nations support the possible bid of the Philippines, which is culturally Asian, Oceanic, and Latin. Qatar and Iran, on the other hand, have fragmented support in the Middle East. Egypt, Israel, and Madagascar are also vying for the position but have yet to express a direct or indirect proposal. Both Qatar and Egypt lost in the 2017 bid against France.

The list of the Directors-General of UNESCO since its establishment in 1946 is as follows:

Audrey Azoulay	France	2017–present
Irina Bokova	Bulgaria	2009–2017
Koïchiro Matsuura	Japan	1999–2009
Federico Mayor Zaragoza	Spain	1987–99
Amadou-Mahtar M'Bow	Senegal	1974–87
René Maheu	France	1961–74; acting 1961
Vittorino Veronese	Italy	1958–61
Luther Evans	United States	1953–58
John Wilkinson Taylor	United States	acting 1952–53
Jaime Torres Bodet	Mexico	1948–52
Julian Huxley	United Kingdom	1946–48

General Conference

This is the list of the sessions of UNESCO General Conference held since 1946:

Session	Location	Year	Chaired by	from
39th	Paris	2017	Zohour Alaoui	Morocco
38th	Paris	2015	Stanley Mutumba Simataa	Namibia
37th	Paris	2013	Hao Ping	China
36th	Paris	2011	Katalin Bogyay	Hungary
35th	Paris	2009	Davidson Hepburn	Bahamas
34th	Paris	2007	George N. Anastassopoulos	Greece
33rd	Paris	2005	Musa Bin Jaafar Bin Hassan	Oman
32nd	Paris	2003	Michael Omolewa	Nigeria
31st	Paris	2001	Ahmad Jalali	Iran
30th	Paris	1999	Jaroslava Moserová	Czech Republic
29th	Paris	1997	Eduardo Portella	Brazil
28th	Paris	1995	Torben Krogh	Denmark
27th	Paris	1993	Ahmed Saleh Sayyad	Yemen
26th	Paris	1991	Bethwell Allan Ogot	Kenya
25th	Paris	1989	Anwar Ibrahim	Malaysia
24th	Paris	1987	Guillermo Putzeys Alvarez	Guatemala
23rd	Sofia	1985	Nikolai Todorov	Bulgaria
22nd	Paris	1983	Saïd Tell	Jordan
4th	Paris	1982		
21st	Belgrade	1980	Ivo Margan	Yugoslavia
20th	Paris	1978	Napoléon LeBlanc	Canada
19th	Nairobi	1976	Taaita Toweett	Kenya
18th	Paris	1974	Magda Jóború	Hungary
3rd	Paris	1973		
17th	Paris	1972	Toru Haguiwara	Japan
16th	Paris	1970	Atilio Dell'Oro Maini	Argentina
15th	Paris	1968	William Eteki Mboumoua	Cameroon
14th	Paris	1966	Bedrettin Tuncel	Turkey
13th	Paris	1964	Norair Sisakian	Soviet Union
12th	Paris	1962	Paulo de Berrêdo Carneiro	Brazil
11th	Paris	1960	Akale-Work Abte-Wold	Ethiopia
10th	Paris	1958	Jean Berthoin	France
9th	N. Delhi	1956	Abul Kalam Azad	India

8th	Monte-video	1954	Justino Zavala Muñiz	Uruguay
2nd	Paris	1953		
7th	Paris	1952	Sarvepalli Radhakrishnan	India
6th	Paris	1951	Howland H. Sargeant	United States
5th	Florence	1950	Stefano Jacini	Italy
4th	Paris	1949	Edward Ronald Walker	Australia
1st	Paris	1948		
3rd	Beirut	1948	Hamid Bey Frangie	Lebanon
2nd	Mexico	1947	Manuel Gual Vidal	Mexico
1st	Paris	1946	Léon Blum	France

OFFICES

The Garden of Peace, UNESCO headquarters, Paris. Donated by the Government of Japan, this garden was designed by American-Japanese sculptor artist Isamu Noguchi in 1958 and installed by Japanese gardener Toemon Sano.

UNESCO headquarters are located at Place de Fontenoy in Paris, France. UNESCO's field offices across the globe are categorized into four primary office types based upon their function and geographic coverage: cluster offices, national offices, regional bureaus and liaison offices.

Field offices by region

The following list of all UNESCO Field Offices is organized geographically by UNESCO Region and identifies the members states and associate members of UNESCO which are served by each office.

Africa

- Abidjan – National Office to Côte d'Ivoire
- Abuja – National Office to Nigeria
- Accra – Cluster Office for Benin, Côte d'Ivoire, Ghana, Liberia, Nigeria, Sierra Leone and Togo
- Addis Ababa – Liaison Office with the African Union and with the Economic Commission for Africa

- Bamako – Cluster Office for Burkina Faso, Guinea, Mali and Niger
- Brazzaville – National Office to the Republic of the Congo
- Bujumbura – National Office to Burundi
- Dakar – Regional Bureau for Education in Africa and Cluster Office for Cape Verde, Gambia, Guinea-Bissau, and Senegal
- Dar es Salaam – Cluster Office for Comoros, Madagascar, Mauritius, Seychelles and Tanzania
- Harare – Cluster Office for Botswana, Malawi, Mozambique, Zambia and Zimbabwe
- Juba – National Office to South Sudan
- Kinshasa – National Office to the Democratic Republic of the Congo
- Libreville – Cluster Office for the Republic of the Congo, Democratic Republic of the Congo, Equatorial Guinea, Gabon and Sao Tome and Principe
- Maputo – National Office to Mozambique
- Nairobi – Regional Bureau for Sciences in Africa and Cluster Office for Burundi, Djibouti, Eritrea, Kenya, Rwanda, Somalia, South Sudan and Uganda
- Windhoek – National Office to Namibia
- Yaoundé – Cluster Office to Cameroon, Central African Republic and Chad

Arab States

- Amman – National Office to Jordan
- Beirut – Regional Bureau for Education in the Arab States and Cluster Office to Lebanon, Syria, Jordan, Iraq and Palestine
- Cairo – Regional Bureau for Sciences in the Arab States and Cluster Office for Egypt, Libya and Sudan
- Doha – Cluster Office to Bahrain, Kuwait, Oman, Qatar, Saudi Arabia, United Arab Emirates and Yemen

- Iraq – National Office for Iraq (currently located in Amman, Jordan)
- Khartoum – National Office to Sudan
- Manama - Arab Regional Centre for World Heritage
- Rabat – Cluster Office to Algeria, Mauritania, Morocco and Tunisia
- Ramallah – National Office to the Palestinian Territories

Asia and Pacific

- Apia – Cluster Office to Australia, Cook Islands, Fiji, Kiribati, Marshall Islands, Federated States of Micronesia, Nauru, New Zealand, Niue, Palau, Papua New Guinea, Samoa, Solomon Islands, Tonga, Tuvalu, Vanuatu and Tokelau (Associate Member)
- Bangkok – Regional Bureau for Education in Asia and the Pacific and Cluster Office to Thailand, Burma, Laos, Singapore and Vietnam
- Beijing – Cluster Office to North Korea, Japan, Mongolia, the People's Republic of China and South Korea
- Dhaka – National Office to Bangladesh
- Hanoi – National Office to Vietnam
- Islamabad – National Office to Pakistan
- Jakarta – Regional Bureau for Sciences in Asia and the Pacific and Cluster Office to the Philippines, Brunei, Indonesia, Malaysia, and East Timor
- Manila - National Office to the Philippines
- Kabul – National Office to Afghanistan
- Kathmandu – National Office to Nepal
- New Delhi – Cluster Office to Bangladesh, Bhutan, India, Maldives, Nepal and Sri Lanka
- Phnom Penh – National Office to Cambodia
- Tashkent – National Office to Uzbekistan
- Tehran – Cluster Office to Afghanistan, Iran, Pakistan and Turkmenistan

Europe and North America

- Almaty – Cluster Office to Kazakhstan, Kyrgyzstan, Tajikistan and Uzbekistan

- Brussels – Liaison Office to the European Union and its subsidiary bodies in Brussels
- Geneva – Liaison Office to the United Nations in Geneva
- New York City – Liaison Office to the United Nations in New York
- Moscow – Cluster Office to Armenia, Azerbaijan, Belarus, Moldova and Russia
- Venice – Regional Bureau for Sciences and Culture in Europe

Latin America and the Caribbean

- Brasilia – National Office to Brazil
- Guatemala City – National Office to Guatemala
- Havana – Regional Bureau for Culture in Latin America and the Caribbean and Cluster Office to Cuba, Dominican Republic, Haiti and Aruba
- Kingston – Cluster Office to Antigua and Barbuda, Bahamas, Barbados, Belize, Dominica, Grenada, Guyana, Jamaica, Saint Kitts and Nevis, Saint Lucia, Saint Vincent and the Grenadines, Suriname and Trinidad and Tobago as well as the associate member states of British Virgin Islands, Cayman Islands, Curaçao and Sint Maarten
- Lima – National Office to Peru
- Mexico City – National Office to Mexico
- Montevideo – Regional Bureau for Sciences in Latin America and the Caribbean and Cluster Office to Argentina, Brazil, Chile, Paraguay and Uruguay
- Port-au-Prince – National Office to Haiti
- Quito – Cluster Office to Bolivia, Colombia, Ecuador and Venezuela
- San José – Cluster Office to Costa Rica, El Salvador, Guatemala, Honduras, Mexico, Nicaragua and Panama
- Santiago de Chile – Regional Bureau for Education in Latin America and the Caribbean and National Office to Chile

CONTROVERSIES

New World Information and Communication order

UNESCO has been the centre of controversy in the past, particularly in its relationships with the United States, the United Kingdom, Singapore and the former Soviet Union. During the 1970s and 1980s, UNESCO's support for a "New World Information and Communication Order" and its MacBride report calling for democratization of the media and more egalitarian access to information was condemned in these countries as attempts to curb freedom of the press. UNESCO was perceived as a platform for communists and Third World dictators to attack the West, in contrast to accusations made by the USSR in the late 1940s and early 1950s. In 1984, the United States withheld its contributions and withdrew from the organization in protest, followed by the United Kingdom in 1985. Singapore withdrew also at the end of 1985, citing rising membership fees. Following a change of government in 1997, the UK rejoined. The United States rejoined in 2003, followed by Singapore on 8 October 2007.

Israel

Israel was admitted to UNESCO in 1949, one year after its creation. Israel has maintained its membership since 1949. In 2010, Israel designated the Cave of the Patriarchs, Hebronand Rachel's Tomb, Bethlehem as National Heritage Sites and announced restoration work, prompting criticism from the United States and protests from Palestinians. In October 2010, UNESCO's Executive Board voted to declare the sites as "al-Haram al-Ibrahimi/Tomb of the Patriarchs" and "Bilal bin Rabah Mosque/Rachel's Tomb" and stated that they were "an integral part of the occupied Palestinian Territories" and any unilateral Israeli action was a violation of international law. UNESCO described the sites as significant to "people of the Muslim, Christian and Jewish traditions", and accused Israel of highlighting only the Jewish character of the sites. Israel in turn accused UNESCO of "detach[ing] the Nation of Israel from its heritage", and accused it of being politically motivated. The Rabbi of the Western Wall claimed that Rachel's tomb had not previously been declared a holy Muslim site. Israel partially suspended ties with UNESCO. Israeli Deputy Foreign Minister Danny Ayalon declared that the resolution was a "part of Palestinian escalation".Zevulun Orlev, chairman of the Knesset Education and Culture Committee, referred to the resolutions as an attempt to undermine the mission of UNESCO as a scientific and cultural organization that promotes cooperation throughout the world.

On 28 June 2011, UNESCO's World Heritage Committee, at Jordan's insistence, censured Israel's decision to demolish and rebuild the Mughrabi Gate Bridge in Jerusalem for safety reasons. Israel stated that Jordan had signed an agreement with Israel stipulating that the existing bridge must be dismantled for safety reasons; Jordan disputed the agreement, saying that it was only signed under U.S. pressure. Israel was also unable to address the UNESCO committee over objections from Egypt.

In January 2014, days before it was scheduled to open, UNESCO Director-General, Irina Bokova, "indefinitely postponed" and effectively cancelled an exhibit created by the Simon Wiesenthal Center entitled "The People, The Book, The Land: The 3,500-year relationship between the Jewish people and the Land of Israel." The event was scheduled to run from 21 January through 30 January in Paris. Bokova cancelled the event after representatives of Arab states at UNESCO argued that its display would "harm the peace process".The author of the exhibition, Professor Robert Wistrich of the Hebrew University's Vidal Sassoon International Center for the Study of Anti-Semitism, called the cancellation an "appalling act," and characterized Bokova's decision as "an arbitrary act of total cynicism and, really, contempt for the Jewish people and its history." UNESCO amended the decision to cancel the exhibit within the year, and it quickly achieved popularity and was viewed as a great success.

Occupied Palestine Resolution

On 13 October 2016, UNESCO passed a resolution on East Jerusalem that condemned Israel for "aggressions" by Israeli police and soldiers and "illegal measures" against the freedom of worship and Muslims' access to their holy sites, while also recognizing Israel as the occupying power. Palestinian leaders welcomed the decision. While the text acknowledged the "importance of the Old City of Jerusalem and its walls for the three monotheistic religions", it referred to the sacred hilltop compound in Jerusalem's Old City only by its Muslim name "Al-Haram al-Sharif", Arabic for Noble Sanctuary. In response, Israel denounced the UNESCO resolution for its omission of the words "Temple Mount" or "Har HaBayit," stating that it denies Jewish ties to the key holy site. After receiving criticism from numerous Israeli politicians and diplomats, including Benjamin Netanyahu and Ayelet Shaked, Israel froze all ties with the organization. The resolution was condemned by Ban ki-Moon and the Director-General of UNESCO, Irina Bokova, who said that Judaism, Islam and Christianity have clear historical connections to Jerusalem and "to deny, conceal or erase any of the Jewish, Christian or Muslim traditions undermines the integrity of the site. Al-Aqsa Mosque is also Temple Mount, whose Western Wall is the holiest place in Judaism." It was also rejected by the Czech Parliament which said the resolution reflects a "hateful anti-Israel sentiment", and hundreds of Italian Jews demonstrated in Rome over Italy's abstention. On 26 October, UNESCO approved a reviewed version of the resolution, which also criticized Israel for its continuous "refusal to let the body's experts access Jerusalem's holy sites to determine their conservation status." Despite containing some softening of language following Israeli protests over a previous version, Israel continued to denounce the text. The resolution refers to the site Jews and Christians refer to as the Temple Mount, or Har HaBayit in Hebrew, only by its Arab name — a significant semantic decision also adopted by UNESCO's executive board, triggering condemnation from Israel and its allies. U.S. Ambassador Crystal Nix Hines stated: "This item should have been defeated. These politicized and one-sided resolutions are damaging the credibility of UNESCO."

In October 2017, the United States and Israel announced they would withdraw from the organization, citing in-part anti-Israel bias.

PRODUCTS OR SERVICES

- UNESDOC – Contains over 146,000 UNESCO documents in full text published since 1945 as well as metadata from the collections of the UNESCO Library and documentation centres in field offices and institutes.

Information processing tools

UNESCO develops, maintains and disseminates, free of charge, two interrelated software packages for database management (CDS/ISIS [not to be confused with UK police software package ISIS]) and data mining/statistical analysis (IDAMS).

- CDS/ISIS – a generalised information storage and retrieval system. The Windows version may run on a single computer or in a local area network. The JavaISIS client/server components allow remote database management over the Internet and are available for Windows, Linux and Macintosh. Furthermore, GenISIS allows the user to produce HTML Web forms for CDS/ISIS database searching. The ISIS_DLL provides an API for developing CDS/ISIS based applications.
- OpenIDAMS – a software package for processing and analysing numerical data developed, maintained and disseminated by UNESCO. The original package was proprietary but UNESCO has initiated a project to provide it as open-source.
- IDIS – a tool for direct data exchange between CDS/ISIS and IDAMS

23

World Tourism Organization

The World Tourism Organization (UNWTO) is the United Nations agency responsible for the promotion of responsible, sustainable and universally accessible tourism. It is the leading international organization in the field of tourism, which promotes tourism as a driver of economic growth, inclusive development and environmental sustainability and offers leadership and support to the sector in advancing knowledge and tourism policies worldwide. It serves as a global forum for tourism policy issues and a practical source of tourism knowledge. It encourages the implementation of the Global Code of Ethics for Tourism to maximize the contribution of tourism to socio-economic development, while minimizing its possible negative impacts, and is committed to promoting tourism as an instrument in achieving the United Nations Sustainable Development Goals (SDGs), geared towards eliminating poverty and fostering sustainable development and peace worldwide.

UNWTO generates market knowledge, promotes competitive and sustainable tourism policies and instruments, fosters tourism education and training, and works to make tourism an effective tool for development through technical assistance projects in over 100 countries around the world.

UNWTO's membership includes 156 countries, 6 territories and over 500 affiliate members representing the private sector, educational institutions, tourism associations and local tourism authorities. Its headquarters are located in Madrid.

ORGANIZATIONAL AIMS

The objectives of the UNWTO are to promote and develop sustainable tourism to contribute to economic development, international understanding, peace, prosperity and universal respect for, and observance of, human rights and fundamental freedoms for all, without distinction as to race, sex, language or religion. In pursuing these aims, UNWTO pays particular attention to the interests of developing countries in the field of tourism.

HISTORY

The origin of UNWTO stems back to 1920 when the International Congress of Official Tourist Traffic Associations (ICOTT) was formed at The Hague. Some articles from early volumes of the Annals of Tourism Research, claim that the UNWTO originated from the International Union of Official Tourist Publicity Organizations (IUOTPO), although the UNWTO states that the ICOTT became the International Union of Official Tourist Publicity Organizations first in 1934.

Following the end of the Second World War and with international travel numbers increasing, the IUOTPO restructured itself into the International Union of Official Travel Organizations (IUOTO). A technical, non-governmental organization, the IUOTO was made up of a combination of national tourist organizations, industry and consumer groups. The goals and objectives of the IUOTO were to not only promote tourism in general but also to extract the best out of tourism as an international trade component and as an economic development strategy for developing nations.

Towards the end of the 1960s, the IUOTO realized the need for further transformation to enhance its role on an international level. The 20th IUOTO general assembly in Tokyo, 1967, declared the need for the creation of an intergovernmental body with the necessary abilities to function on an international level in cooperation with other international agencies, in particular the United Nations. Throughout the existence of the IUOTO, close ties had been established between the organization and the United Nations (UN) and initial suggestions had the IUOTO becoming part of the UN. However, following the circulation of a draft convention, consensus held that any resultant intergovernmental organization should be closely linked to the UN but preserve its "complete administrative and financial autonomy".

It was on the recommendations of the UN that the formation of the new intergovernmental tourism organization was based. Resolution 2529 of the XXIVth UN general assembly stated:

In 1970, the IUOTO general assembly voted in favor of forming the World Tourism Organization (WTO). Based on statutes of the IUOTO, and after ratification by the prescribed 51 states, the WTO came into operation on November 1, 1974.

Most recently, at the fifteenth general assembly in 2003, the WTO general council and the UN agreed to establish the WTO as a specialized agency of the UN. The significance of this collaboration, WTO Secretary-General Mr. Francesco Frangialli claimed, would lie in "the increased visibility it gives the WTO, and the recognition that will be accorded to [it]. Tourism will be considered on an equal footing with other major activities of human society".

In 2004, UNWTO established the World Committee on Tourism Ethics, the implementation body for the Global Code of Ethics for Tourism (adopted in 1999). The Committee, whose members are elected due to their professional capacities rather than their nationalities or country affiliations, promotes and disseminates the Code and evaluates and monitors the implementation of its principles. The Committee was permanently headquartered in Rome in 2008.

Taleb Rifai of Jordan became UNWTO Secretary-General in 2010. Under his mandate the Organization introduced Hotel Energy Solutions (HES), a web-based tool to help hotels reduce their carbon footprint whilst increasing profits, worked with Members on research on benefits of easing visa facilitation, and forecast that in 2030 the number of international tourists would reach 1.8 billion. It reached 1 billion in 2012.

Taleb Rifai's mandate has seen focus placed on the people involved in the tourism experience. Two publications under the title "Tourism Stories" were released compiling research and interviews with individuals working in tourism from around the world.

In 2014 the 69th session of the United Nations General Assembly adopted by consensus the resolution entitled 'Promotion of sustainable tourism, including ecotourism, for poverty eradication and environment protection'. This was followed in 2015 by the adoption of 2017 as the International Year of Sustainable Tourism for Development, "Recognizing the important role of sustainable tourism as a positive instrument towards the eradication of poverty, the protection of the environment, the improvement of quality of life and the economic empowerment of women and youth and its contribution to the three dimensions of sustainable development, especially in developing countries". The United Nations also recognized tourism in the Sustainable Development Goals, approved at the same 70th Session of its General Assembly. Tourism is included as a target in Goals 8, 12 and 14.

MEMBERS

As of July 2017, membership of the UNWTO included 156 states, six territories (Flemish Community (1997), Puerto Rico (2002), Aruba (1987), Hong Kong (1999), Macau (1981), Madeira (1995)), and two permanent observers (Holy See (1979), Palestine (1999)). Seventeen state members have withdrawn from the organization for different periods in the past: Australia, Bahamas, Bahrain, Belgium, Canada, Costa Rica, El Salvador, Grenada, Honduras, Kuwait, Latvia, Malaysia, Myanmar, Panama, Philippines, Qatar, Thailand, United Kingdom and Puerto Rico (as an associate member). The Netherland Antilles was an associate member before its dissolution.

Non-members are: Antigua and Barbuda, Barbados, Belgium, Belize, Comoros, Denmark, Dominica, Estonia,

Finland, Grenada, Guyana, Iceland, Ireland, Kiribati, Latvia, Liechtenstein, Luxembourg, Marshall Islands, Micronesia, Nauru, New Zealand, Palau, Saint Kitts and Nevis, Saint Lucia, Saint Vincent and the Grenadines, Samoa, Singapore, Solomon Islands, Somalia, South Sudan, Suriname, Sweden, Tonga, Tuvalu, United Kingdom, United States.

The United Arab Emirates (UAE) rejoined the organization in May 2013, 26 years after having left UNWTO.

Additionally, and uniquely for a United Nations specialized agency, UNWTO has over 500 affiliate members, representing the private sector, educational institutions, tourism associations and local tourism authorities, non-governmental entities with specialised interests in tourism, and commercial and non-commercial bodies and associations with activities related to the aims of UNWTO or falling within its competence.

SECRETARIES-GENERAL

Name	Years of Tenure
Robert Lonati	1975–1985
Willibald Pahr	1986–1989
Antonio Enriquez Savignac	1990–1996
Francesco Frangialli	1997–2009
Taleb Rifai	2010–2017
Zurab Pololikashvili	2018–

STRUCTURE

General Assembly

The General Assembly is the principal gathering of the World Tourism Organization. It meets every two years to approve the budget and programme of work and to debate topics of vital importance to the tourism sector. Every four years it elects a Secretary-General. The General Assembly is composed of full members and associate members. Affiliate members and representatives of other international organizations participate as observers. The World Committee on Tourism Ethics is a subsidiary organ of the General Assembly.

Executive Council

The Executive Council is UNWTO's governing board, responsible for ensuring that the Organization carries out its work and adheres to its budget.

It meets at least twice a year and is composed of members elected by the General Assembly in a ratio of one for every five full members.

As host country of UNWTO's headquarters, Spain has a permanent seat on the Executive Council. Representatives of the associate members and affiliate members participate in Executive Council meetings as observers.

Committees

Specialized committees of UNWTO members advise on management and programme content. These include: the Programme Committee, the Committee on Budget and Finance, the Committee on Statistics and the Tourism Satellite Account, the Committee on Market and Competitiveness, the Sustainable Development of Tourism Committee, the World Committee on Tourism Ethics, the Committee on Poverty Reduction and the Committee for the Review of applications for affiliate membership.

Secretariat

The Secretariat is responsible for implementing UNWTO's programme of work and serving the needs of members and affiliate members. The group is led by Secretary-General, Taleb Rifai of Jordan, who supervises about 110 full-time staff at UNWTO's Madrid headquarters. The Secretariat also includes a regional support office for Asia-Pacific in Osaka, Japan, financed by the Japanese Government, and a liaison office in Geneva as UNWTO's representation to the UN System, the World Trade Organization, and other diplomatic organizations in Switzerland.

Official languages

The official languages of UNWTO are Arabic, English, French, Russian and Spanish.

PUBLICATIONS

UNWTO research concluded that, by improving visa processes and entry formalities, G20 economies could boost their international tourist numbers by 122 million, tourism exports by US$2016 billion and employment by 5 million.

The Organization's latest UNWTO Visa Openness Report, published in 2016, shows the highest ever percentage of international tourists not requiring a visa to travel - 39% compared with 23% in 2008. The report concluded that the 30 countries whose citizens were least affected by visa restrictions in 2015 were (based on the data compiled by the UNWTO, based on information from national official institutions):

24

United Nations Industrial Development Organization (UNIDO)

The United Nations Industrial Development Organization (UNIDO), French/Spanish acronym ONUDI, is a specialized agency in the United Nations system, headquartered in Vienna, Austria. The Organization's primary objective is the promotion and acceleration of industrial development in developing countries and countries with economies in transition and the promotion of international industrial cooperation. It is also a member of the United Nations Development Group.

OVERVIEW

UNIDO believes that competitive and environmentally sustainable industry has a crucial role to play in accelerating economic growth, reducing poverty and achieving the Millennium Development Goals. The Organization therefore works towards improving the quality of life of the world's poor by drawing on its combined global resources and expertise in the following three interrelated thematic areas:

- Poverty reduction through productive activities;
- Trade capacity-building; and
- Energy and environment.

Activities in these fields are strictly aligned with the priorities of the current United Nations Development Decade and related multilateral declarations, and reflected in the long-term vision statement, business plan and mid-term programme frameworks of UNIDO.

In order to fulfill these objectives, UNIDO

- assists developing countries in the formulation of development, institutional, scientific and technological policies and programmes in the field of industrial development;
- analyzes trends, disseminates information and coordinates activities in their industrial development;
- acts as a forum for consultations and negotiations directed towards the industrialization of developing countries; and
- provides technical cooperation to developing countries for implementing their development plans for sustainable industrialization in their public, cooperative and private sectors.

UNIDO thus works largely in developing countries, with governments, business associations and individual companies. The Organization's "service modules" are Industrial Governance and Statistics, Investment and Technology Promotion, Industrial Competitiveness and Trade, Private sector Development, Agro-Industries, Sustainable energy and Climate Change, Montreal Protocol, and Environmental management.

UNIDO was established as a UN programme in 1966 with headquarters in Vienna, Austria, and became a specialized agency of the United Nations in 1985. In 2004, UNIDO established the UNIDO Goodwill Ambassador programme.

In 2009, UNIDO created a new flagship publication, *Making It: Industry for Development.*

FACTS AND FIGURES

As of January 2017, 168 States are Members of UNIDO. The organization employs some 670 staff at Headquarters and in field representations in about 80 countries, and draws on the services of some 2,800 international and national experts (approx. 50% from developing countries) annually, who work in project assignments throughout the world.

The estimated total volume of UNIDO operations for the biennium 2012–2013 is €460 million, the value of technical cooperation delivery in 2012 amounted to $189.2 million.

UNIDO's headquarters are located at the Vienna International Centre, the UN campus that also hosts the International Atomic Energy Agency, the United Nations Office on Drugs and Crime and the Preparatory Commission for the Comprehensive Test Ban Treaty Organization.

THEMATIC FOCUS

UNIDO explains its thematic focus areas as follows:

Poverty reduction through productive activities

As a primary driver of economic growth and employment creation, the private sector has a central role in poverty reduction and the achievement of the Millennium Development Goals. Private sector-led industrial development makes a significant contribution to bringing about the much needed structural changes that can set the economies of poor countries on a path of sustained economic growth. UNIDO's services therefore focus on encouraging the creation of decent employment and income to overcome poverty. Now, these services are customized for developing countries and range from industrial policy advice to entrepreneurship and SME development, and from investment and technology promotion to the provision of rural energy for productive uses.

Trade capacity-building

The technical ability of developing countries to produce competitive exportable products that comply with international standards is key to their successful participation in international trade. UNIDO is one of the largest providers of trade-related development services, offering focused and neutral advice and technical cooperation in the areas of competitiveness, industrial modernization and upgrading, compliance with international trade standards, testing methods and metrology.

Energy and environment

Fundamental changes in the way societies produce and consume are indispensable for achieving global sustainable development and fighting climate change. UNIDO therefore promotes sustainable patterns of industrial consumption and production to de-link the processes of economic growth and environmental degradation. UNIDO is a leading provider of services for improved industrial energy efficiency and the promotion of renewable sources of energy. It also assists developing countries in implementing multilateral environmental agreements and in simultaneously reaching their economic and environmental goals.

UNIDO organizes the Global Renewable Energy Forum in October 2009.

HISTORICAL BACKGROUND

Origins

The origins of the United Nations Industrial Development Organization (UNIDO) can be traced to a series of studies on a programme of rapid industrialization of developing countries that the United Nations Secretariat carried out during the early 1950s at the request of the United Nations Economic and Social Council (ECOSOC). These studies culminated in a programme of work on industrialization and productivity prepared by the United Nations Secretary-General in 1956 and endorsed the next year by ECOSOC and the General Assembly. At that time, it was first suggested that a special body to deal with the problems of industrialization be established, whose political organs could relieve ECOSOC and the General Assembly of the detailed consideration of those questions and whose secretariat could carry out more substantive work than the existing Industry Section of the Bureau of Economic Affairs within the Secretariat. The Industry Section of the Secretariat became a branch in 1959, and in 1962 it became the *Industrial Development Centre*, headed by a *Commissioner for Industrial Development.*

Special organ of the United Nations

In the aftermath, proposals for further institutionalizing industrial development-related issues within the UN were considered by various advisory groups and inter-organizational organs. Subsequently, the United Nations General Assembly created the UNIDO in November 1966 as a special organ of the United Nations. In January 1967, the Organization was formally established with Headquarters in Vienna, Austria. Compared to the Industrial Development Centre, UNIDO's creation was intended to broaden the work of its predecessor. Besides normative activities, such as acting as a forum for discussions, analytical functions and information dissemination, UNIDO became involved in operational activities, i.e. in technical co-operation activities.

Conversion into a specialized agency

The setting up of UNIDO as a special organ had nonetheless been a compromise solution. The developing countries (the Group of 77) had in the first instance promoted the idea of a specialized agency with its own political decision-making governing bodies and autonomy in budgetary matters. The same position was advocated by several high-level expert groups and intergovernmental committees during the following years. In the context of the General Assembly's adoption of the *Declaration and Programme of Action on the Establishment of a New International Economic Order and of the Charter of Economic Rights and Duties of States*, UNIDO's second General Conference, held in 1975 in Lima, Peru, adopted the *Lima Declaration on Industrial Development and Cooperation.* For the first time, industrial development objectives were quantified internationally — the Lima Target anticipated the developing countries to attain a twenty-five per cent share of world industrial production by the year of 2000. As part of the institutional arrangements of the Lima Plan of Action, and with a view to assisting in the establishment of a New International Economic Order, it was recommended to the General Assembly that UNIDO be converted into a specialized agency.

An intergovernmental committee prepared a draft constitution, which was adopted in Vienna in 1979. However, the objections and doubts of industrialized countries as to the necessity of a specialized agency contributed to delaying the ratification process. In order to ensure that the new organization would start up with a membership including substantially all significant States, the General Assembly, by resolutions adopted in 1982 and 1984, called for a series of formal consultations among prospective Member States, which eventually led to a general agreement that the new UNIDO Constitution should enter into force. All necessary formal requirements were fulfilled in 1985, and in December of the same year, UNIDO finally became the sixteenth Specialized Agency of the United Nations with Headquarters in Vienna.

Crisis and reform during the 1990s

During the subsequent years, UNIDO continuously expanded particularly its operational activities. However, several developments outside and inside the Organization led to a crisis, which reached a breaking point in 1997 when UNIDO faced the risk of closure: After the end of the Cold War and the triumph of the market economic system over the command economic system, and in view of the Washington Consensus that limited the role of industrial policy in economic development processes, some Member States felt that industrial development could be supported more effectively and efficiently by the private sector. As a result, Canada, the United States (UNIDO's then largest donor), and Australia subsequently withdrew from the Organization between 1993 and 1997. Simultaneously, the continued slowdown in the economies of some major industrialized countries as well as the financial turmoil of the 1997 Asian financial crisis caused multilateral development assistance to decline. In addition, a weak management structure and lack of focus and integration of UNIDO's activities contributed to aggravate the crisis.

UNIDO's Member States responded by adopting a stringent Business Plan on the Future Role and Functions of the Organization in June 1997. Activities laid out in the Business Plan are based on the clear comparative advantages of UNIDO, while avoiding overlap and duplication with other multilateral institutions. A key point was that activities should be integrated into packages of services, rather than being provided on a stand-alone basis. The Organization radically reformed itself on the basis of this business plan and streamlined its services, human and financial resources as well as internal processes during the following years.

Post-reform role

On the basis of sound finances and in a second wave of programmatic reforms in 2004, UNIDO further focused its activities and technical services directly responding to international development priorities. In an independent assessment of 23 international organizations against a large numbers of criteria, UNIDO was assessed 6th best overall and as best in the group of specialized agencies. In regard of the current UN Reform debate, it can be observed that UNIDO is actively contributing to UN system-wide coherence and cost efficiency.

GOVERNANCE

Membership

Members of the UN, or of UN specialized agencies, or of the IAEA, are eligible for membership with UNIDO. The process of becoming a Member of the Organization is achieved by becoming a party to the Constitution. Observer status is open, upon request, to those enjoying such status in the General Assembly of the United Nations, unless the UNIDO General Conference decides otherwise. The Conference has the authority to invite other observers to participate in the work of the Organization in accordance with the relevant rules of procedure and the provisions of the Constitution.

As of May 17th, 2018, 168 States are Members± of UNIDO, all of them being UN members. UNIDO Members are divided into four lists. List A consists of all UNIDO countries in the African + Asian Groups of UN (along with Israel, while excluding Cyprus and Japan). List B consists of all UNIDO countries in WEOG group of UN (along with Cyprus and Japan, and excluding Israel). List C consists of all UNIDO countries in GRULAC group of UN. List D consists of all UNIDO countries in the Eastern European group of UN.

The lists, originally defined in General Assembly resolution 2152 and the UNIDO Constitution serve to balance geographical distribution of member states' representation on the Industrial Development Board and the Programme and Budget Committee.

UNIDO is the one of the two UN specialized agencies where members are separated into groups while the other is IFAD. UNIDO List B, is similar to IFAD List A – which comprises primarily developed countries, while the set of the rest of UNIDO members is similar to the set of the rest of IFAD members – which comprise primarily developing countries.

The full lists are as follows:

List A (100 members): Afghanistan, Algeria, Angola, Bahrain, Bangladesh, Benin, Bhutan, Botswana, Burkina Faso, Burundi, Cambodia, Cameroon, Cape Verde, Central African Republic, Chad, China, Comoros, Congo, Ivory Coast, DR Congo, Djibouti, Egypt, Equatorial Guinea, Eritrea, Ethiopia, Fiji, Gabon, Gambia, Ghana, Guinea, Guinea-Bissau, India, Indonesia, Iran, Iraq, Israel, Jordan, Kazakhstan, Kenya, Kiribati, North Korea, South Korea, Kuwait, Kyrgyzstan, Laos, Lebanon, Lesotho, Liberia, Libya, Madagascar, Malawi, Malaysia, Maldives, Mali, Marshall Islands, Mauritania, Mauritius, Mongolia, Morocco, Mozambique, Myanmar, Namibia, Nepal, Niger, Nigeria, Oman, Pakistan, State of Palestine, Papua New Guinea, Philippines, Qatar, Rwanda,

Samoa, Sao Tome and Principe, Saudi Arabia, Senegal, Seychelles, Sierra Leone, Somalia, South Africa, Sri Lanka, Sudan, Swaziland, Syria, Tajikistan, Thailand, Timor-Leste, Togo, Tonga, Tunisia, Tuvalu, Uganda, United Arab Emirates, Tanzania, Turkmenistan, Uzbekistan, Vanuatu, Vietnam, Yemen, Zambia, Zimbabwe.

List B (21 members): Austria, Cyprus, Finland, Germany, Ireland, Italy, Japan, Luxembourg, Malta, Monaco, Netherlands , Norway, Spain, Sweden, Switzerland, Turkey.

List C (32 members): Argentina, Bahamas, Barbados, Belize, Bolivia, Brazil, Chile, Colombia, Costa Rica, Cuba, Dominica, Dominican Republic, Ecuador, El Salvador, Grenada, Guatemala, Guyana, Haiti, Honduras, Jamaica, Mexico, Nicaragua, Panama, Paraguay, Peru, Saint Kitts and Nevis, Saint Lucia, Saint Vincent and the Grenadines, Suriname, Trinidad and Tobago, Uruguay, Venezuela.

List D (20 members): Albania, Armenia, Azerbaijan, Belarus, Bosnia and Herzegovina, Bulgaria, Croatia, Czech Republic, Georgia, Hungary, Montenegro, Poland, Republic of Moldova, Romania, Russian Federation, Serbia, Slovakia (denounced, effective 31 December 2017), Slovenia, Macedonia, Ukraine.

Signatory states that have not finished their ratification procedures are: Antigua and Barbuda (1982).

Former UNIDO members are Australia (1985–97, List B), Belgium, (1985-2015, List B), Canada (1985–93, List B), France (1982–2014, List B), Lithuania (1991–2012, List D), New Zealand (1984–2013, List B), Portugal (1984–2014, List B), United Kingdom (1985–2012, List B), the United States (1985–96, List B), Belgium (1981–2015), Denmark (1985-2016, List B) and Greece (1985-2016, List B). Slovakia denounced the convention in December 2016 and will cease to be a UNIDO member on 31 December 2017.

The Holy See and the Sovereign Military Order of Malta have observer status with UNIDO.

Other UN member states that have not signed, ratified, or denounced the constitution are Andorra, Brunei, Estonia,

Iceland, Latvia, Liechtenstein, Micronesia, Nauru, Palau, San Marino, Singapore, Solomon Islands, and South Sudan.

Policy-making organs

The policy-making organs (or governing bodies) of UNIDO are based on their predecessors that were effective prior to UNIDO becoming a specialized agency. Thus, the General Conference, the Industrial Development Board (IDB) and the Programme and Budget Committee (PBC) are anchored in the Constitution.

Substantive decisions of the policy-making organs are generally taken by consensus. A vote takes place when no consensus can be reached or on specific request of a member of the policy-making organ

General Conference

The Conference is the highest policy-making organ of the Organization and consists of all Member States of UNIDO. It meets every two years and approves the programme and budgets, establishes the scale assessments for regular budget expenditures for the forthcoming biennium and, every second time, appoints the Director-General for a period of four years.

Industrial Development Board (IDB)

The Board meets once in Conference years and twice in other years, and consists of 53 Member States of the Organization that are elected for a four-year term. It acts as a preparatory body for the Conference and reviews the implementation of the approved programme of work and of the corresponding regular and operational budgets for the forthcoming biennium. Among its other main functions, the Board recommends to the Conference a scale of assessments, as well as a candidate for the post of Director-General.

Programme and Budget Committee (PBC)

The Committee consists of 27 Member States of the Organization that are elected for a two-year term and meets at least once a year to consider, inter alia, the proposals of the Director-General for the programme of work and corresponding estimates for the regular and operational budgets.

Secretariat

The Secretariat of UNIDO is based in Vienna (Austria) and maintains representative offices in Brussels (Belgium), Geneva (Switzerland) and New York City (USA). As of 2013, UNIDO's organizational structure comprises The Office of the Director-General (ODG), the Programme Development and Technical Cooperation Division (PTC), the Office of the Deputy to the Director General (DDG), the Programme Support and General Management Division (PSM) as well as offices of Internal Oversight and Legal Services.

The current (2013) Director-General of UNIDO, Mr. Li Yong (China), was elected by Member States in June 2013.

COUNTRY LEVEL REPRESENTATION

Field representation

UNIDO's system of field representation includes four categories of offices:

- Regional offices, which cover the country of their location as well as a number of countries in the same region, in which the Organization assumes the status of a non-resident agency
- Country Offices, which cover their host country
- Focal point offices maintained within national governments
- UNIDO Desks in UNDP offices.

Technical offices at country level

In order to provide additional support to UNIDO's technical activities, different types of technical offices have been established. These include:

- *Investment and Technology Promotion Offices (ITPOs)*, which promote investment and technology flows to developing countries and countries with economies in transition, being financed by their host countries

- *International Technology Centres*, which act as catalysts for technology upgrading and assist in managing technology change
- In collaboration with the United Nations Environment Programme (UNEP), UNIDO set up a global network of *National Cleaner Production Centres (NCPCs)*, aiming at building national capacities in clean production technologies, fostering dialogue between industry and government and enhancing investments for transfer and development of environmentally sound technologies.
- UNIDO's *Industrial Subcontracting and Partnership Exchanges (SPX)* facilitate production linkages between small, medium and large manufacturing firms and link up with global markets and supply chain networks.
- UNIDO *Centres for South-South Cooperation* as part of a major UNIDO South-South cooperation initiative in several of the more advanced developing countries.

25

World Bank Group (WBG)

The World Bank Group (WBG) (French: *Groupe de la Banque mondiale*) is a family of five international organizations that make leveraged loans to developing countries. It is the largest and most well-known development bank in the world and is an observer at the United Nations Development Group. The bank is based in Washington, D.C. and provided around $61 billion in loans and assistance to "developing" and transition countries in the 2014 fiscal year. The bank's stated mission is to achieve the twin goals of ending extreme poverty and building shared prosperity. Total lending as of 2015 for the last 10 years through Development Policy Financing was approximately $117 billion. Its five organizations are the International Bank for Reconstruction and Development (IBRD), the International Development Association (IDA), the International Finance Corporation (IFC), the Multilateral Investment Guarantee Agency (MIGA) and the International Centre for Settlement of Investment Disputes (ICSID). The first two are sometimes collectively (and confusingly) referred to as the World Bank.

The World Bank's (the IBRD and IDA's) activities are focused on developing countries, in fields such as human development (e.g. education, health), agriculture and rural development (e.g. irrigation and rural services), environmental protection (e.g. pollution reduction, establishing and enforcing regulations), infrastructure (e.g. roads, urban regeneration, and electricity), large industrial construction projects, and governance (e.g. anti-corruption, legal institutions development). The IBRD and IDA provide loans at preferential rates to member countries, as well as grants to the poorest countries. Loans or grants for specific projects are often linked to wider policy changes in the sector or the country's economy as a whole. For example, a loan to improve coastal environmental management may be linked to development of new environmental institutions at national and local levels and the implementation of new regulations to limit pollution.

The World Bank has received various criticisms over the years and was tarnished by a scandal with the bank's then President Paul Wolfowitz and his aide, Shaha Riza, in 2007.

HISTORY

Founding

The WBG came into formal existence on 27 December 1945 following international ratification of the Bretton Woods agreements, which emerged from the United Nations Monetary and Financial Conference (1–22 July 1944). It also provided the foundation of the Osiander Committee in 1951, responsible for the preparation and evaluation of the World Development Report. Commencing operations on 25 June 1946, it approved its first loan on 9 May 1947 (US$250M to France for postwar reconstruction, in real terms the largest loan issued by the Bank to date).

MEMBERSHIP

All of the 193 UN members and Kosovo that are WBG members participate at a minimum in the IBRD. As of May 2016, all of them also participate in some of the other four organizations: IDA, IFC, MIGA, ICSID.,

WBG members by the number of organizations which they participate in:

1. only in IBRD: None
2. IBRD and one other organization: San Marino, Nauru, Tuvalu, Brunei

3. IBRD and two other organizations: Antigua and Barbuda, Suriname, Venezuela, Namibia, Marshall Islands, Kiribati
4. IBRD and three other organizations: India, Mexico, Belize, Jamaica, Dominican Republic, Brazil, Bolivia, Uruguay, Ecuador, Dominica, Saint Vincent and the Grenadines, Guinea-Bissau, Equatorial Guinea, Angola, South Africa, Seychelles, Libya, Somalia, Ethiopia, Eritrea, Djibouti, Bahrain, Qatar, Iran, Malta, Bulgaria, Poland, Russia, Belarus, Kyrgyzstan, Tajikistan, Turkmenistan, Thailand, Laos, Vietnam, Palau, Tonga, Vanuatu, Maldives, Bhutan, Myanmar
5. All five WBG organizations: the rest of the 138 WBG members

Non-members are: Andorra, Cuba, Liechtenstein, Monaco, State of Palestine, Vatican City, Taiwan, and North Korea.

ORGANIZATIONAL STRUCTURE

The World Bank Sign on the building

Together with four affiliated agencies created between 1957 and 1988, the IBRD is part of the World Bank Group. The Group's headquarters are in Washington, D.C. It is an international organization owned by member governments; although it makes profits, these profits are used to support continued efforts in poverty reduction.

Technically the World Bank is part of the United Nations system, but its governance structure is different: each institution in the World Bank Group is owned by its member governments, which subscribe to its basic share capital, with votes proportional to shareholding. Membership gives certain voting rights that are the same for all countries but there are also additional votes which depend on financial contributions to the organization. The President of the World Bank is nominated by the President of the United States and elected by the Bank's Board of Governors. As of 15 November 2009 the United States held 16.4% of total votes, Japan 7.9%, Germany 4.5%, the United Kingdom 4.3%, and France 4.3%. As changes to the Bank's Charter require an 85% super-majority, the US can block any major change in the Bank's governing structure.

World Bank Group agencies

The World Bank Group consists of

- the International Bank for Reconstruction and Development (IBRD), established in 1945, which provides debt financing on the basis of sovereign guarantees;
- the International Finance Corporation (IFC), established in 1956, which provides various forms of financing without sovereign guarantees, primarily to the private sector;
- the International Development Association (IDA), established in 1960, which provides concessional financing (interest-free loans or grants), usually with sovereign guarantees;
- the International Centre for Settlement of Investment Disputes (ICSID), established in 1965, which works with governments to reduce investment risk;
- the Multilateral Investment Guarantee Agency (MIGA), established in 1988, which provides insurance against certain types of risk, including political risk, primarily to the private sector.

The term "World Bank" generally refers to just the IBRD and IDA, whereas the term World Bank Group or WBG is used to refer to all five institutions collectively.

The World Bank Institute is the capacity development branch of the World Bank, providing learning and other capacity-building programs to member countries.

The IBRD has 189 member governments, and the other institutions have between 153 and 184 members. The institutions of the World Bank Group are all run by a Board of Governors meeting once a year. Each member country appoints a governor, generally its Minister of Finance. On a daily basis the World Bank Group is run by a Board of 25 Executive Directors to whom the governors have delegated certain powers. Each Director represents either one country (for the largest countries), or a group of countries. Executive Directors are appointed by their respective governments or the constituencies.

The agencies of the World Bank are each governed by their Articles of Agreement that serve as the legal and institutional foundation for all of their work.

The activities of the IFC and MIGA include investment in the private sector and providing insurance respectively.

Presidency

Traditionally, the Bank President has always been a U.S. citizen nominated by the President of the United States, the largest shareholder in the bank. The nominee is subject to confirmation by the Board of Governors, to serve for a five-year, renewable term.

Current President

On 16 April 2012, The World Bank announced that Jim Yong Kim would be its next President. Kim assumed office on 1 July 2012.

Independent Evaluation group

The Independent Evaluation Group (IEG) (formerly known as the Operations Evaluation Department (OED)) plays an important check and balance role in the World Bank. Similar in its role to the US Government's Government Accountability

Office (GAO), it is an independent unit of the World Bank that reports evaluation findings directly to the Bank's Board of Executive Directors. Caroline Heider is the Director-General, Evaluation, whose evaluations provide an objective basis for assessing the results of the Bank's work, and ensuring accountability of World Bank management to the member countries (through the World Bank Board) in the achievement of its objectives.

Extractive Industries Review

After longstanding criticisms from civil society of the Bank's involvement in the oil, gas, and mining sectors, the World Bank in July 2001 launched an independent review called the *Extractive Industries Review* (EIR – not to be confused with Environmental Impact Report). The review was headed by an "Eminent Person", Dr. Emil Salim (former Environment Minister of Indonesia). Dr. Salim held consultations with a wide range of stakeholders in 2002 and 2003. The EIR recommendations were published in January 2004 in a final report entitled "Striking a Better Balance". The report concluded that fossil fuel and mining projects do not alleviate poverty, and recommended that World Bank involvement with these sectors be phased out by 2008 to be replaced by investment in renewable energy and clean energy. The World Bank published its Management Response to the EIR in September 2004. following extensive discussions with the Board of Directors. The Management Response did not accept many of the EIR report's conclusions. However, the EIR served to alter the World Bank's policies on oil, gas and mining in important ways, as has been documented by the World Bank in a recent follow-up report. One area of particular controversy concerned the rights of indigenous peoples. Critics point out that the Management Response weakened a key recommendation that indigenous peoples and affected communities should have to provide 'consent' for projects to proceed – instead, there would be 'consultation'. Following the EIR process, the World Bank issued a revised Policy on Indigenous Peoples.

Impact evaluations

In recent years there has been an increased focus on measuring results of World Bank development assistance through impact evaluations. An impact evaluation assesses the changes in the well-being of individuals that can be attributed to a particular project, program or policy. Impact evaluations demand a substantial amount of information, time and resources. Therefore, it is important to select carefully the public actions that will be evaluated. One of the important considerations that could govern the selection of interventions (whether they be projects, programs or policies) for impact evaluation is the potential of evaluation results for learning. In general, it is best to evaluate interventions that maximize the possibility of learning from current poverty reduction efforts and provide insights for midcourse correction, as necessary.

Access to Information

The World Bank Policy on Access to Information sets forth a ground-breaking change in how the World Bank makes information available to the public. Now the public can get more information than ever before—information about projects under preparation, projects under implementation, analytic and advisory activities, and Board proceedings.

Over the past 15 years, the World Bank's policy on disclosing information has evolved gradually. Until now, the World Bank's approach has been to spell out what documents the World Bank discloses. The new World Bank Policy on Access to Information effective 1 July 2010, is a pivotal shift in the World Bank's approach to making information available to the public. Under the new policy, the World Bank will disclose any information in its possession that is not on a list of exceptions. This policy positions the World Bank as a leader in transparency and accountability among international institutions.

AIDS funding

The World Bank is a major source of funding for combating AIDS in poor countries. In the past six years, it has committed about $2 billion through grants, loans, and credits for programs to fight HIV/AIDS.

CRITICISM

A young World Bank protester in Jakarta, Indonesia.

The World Bank has long been criticized by a range of non-governmental organizations and academics, notably including its former Chief Economist Joseph Stiglitz, who is equally critical of the International Monetary Fund, the US Treasury Department, and US and other developed country trade negotiators. Critics argue that the so-called free market reform policies – which the Bank advocates in many cases – in practice are often harmful to economic development if implemented badly, too quickly ("shock therapy"), in the wrong sequence, or in very weak, uncompetitive economies. World Bank loan agreements can also force procurements of goods and services at uncompetitive, non free-market, prices.

In *Masters of Illusion: The World Bank and the Poverty of Nations* (1996), Catherine Caufield argues that the assumptions and structure of the World Bank operation ultimately harms developing nations rather than promoting them. In terms of assumption, Caufield first criticizes the highly homogenized and Western recipes of "development" held by the Bank. To the World Bank, different nations and regions are indistinguishable, and ready to receive the "uniform remedy of development". The danger of this assumption is that to attain even small portions of success, Western approaches to life are adopted and traditional economic structures and values are abandoned. A second assumption is that poor countries cannot modernize without money and advice from abroad.

A number of intellectuals in developing countries have argued that the World Bank is deeply implicated in contemporary modes of donor and NGO driven imperialism and that its intellectual contribution functions, primarily, to seek to blame the poor for their condition.

Defenders of the World Bank contend that no country is forced to borrow its money. The Bank provides both loans and grants. Even the loans are concessional since they are given to countries that have no access to international capital markets. Furthermore, the loans, both to poor and middle-income countries, are at below market-value interest rates. The World Bank argues that it can help development more through loans than grants, because money repaid on the loans can then be lent for other projects.

Criticism was also expressed towards the IFC and MIGA and their way of evaluating the social and environmental impact of their projects. Critics state that even though IFC and MIGA have more of these standards than the World Bank they mostly rely on private-sector clients to monitor their implementation and miss an independent monitoring institution in this context. This is why an extensive review of the institutions' implementation strategy of social and environmental standards is demanded.

Allegations of corruption

The World Bank's Integrity Vice Presidency (INT) is charged with investigation of internal fraud and corruption, including complaint intake, investigation and investigation reports.

Investments

The World Bank Group has also been criticized for investing in projects with human rights issues.

The Compliance Advisor/Ombudsman (CAO) criticized a loan given to the palm oil company Dinant by the World Bank after the 2009 Honduran coup d'état. There have been numerous killings of peasants in the region where Dinant was operating.

Other controversial investments include loans for the Chixoy Hydroelectric Dam in Guatemala while it was under military dictatorship, and a loan to Goldcorp (then Glamis Gold) for the construction of the Marlin Mine.

Bibliography

Alcock, A. *History of the International Labour Organization,* London, 1971.

Allchin, Bridget: *Origins of a Civilization: The Prehistory and Early Archaeology of South Asia.* New Delhi, New York: Viking, 1997.

Allison, Graham: *Nuclear Terrorism: The Ultimate Preventable Catastrophe,* New York: Times Books, 2004.

Arif. S.M.: *Islamic Fundamentalism and Jihad,* MD Pub, Delhi, 2010.

Ayesha Siddiqa-Agha: *Military Inc.: Inside Pakistan's Military Economy,* London: Pluto, 2007.

Bade, Klaus J.: *Migration in European History,* Oxford: Blackwell, 2003.

Barros, James. *The Corfu incident of 1923: Mussolini and the League of Nations,* Princeton UP, 2015.

Bendiner, Elmer. *A Time of Angels: The Tragi-comic History of the League of Nations,* 1975.

Bernard Wood: *Development Dimension of Conflict Prevention and Peace-building,* New York: UNDP,. 2003.

Borowy, Iris. *Coming to terms with world health: the League of Nations Health Organisation 1921–1946,* Peter Lang, 2009.

Briggs, Asa: *Iron Bridge to Crystal Palace: Impacet and Images of the Industrial Revolution.* London: 1979.

Bruce, Hoffman: *Inside Terrorism,* New York: Columbia University Press, 1998.

Burkman, Thomas W. *Japan and the League of Nations: Empire and world order, 1914–1938,* U of Hawaii Press, 2008.

Channon, John: *The Penguin Historical Atlas of Russia,* Penguin, 1995.

Chopra, Surendra and Kusum Lata Chadda: *Islamic Fundamentalism, Pakistan and the Muslim World* : Kanishka, Delhi, 2009.

Clavin, Patricia. *Securing the world economy: the reinvention of the League of Nations, 1920–1946,* Oxford UP, 2013.

Cowan, Ruth Schwartz: *A Social History of American Technology.* New York: Oxford University Press, 1996.

Curtin, Philip D.: *Cross-Cultural Trade in World History.* Cambridge, U.K.: Cambridge University Press, 1984.

Dittmer, L.: *The Strategic Triangle: An Elementary Game-Theoretical Analysis,* Cambridge, Cambridge University Press, 1981.

Elvin, Mark: *The Retreat of the Elephants: An Environmental History of China,* New Haven: Yale University Press, 2004.

Endres, A.; Fleming, G. *International Organizations and the Analysis of Economic Policy, 1919–1950,* Cambridge, 2002.

Ewing, K. *Britain and the ILO,* London, 1994.

Galenson, Walter. *The International Labor Organization: An American View,* Madison, 1981.

Jeevan Nair : *Encyclopaedia of Indian Government and Politics*, 2000.

Johnston, G.A. *The International Labour Organization: Its Work for Social and Economic Progress,* London, 1970.

Jones, W.H.: *The Government and Politics of India*, London, Hutchinson, 1971.

Kegan, K. : *Money and the Mechanism of Exchange,* MacMillan, London, 1890.

Kenneth C. Wheare: *Federal Government,* New York, Oxford University Press, 1953.

Knutsen T.: *A History of International Relations Theory*, Manchester University Press, Manchester, 1992.

Lawrence H. White: *The Theory of Monetary Institutions,* Oxford, Blackwell, 1999.

Leslie, J.: *Toward Empowerment: Women and Politics in India,* Colorado, Westview Press, 1992.

MacKinley, A.C.: *The Econometrics of Financial Markets,* Princeton University Press, 1996.

Maheshwari, Shriram: *Rural Development in India: A Public Policy Approach,* New Delhi, Sage, 1995.

Martin, L. J. and Hiebert, R. E.: *Current Issues in International Communication*, White Plains, NY: Longman, 1990.

McCallum, J. : *Global Disequilibrium*, London, MacMillan, 1992.

Mclean, I.: *Democracy and New Technology*, Cambridge, Polity Press, 1989.

Mishra, Jayashri: *Social and Economic Conditions under the Imperial Rashtrakutas*, New Delhi, Commonwealth, 1992.

Morse, David. *The Origin and Evolution of the ILO and its Role in the World Community,* Ithaca, 1969.

Narula, Sanjay : *Indian Politics,* New Delhi, Murari Lal and Sons, 2007.

Nehru, Jawaharlal , *Towards A Socialistic Order,* New Delhi, 1956.

Patnaik, Naveen: *A Second Paradise: Indian Courtly Life, 1590-1947,* Garden City, New Jersey, Doubleday, 1985.

Polak, J.J. : *The New International Monetary System,* New York, Columbia University Press, 1978.

Probyn, Mr. : *Indian Coinage and Currency,* Effingham Wilson, London, 1897.

Pruthi, R.K. : *Indian Political Thought,* New Delhi, Mohit Pub., 2007.

Quincy W.: *The Study of International Relations,* Apleton-Century-Crofts, N.Y., 1955

Ranade, Sudhanshu: *Rural Banking Adrift,* Bombay, Jaico Publishing House, 1984.

Robert Smith: *Modern Labor Economics,* Harper Collins, 1994.

Robert Z. Aliber: *The International Market for Foreign Exchange,* New York, Praeger, 1969.

Saksena, N.S.: *India: Towards Anarchy, 1967-1992,* New Delhi, Abhinav, 1993.

Schmidhauser, R.: *Supreme Court: Its Politics, Personalities and Procedures,* New York, Holt, 1960.

Somiah, C.G.: *The Honest always Stand Alone.* New Delhi: Niyogi Books, 2010.

Swoboda, A. : *Monetary Problems of the International Economy,* Chicago, University of Chicago Press, 1969.

Tomlinson, B. R.: *The Economy of Modern India, 1860–1970.* New York: Cambridge University Press, 1993.

Victor G. : *Law as a Political Instrument,* New York, Random House, 1955.

Viotti P. & Kauppi M.: *International Relations Theory,* N.Y,Macmillan,1987

Warwick, D. P.: *A Theory of Public Bureaucracy,* Cambridge, MA: Harvard University Press, 1975.

Yearwood, Peter J. *Guarantee of Peace: The League of Nations in British Policy 1914–1925,* Oxford UP, 2009.

Zaidi,A.M. and S.G. Zaidi: *The Foundations of Indian Economic Planning,* New Delhi, 1979.

Index

W

❑❑❑